THE NEW PARADOX FOR JAPANESE WOMEN:
GREATER CHOICE, GREATER INEQUALITY

The LTCB International Library Trust

The LTCB (Long-Term Credit Bank of Japan) International Library Trust, established in July 2000, is the successor to the LTCB International Library Foundation. It carries on the mission that the foundation's founders articulated as follows:

> The world is moving steadily toward a borderless economy and deepening international interdependence. Amid economic globalization, Japan is developing ever-closer ties with nations worldwide through trade, through investment, and through manufacturing and other localized business operations.
>
> Japan's global activity is drawing attention to its political, economic, and social systems and to the concepts and values that underlie those systems. But the supply of translations of Japanese books about those and other Japan-related subjects has not kept pace with demand.
>
> The shortage of foreign-language translations of Japanese books about Japanese subjects is attributable largely to the high cost of translating and publishing. To address that issue, the LTCB International Library Foundation funds the translation and the distribution of selected Japanese works about Japan's politics, economy, society, and culture.

International House of Japan, Inc., manages the publishing activities of the LTCB International Library Trust, and Chuo Mitsui Trust and Banking Company, Ltd., manages the trust's financial assets.

LTCB International Library Selection No. 26

LTCB International Library Trust/International House of Japan

The New Paradox for Japanese Women: Greater Choice, Greater Inequality

Tachibanaki Toshiaki

Translated by Mary E. Foster

Translation Notes

The Hepburn system of romanization is used for Japanese terms, including the names of persons and places. Except for familiar place names, long vowels are indicated by a macron. The local custom of placing the family name first has been followed for the names of Japanese persons.

Japanese government agency names current as of January 1, 2010, have been used regardless of the publication date of the statistics cited. All organization names have been rendered in American English spelling.

At the author's request, the Japanese book has been slightly abridged for the English edition.

This book was originally published in 2008 by Toyo Keizai, Inc., under the title Jojo kakusa. English translation rights are reserved by the International House of Japan, Inc., under contract with Tachibanaki Toshiaki and through the courtesy of Toyo Keizai, Inc.

First English edition published March 2010 by the International House of Japan, Inc.
5-11-16 Roppongi, Minato-ku, Tokyo 106-0032, Japan
Tel: +81-3-3470-3211 or +81-3-3470-9059   Fax: +81-3-3470-3170
E-mail: ihj@i-house.or.jp

Printed in Japan
ISBN 978-4-924971-28-8

Contents

—

Tables and Figures

Tables

Figures

Preface to the English Edition

Japan suffers today from a high inequality in income distribution and a lack of equal opportunity. Simply put, Japan is a class society (*kakusa shakai*). Many Japanese do not accept such a judgment, however, as it has been widely believed that Japan enjoys social equality. In 2005 I published *Confronting Income Inequality in Japan* (MIT Press) and refuted that belief. Great controversy then erupted surrounding the issue of inequality in Japan, and this is still a major debate, not only in academia but also in the political arena.

To date, much attention has been given to inequality among men or among households. This book is concerned with disparities among women, to which little attention has been paid. One of the reasons why women have been ignored in the literature is that there is a large number of nonworking women or full-time homemakers, who do not receive any income, and it is not easy to discuss inequality in such a case. The number of working women is increasing, however, and it is natural to conceive of disparities in income and other areas among them.

Education, occupation, family background, employment status (for example, full-time or part-time work), marital status, and children all exert an impact on female employment and income. This book examines that impact. At the same time, it is interesting to inquire how educational and occupational attainments, employment situation, marital status, and birth figures differ among women. This book is concerned with such differentials.

This English edition is published as part of the LTCB International Library Trust translation series. I am grateful to the Selection Committee and the General Policy Committee of the LTCB International Library Trust for enabling me to have my Japanese book, entitled *Jojo kakusa*, translated into English and published.

A painstaking and excellent job of translation has been performed by Mary Foster. I recognize that her superb job went beyond the role of a translator. If readers of this book should find it to be easy to read, they would be in her deep debt. I also thank Saji Yasuo, publication officer, for his skillful management and coordination of the project.

Tachibanaki Toshiaki
January 2010

Preface to the Japanese Edition

*T*he *New Paradox for Japanese Women: Greater Choice, Greater
Inequality* aims to shed light on the social inequalities existing among Japanese women today. Japan has long been considered
a society where all people are middle class. It is generally agreed
today, though, that Japan has become a society of increasing social
inequality. This is evidenced by the widening gap between rich and
poor and the development of rigid social classes. This book is the
first to discuss the phenomenon of increasing social inequality
among women in Japan.

The discussion of social disparities has traditionally focused on
households; it has centered on comparisons of household income
or the financial status or social class of the householder, who was a
man in most cases. It was natural for research into social inequalities
to focus on men because they have been the main breadwinners in
Japan. Women make up half the population, though, and today more
than half of married women work while another sizable portion of
them desire to be full-time homemakers. This fact alone suggests
that there are disparities among women as well. This book attempts
to address that very question.

There are wage gaps among working women and a variety of
other disparities that derive from their work situations. For example, some women have full-time work while others work part-time.
Some are on the management track while others are on the clerical track at their workplaces. Disparities also arise between women
who receive promotions at work and those who do not. Considering

inequalities from these kinds of perspectives is particularly important in the case of women. Why do such disparities arise? Should they be tolerated? This book addresses such questions.

Disparities among women can also be discussed from the perspective of education. All women, whether or not they are in the work force, receive education, but how much education do they receive? Little study has been made of the education gap among women so I offer an extensive discussion of that in these pages. What kinds of families do highly educated women come from? Is their high level of education helping them? These are all questions of interest.

This book also discusses what should be used as the basis for determining a woman's social class. Social mobility has long been discussed in relation to father and son, but looking at it in relation to father and daughter is also very meaningful.

Marriage, childbirth, and childrearing are key life events for a woman, and they have been the subject of much sociological analysis. Very little research, though, has discussed these matters from the perspective of inequality. This book attempts to consider these events from that perspective. I focus particularly on the disparities that arise between highly educated and lesser-educated women in relation to employment, marriage, childbirth, and childrearing.

The book examines disparities among women in relation to these various issues, but it also gives considerable attention to men's influence on inequalities as well. How do men impact social disparities among women? First, before Japan became affluent, many families sent their sons to university even if it was a financial strain on the family, but they educated their daughters only through high school or, at most, junior college. Families sacrificed their daughters' education for that of their sons. Second, a woman's social class is determined based solely on her husband's situation if she is a full-time homemaker. These two examples show that men have a great influence on social disparities among women. The impact of men is actually the hardest to analyze and may become a topic of debate in the future.

Some of the inequalities I have mentioned here are justifiable and others are not. A key recommendation of this book is that those inequalities that are not justifiable be corrected.

I have cited much survey data in these pages. Two publications have been particularly helpful in this regard and I would like to make special mention of them here: *Danjo kyōdō sankaku tōkei dēta bukku 2006* (Gender equality data book, 2006) edited by the National Women's Education Center and *Heisei 17 nen dai 13 kai shusshō dōkō kihon chōsa, dai I to dai II hōkokusho* (Report on the thirteenth Japanese national fertility survey, 2005, volumes I and II) by the National Institute of Population and Social Security Research.

Yahagi Tomoko of Toyo Keizai Inc. inspired me to write this book. She enthusiastically proposed that I take up the question of social disparities among women, as I was one of the first commentators to note the widening inequalities in Japanese society. *The New Paradox for Japanese Women* is my response to her suggestion. I would like to thank Ms. Yahagi for her encouragement to write this book and for her skillful editing. Of course, all responsibility for the content of this book lies solely with the author.

Tachibanaki Toshiaki

May 2008

Chapter One

The Gender Gap

Although the main focus of this book is inequalities among women, it is also important to compare women with the other gender, namely, men. When we detect a gap among women, we must determine whether this has been affected by a disparity with men—has resulted from a gender gap—or whether it is solely due to factors unique to women.

A simple example will serve to illustrate this concept. Research has shown a disparity among women in terms of occupation or job: women hold few managerial, specialized, or management-track positions but are concentrated in non-managerial, secretarial, or clerical-track jobs. This situation, however, is related to the level and type of education that women receive. A smaller percentage of women go on to higher education than do men, and many men are trained in the social and natural sciences. The percentage of women who attend four-year universities is still low, and those who do tend to major in the humanities and arts. It is easier, therefore, for men to find managerial, specialized, and management-track positions. Women, on the other hand, generally acquire an education that makes them poorly suited for such positions. Thus, the disparity in occupation noted among women is in fact affected by the disparity in education between men and women.

In addition to education, other gaps between men and women result in inequalities among women. In this chapter, therefore, I would like to discuss the gender gap before moving on to the "woman-woman" gap.

The Gender Gap and Demographics

Female longevity

It is well established that women live longer than men, but let's look at how life expectancy at birth has changed in Japan since World War II. As shown in table 1-1, the average life expectancy at birth for both sexes hovered around sixty in 1950–52, a few years after the war ended. In 2004, the average life expectancy had lengthened to somewhat over 85.5 for women and slightly over 78.5 for men. Life expectancy has increased for both sexes, but the gender gap in life expectancy has risen from 3.40 years to 6.95 years.

Among the reasons why women live longer than men, the physical factor is key: women are physically designed for longevity. There are major social factors as well. Women are not generally engaged in

Table 1-1 Average life expectancy at birth by sex (1950–2004)

(Years old; years)

Year	Female	Male	Difference = female – male
1950–52	62.97	59.57	3.40
1955	67.75	63.60	4.15
1960	70.19	65.32	4.87
1965	72.92	67.74	5.18
1970	74.66	69.31	5.35
1975	76.89	71.73	5.16
1980	78.76	73.35	5.41
1985	80.48	74.78	5.70
1990	81.90	75.92	5.98
1995	82.85	76.38	6.47
2000	84.60	77.72	6.88
2001	84.93	78.07	6.86
2002	85.23	78.32	6.91
2003	85.33	78.36	6.97
2004	85.59	78.64	6.95

Sources: For all years except 2004: Based on National Institute of Population and Social Security Research, *Jinkō no dōkō, Nihon to sekai: jinkō tōkei shiryōshū, 2005* (Population trends in Japan and the world: Population statistics of Japan, 2005). For 2004: Based on Ministry of Health, Labor, and Welfare, *Abridged Life Tables for Japan, 2004.*

heavy physical labor and a much higher percentage of men smoke cigarettes and drink alcohol, resulting in a higher morbidity rate. The suicide rate is also higher for men. As more and more women enter the work force, however, the number of women who overwork, smoke, and drink is increasing, and the rise in female longevity is decreasing, as evidenced in the slight narrowing in very recent years in the gender gap in average life expectancy at birth.

Fertility rate

In that having children involves activities that only women can perform, such as pregnancy, childbirth, and, in many cases, childrearing, the fertility rate relates only to women, and no comparison with men can be made. It is true that men also can be involved in childrearing, but nonetheless having children still has a greater impact on women.

Table 1-2 gives trends in the total fertility rate (the average number of children born to a woman over her lifetime) from 1950 until 2005. We can see that the rate has dropped dramatically, falling from 3.65 after the war to 1.26 in 2005. A woman's lifestyle used to change greatly after she gave birth (for example, leaving the work force to be a full-time homemaker), but women have increasingly been released from the sole life path of childbearing and childrearing so that the range

Table 1-2 Total fertility rate

Year	Total fertility rate
1950	3.65
1955	2.37
1960	2.00
1965	2.14
1970	2.13
1975	1.91
1980	1.75
1985	1.76
1990	1.54
1995	1.42
2000	1.36
2005	1.26

Source: Based on National Institute of Population and Social Security Research, *Jinkō tōkei shiryōshū* (Population statistics of Japan).

of options open to them has broadened. It is now easy for women to continue to work while they bear and raise children. In this sense, the decline in the fertility rate has had a major impact on society.

The reverse might also be said, however. That is, if a woman wants to be economically independent and to continue working, or feels that childbearing and childrearing are too heavy a burden, she might very well refrain from having children. We must be careful in our analysis when two such differing interpretations are possible.

Age at marriage

Let's turn next to marriage. Table 1-3 gives statistics for the average age of men and women at time of marriage, as well as the age difference between the bride and the groom. From this table, we can see that the age at first marriage is increasing for both men and women, but the rise for women is particularly striking. A woman's marrying later affects her life path in various ways, for example, increasing her number of years in the work force before getting married and having children. However, with the increase in women's education level, women are entering the work force when they are older, so we must take with a grain of salt the statement that their years at work have risen.

Table 1-3 Mean age of bride and groom at marriage and their age difference

(Years old; years)

Year	All marriages		First marriages		Age difference (groom – bride)	
	Bride	Groom	Bride	Groom	All marriages	First marriages
1970	24.6	27.6	24.2	26.9	3.0	2.7
1980	25.9	28.7	25.2	27.8	2.8	2.6
1990	26.9	29.7	25.9	28.4	2.8	2.5
2000	28.2	30.4	27.0	28.8	2.2	1.8
2005	29.2	31.5	27.8	29.6	2.3	1.8

Source: Based on Statistics and Information Department, Ministry of Health, Labor, and Welfare, Vital Statistics of Japan.

If a woman marries later, her age at childbirth will be higher as well, and this affects the fertility rate. In fact, it is widely thought that one reason for the declining fertility rate in Japan is that women are marrying later. We must hold off on drawing such a conclusion, however. The impact of later marriage may well be offset by an increase in out-of-wedlock childbirth, as well as advances in medicine making it possible for women to give birth later in life.

Divorce

Obviously, there is no gender gap in the number of divorces as divorce is the separation of a couple. What is important here, rather, is that divorce is on the rise. As shown in figure 4-9 and table 4-8 on page 127, Japan's divorce rate has been on a steady climb over the past thirty to forty years and stood at 2 to 3 per 1,000 population annually in 2004, which is on a par with major European countries like Britain, Sweden, and France.

Table 4-8 presents some interesting data. Past figures for South Korea are not given here, but the divorce rates in the East Asian countries of Japan and South Korea have been on a dramatic rise in recent years. In contrast, the divorce rate in the United States, while without question very high, has been on the decline for the past decade. The rates for Britain and France are also declining slightly. It is not known exactly why the past rising divorce rates in these countries have been reversed. Nonetheless, the number of divorces has peaked and is proceeding to decrease in the West while, in contrast, divorce is increasing rapidly in East Asia. Of course, the rates for East Asia may also slow at some point, especially since Japan's social and economic trends often follow those of the United States with a lag of about twenty to thirty years.

An interesting question in relation to divorce is the matter of which spouse lodges for divorce and the reasons for divorce. According to figure 1-1, in 2004 a total of 67,688 divorces were filed in Japan, and about 70 percent of those were initiated by wives. As women, with their lower level of economic independence, are more likely to suffer from a divorce than men are, we can conclude that

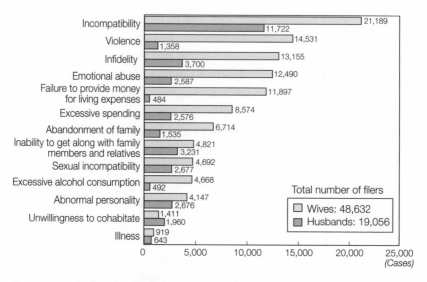

Fig. 1-1 Number of divorce cases by reason for filing for divorce and by filing spouse (2004)

Note: In each case, multiple reasons were indicated as the reason for filing for divorce. The top three reasons reported by the filer are included in the figures for reason for filing. Figures for "other" and "not reported" were wives: 4,628; husbands: 3,218.

Source: Based on Supreme Court of Japan, *Heisei 16 nen shihō tōkei nenpō* (Annual report of judicial statistics, 2004).

women have a comparatively higher level of dissatisfaction with married life than men do.

A gender gap is particularly evident in regard to the reason for filing for divorce. For both men and women, the most frequent reason given is incompatibility, but the next most frequent reasons stated by women filers are violence, infidelity, emotional abuse, failure to provide money for living expenses, and excessive spending. This reveals the existence of domestic violence and other problems specific to men, such as extramarital affairs and failure as the family provider. This would seem to imply that men are more violent and less responsible than women.

Let me make a few comments, though, that may serve to exonerate men. Regarding extramarital affairs, let me point out that a man cannot have an affair alone; there is definitely a female counterpart involved. Might I suggest that both the man and the woman are responsible for having an affair and therefore it is not just the man who is in the wrong? Turning to the issue of providing money for living expenses, since this problem arises where the husband is the sole breadwinner, there is a good chance that it will decline as Japan enters the era of gender equality and wives also work outside of the home. Of course, this issue will not disappear completely as long as men have higher earnings than women.

Child custody

In figure 1-2, we can see changing trends in custody rights for divorcing couples with children. Interesting here is the shift that occurred around 1965. Prior to that time, the husband was awarded custody of the children more often than the wife was. After around 1965, however, the wife came to be awarded custody. Today custody is given to the wife in the vast majority of cases. In fact, the wife is awarded custody in more than 80 percent of cases whereas the husband is awarded custody in only about 15 percent. In other words, custody is given to the wife over five times more than to the husband.

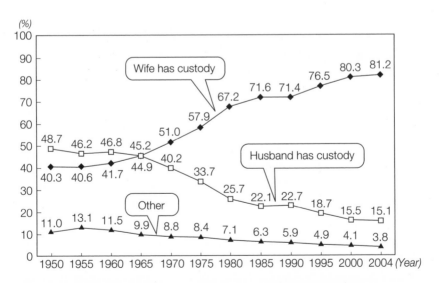

Fig. 1-2 Divorce cases by spouse with custody (1950–2004)

Source: Based on Statistics and Information Department, Ministry of Health, Labor, and Welfare, *Vital Statistics of Japan*.

Why did this dramatic shift occur? First, years ago, generally the wife did not work and custody was awarded to the husband because he had the economic means to raise the children. With the increase over the past twenty years in the percentage of working wives, however, some women now also have the economic means to raise the children.

Second, Japan was a patriarchal society before World War II, and this continued after the war for a time as well so that it was considered natural to award the custody of the children to the husband. It was an age in which the husband ruled the household and the wife followed. Times have changed, however, and the idea of gender equality has become widespread for a major impact on child custody.

Third, in any era, the mother plays the central role in rearing children with the mother-child bond tending to be stronger than the father-child bond. As the reasons for paternal custody gradually weakened, the mother-child bond came to the fore. Also, more and more divorcing couples have recognized that it is better for the children to be raised by the mother than by a father who is unaccustomed to childrearing.

One-person households

Having looked at marriage, divorce, and child custody, next let's investigate the alternative case of one-person households.

We can see trends in family type since 1960 in table 1-4. Particularly striking is the increase in one-person households from 16.1 percent in 1960 to 27.6 percent in 2000. First we should note the distinction between one-person households and unmarried persons. A one-person household is a household where the person does not share housing with another person; an unmarried person is a person who has no spouse. Thus, people who have a spouse but live alone (the typical example in Japan would be people who are transferred by their employer to a different work location, but are not accompanied by their family) fall under the category of one-person households. It is noteworthy that women make up 46.0 percent, or almost half, of one-person households. I will argue in a later chapter that this phenomenon has had a significant impact on inequalities among women.

Table 1-4 gives us several other pieces of information. First, households composed solely of a married couple have almost tripled from 7.3 percent in 1960 to 18.9 percent in 2000. In contrast, households composed of a married couple and child(ren) declined slightly from 38.2 percent to 31.9 percent. Second, "other relatives" households dropped by more than half from 30.5 percent to 13.6 percent. Most of these "other relatives" households are three-generation households, so this tells us that such households have decreased dramatically in Japan.

Table 1-4 Households by family type (1960–2000) and female householders (2000)

(1,000 households; %; persons)

			1960		1980		1990		2000			
			No.	%	No.	%	No.	%	No.	%	Female house-holders (No.)	Female house-holders (%)
Private households			22,231	100.0	35,824	100.0	40,670	100.0	46,782	100.0	9,448	20.2
One-person households			3,579	16.1	7,105	19.8	9,390	23.1	12,911	27.6	5,933	46.0
Relatives households	Nuclear families	Married couple only	1,630	7.3	4,460	12.5	6,294	15.5	8,835	18.9	70	0.8
		Married couple and child(ren)	8,489	38.2	15,081	42.1	15,172	37.3	14,919	31.9	63	0.4
		Mother and child(ren)	1,424	6.4	1,756	4.9	2,328	5.7	3,032	6.5	2,561	84.5
		Father and child(ren)	245	1.1	297	0.8	425	1.0	545	1.2	8	1.5
	Other relatives households		6,790	30.5	7,063	19.7	6,986	17.2	6,347	13.6	758	11.9
Non-relatives households			74	0.3	62	0.2	77	0.2	192	0.4	54	28.1
Average no. of household members			4.14		3.22		2.99		2.67			

Note: Figures for 1960 are based on 1 percent sampling tabulation. Total number of households in 1960 was 22,539,000.

Source: Based on Statistics Bureau, Ministry of Internal Affairs and Communications, *Population Census of Japan*, quoted in National Institute of Population and Social Security Research, *Jinkō no dōkō, Nihon to sekai: jinkō tōkei shiryōshū, 2005* (Population trends in Japan and the world: Population statistics of Japan, 2005).

Looking at trends in one-person households by sex and age, table 1-5 shows that the percentage of female one-person households is increasing among the young and middle-aged age brackets (ages 20–34). Nonetheless, they make up between about 30 and 40 percent of one-person households at most. Male one-person households therefore are more common. Over the two decades from 1980 to 2000, however, the percentage of female one-person households in that age range increased dramatically (for example, the percentage rose from 21.4 to 33.3 percent in the 25–29 age group, and from 25.6 to 30.8 percent in the 30–34 age group). It seems likely that female one-person households will further increase in the future, meaning

Table 1-5 One-person households by sex and age group, and percentage of female households (1980 and 2000)

(1,000 households; %)

	1980				2000			
	Total	Female	Male	Female house-holds (%)	Total	Female	Male	Female house-holds (%)
Total	7,105	3,143	3,962	44.2	12,911	5,933	6,979	46.0
Under age 20	640	268	372	41.9	491	207	284	42.1
20–24	1,795	597	1,198	33.3	1,954	765	1,189	39.2
25–29	1,118	239	878	21.4	1,740	579	1,161	33.3
30–34	640	164	476	25.6	1,117	344	774	30.8
35–39	353	122	231	34.6	758	220	537	29.0
40–44	285	121	164	42.5	606	165	441	27.2
45–49	321	167	155	51.9	732	210	522	28.7
50–54	364	226	138	62.1	925	329	595	35.6
55–59	359	268	91	74.6	803	375	428	46.7
60–64	348	281	67	80.7	753	448	305	59.5
65 and over	881	688	193	78.1	3,032	2,290	742	75.5

Source: Based on Statistics Bureau, Ministry of Internal Affairs and Communications, *Population Census of Japan*.

that the number of women in this generation who are, or who have to be, economically independent is on the rise.

The percentage of female one-person households rises in the senior age bracket because many married women become widowed. We can cite two reasons why there are more female one-person households than male among the elderly. First, women are longer lived and wives are generally a few years younger than their husbands. Second, although women can live on their own, men of that generation have difficulty living alone because they had their wives perform all household chores during their marriage. Therefore, men choose not to live alone in many cases.

Next, table 1-6 tracks trends in unmarried persons by showing marital status by sex and age. Here we find much overlap in trends with one-person households: there are many unmarried men in the younger age brackets and many unmarried women in the older ones. Looking at the statistics for persons age sixty and over, we can confirm that there are many, many cases where women return to the unmarried category when their husbands die, as mentioned in the previous paragraph.

Of particular interest in table 1-6 is the 20–39 age category, or people who are at a marriageable age. We note that the percentage of men who have never married is higher than that of women. The difference between the sexes is 5.0 percentage points in the 20–24 age group, 15.3 points for those 25 to 29, 16.3 points for those 30 to 34, and 11.9 points for those 35 to 39. It is commonly said in Japan now that women are no longer marrying, but the actual statistics tell us that the percentage of men who have never married is higher than that of women.

Why is there this divergence between the facts and popular belief? First, there was no appreciable difference between the male and female population ratios a decade ago. Male births slightly outnumbered female births, but the male-female ratio among adults was near 1.0 because a slightly higher number of boys died in early childhood than girls. With the decrease in the infant mortality rate, however, the sex ratio has exceeded 1.0, with men outnumbering

Table 1-6 Population 15 years of age and over by sex and age group, and of marital status percentages for each (2000)

(1,000 persons; %)

	Female					
	Total no.	Total %	Never married	Married	Widowed	Divorced
Total	55,721	100.0	23.7	58.2	13.0	4.4
Age 15–19	3,654	100.0	99.1	0.9	0.0	0.0
20–24	4,114	100.0	87.9	11.3	0.0	0.7
25–29	4,825	100.0	54.0	43.5	0.1	2.4
30–34	4,340	100.0	26.6	68.9	0.2	4.2
35–39	4,019	100.0	13.8	79.2	0.5	5.6
40–44	3,876	100.0	8.6	83.3	1.2	6.3
45–49	4,448	100.0	6.3	83.7	2.3	7.0
50–54	5,232	100.0	5.3	82.4	4.2	7.3
55–59	4,444	100.0	4.3	80.3	8.1	6.4
60–64	3,986	100.0	3.8	75.7	14.3	5.2
65–69	3,749	100.0	3.9	67.8	23.0	4.3
70–74	3,230	100.0	4.0	56.1	34.9	3.9
75–79	2,525	100.0	3.2	38.7	53.0	3.4
80–84	1,699	100.0	2.2	21.5	71.5	2.6
85 and over	1,580	100.0	1.6	7.7	86.0	1.9

	Male					
	Total no.	Total %	Never married	Married	Widowed	Divorced
Total	52,503	100.0	31.8	61.8	2.7	2.7
Age 15–19	3,834	100.0	99.5	0.4	0.0	0.0
20–24	4,307	100.0	92.9	6.8	0.0	0.2
25–29	3,965	100.0	69.3	29.6	0.0	1.0
30–34	4,437	100.0	42.9	54.9	0.1	2.0
35–39	4,096	100.0	25.7	69.2	0.2	3.0
40–44	3,924	100.0	18.4	76.1	0.3	3.6
45–49	4,468	100.0	14.6	78.8	0.7	4.3
50–54	5,210	100.0	10.1	82.2	1.2	4.9
55–59	4,290	100.0	6.0	85.6	2.2	4.7
60–64	3,750	100.0	3.8	87.2	3.5	4.0
65–69	3,357	100.0	2.5	87.4	5.6	3.1
70–74	2,670	100.0	1.7	86.1	8.7	2.1
75–79	1,626	100.0	1.2	82.4	13.3	1.5
80–84	915	100.0	0.9	76.3	19.8	1.2
85 and over	653	100.0	0.8	59.5	36.3	1.0

Note: "Total no." figures include cases where marital status was not reported.

Source: Based on Statistics Bureau, Ministry of Internal Affairs and Communications, *2000 Population Census of Japan*.

women by a considerable margin. Under the practice of monogamy, many men are unable to marry.

A second factor is that men are slightly older than women at time of marriage. These days, the ranks of the younger age groups are decreasing in number every year because the birthrate is on the decline. Men seek younger women as marriage partners, but there are fewer and fewer women in younger age groups. This also means that more and more men are unable to marry.

Third, there is an imbalance from the perspective of male occupation, as witnessed by the shortage of brides in rural communities, a topic often covered in the Japanese media. The declining birthrate is also well publicized in Japan so the idea that women are refusing to marry has come to be believed more than is the actual case. The Japanese public has come to think that men have a strong desire to marry, but women do not have as strong an incentive to marry as before because of their gains in economic power. This belief in turn has led the Japanese public to conclude that women want to remain single.

The Gender Gap and Work

Labor force participation

Although both men and women of working age participate in the labor force, there is a definite gender gap that can be summarized as follows. First, all men and women in the 20–24 age group who can work do so. For age brackets after that, however, the labor force participation rate for women never reaches 75 percent at its highest, while the rate for men hovers around 95 percent. Second, the female rate traces an M-curve, as it declines during women's marriage and childbearing years of twenty-five to thirty-four and then rises again starting from age thirty-five.

Figure 1-3 shows the labor force participation rate for men and women by age group, illustrating the two points just mentioned. The male rate takes the form of a bell with the rate standing at around 95 percent in almost all age groups, while the female rate traces an M-curve.

However, we can also witness a change in this M-curve for women. Three decades ago, in 1975, there was a sharp dip in the M. As times have changed, however, the curve is becoming more similar to a bell in shape. This signifies that women in the 25–34 age group are no longer resigning from the work force with marriage and childbirth but are continuing to work during those years: the curve in the women's labor force participation rate might well come to have a bell shape like that for men in about a decade.

It is significant that the labor force participation rate for women of all ages outside the 25–34 age group has increased over the past thirty years. This means that the percentage of women who are full-time homemakers is decreasing and the percentage of working women is rising across the board. A decade ago, a division of labor between men and women in which men worked outside the home and women

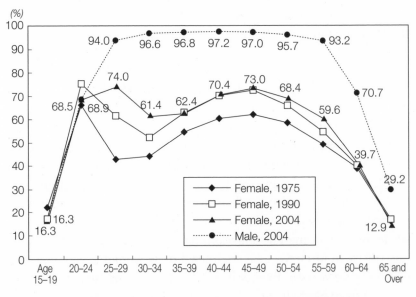

Fig. 1-3 Labor force participation rate by sex and age group (1975–2004)

Note: The statistics for men show less change compared with those for women so only 2004 figures are given for men. Figures for women are given for 2004, and trends for women for all three years are depicted by lines.

Source: Based on Statistics Bureau, Ministry of Internal Affairs and Communications, *Labor Force Survey*.

took care of the home and raised the children was the mainstream, but that arrangement is becoming less common. However, there will always be some women who choose to be full-time homemakers. As a result, women's labor force participation rate will not rise to the same level as that for men. Nonetheless, it is undeniable that the increase in the percentage of working women is influencing Japanese society and economy, including inequalities among women.

Industry and occupation type

It is clear that the employment rate among women has risen. Now let's look at the kinds of industries and occupations in which women are working. Here our main interest is the gender gaps evident in figures 1-4 (industry) and 1-5 (occupation).

Looking at the gender gap by type of industry, we note that there are many women working in the two sectors of (1) services and (2) wholesale/retail trade and restaurants/bars, with women numbering 9.57 million and 8.55 million in 2002, respectively. In fact, about 70 percent of all employed women are in these two sectors. Moreover, the number of women in these two sectors is on the rise, in contrast to agriculture and forestry, which has seen the largest decline in female workers. Manufacturing is next in terms of number of women employed with 4.11 million females engaged in that sector. The number of women in manufacturing increased from 1955 to 1985, but has tapered slightly since then.

What are the trends for male workers? Like women, the number of men working in services has skyrocketed. This sector was the largest employer of men in 2002, with 8.47 million on the payroll. In contrast, manufacturing, which has in the past been the largest, is declining slightly. The sector witnessing the sharpest decline in male workers is agriculture and forestry, as was the case for women as well. A considerable number of male workers are in the construction and the transport and communication sectors, two industries that have almost no women workers.

In other words, changes in Japan's industrial structure (the decline of agriculture and forestry, the rise and subsequent slight decline of manufacturing, and the consistent expansion of services)

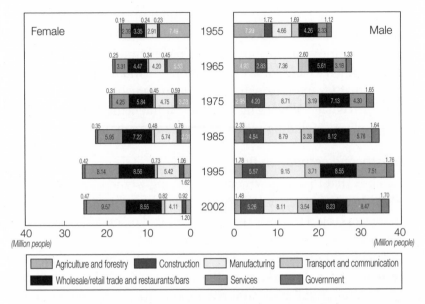

Fig. 1-4 Employed persons by sex and major industry (1955–2002)

Notes: 1. With the 2002 revision of the Japan Standard Industrial Classification (JSIC), the new JSIC has been applied starting from 2003. The figures in this graph are based on the old JSIC and stop at 2002 as no time series comparison can be performed thereafter.

2. "Transport and communication" includes the electricity, gas, heat supply, and water industries. "Wholesale/retail trade and restaurants/bars" includes the finance, insurance, and real estate industries.

Source: Based on Statistics Bureau, Ministry of Internal Affairs and Communications, *Labor Force Survey*.

are having an impact on the industries in which men and women work. One gender disparity, however, is consistent across all survey years: the large number of men in the construction and the transport and communication sectors. Since construction requires considerable physical strength and transport features such work as driving vehicles, it is perhaps natural that they remain male domains. It is also easy to see why many women work in services and in wholesale/retail trade and restaurants/bars, which require minimal physical strength but need a cheerful disposition and people skills.

Gender trends similar to those noted in relation to type of industry are found in occupational choice as well. Many women are in the following occupational categories, ranked in order of number of

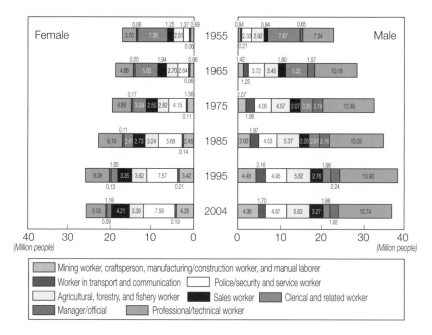

Fig. 1-5 Employed persons by sex and major occupation (1955–2004)

Source: Based on Statistics Bureau, Ministry of Internal Affairs and Communications, *Labor Force Survey*.

female workers: clerical and related worker; mining worker, craftsperson, manufacturing/construction worker, and manual laborer; police/security and sevice worker; and sales worker. In contrast, the vast majority of men are mining workers, craftspersons, manufacturing/construction workers, and laborers, followed by sales workers, professional/technical workers, and clerical and related workers. The gender difference in physical strength is clear.

However, the largest gender gap is seen in the occupational categories of professional/technical worker and manager/official. The vast majority of people in these occupations are men, although there has been a rapid increase in female professional/technical workers from around 1985 that has served to offset the decrease in the number of female mining workers, craftspersons, manufacturing/

construction workers, and manual laborers from around that same time. This rise in female professional/technical workers has had an important impact in producing disparities among women, which we will look at in more detail in later chapters.

Nonregular work

Another significant feature of the labor market in Japan is that men engage in regular work, that is, full-time work, whereas the vast majority of women have nonregular work, that is, work as part-time or temporary workers (*Arbeit*) or as workers dispatched by temporary labor agencies. (See table 8-1 on page 230 for detailed definitions of the various types of employment.)

Looking at table 1-7, we can see that the number of female employees rose by 5.5 million over the fifteen years up to 2002, from 17 million to 22.5 million. That increase in female workers far exceeds the rise in male workers, whose numbers grew by about 3.1 million. This speaks clearly of women's entry into the work force over that period.

The second striking gender difference evident from this table is that women make up 70 to 80 percent of part-time and other nonregular workers. And while the percentage of female part-time and temporary workers declined slightly from a little over 82 percent in 1987 to 77 percent in 2002, the absolute number of female part-time and temporary workers increased considerably—in fact almost doubling—from 5.4 million to 9.3 million. There are many reasons for this rise in the number of women doing nonregular work, and since the working conditions of nonregular workers are, in general, significantly inferior to those of regular workers, this situation also is one cause of inequalities among women, as will be discussed in a later chapter.

A third point is that not only has the number of female nonregular workers increased considerably, but the number of male nonregular workers has as well, from 1.2 million to 2.7 million, due to the increase in the number of part-time workers and freeters* mainly among young men. This has become a serious social problem in Japan today.

* Freeters are young people who do not have regular employment but who work at one or more part-time jobs or at one short-term job after another. The term was coined by combining the English word *free* and the German word *Arbeiter* (laborer).

**Table 1-7 Number of employees by sex and employment type, and
the percentage of women (1987–2002)**

(1,000 persons; %)

		Total no. of employees	Corporate executives	Corporate employees, excl. executives				
				Regular staff	Part-time and temporary workers (*Arbeit*)	Short-term contract workers (*shokutaku*), etc.	Dispatched workers from temporary labor agencies	Other
Female	1987	16,998	619	10,309	5,394	252	49	375
	1992	20,529	895	11,962	6,871	301	114	384
	1997	21,867	877	11,755	8,254	361	204	412
	2002	22,531	939	10,145	9,337	1,169	517	402
Male	1987	29,154	2,471	24,256	1,168	478	38	743
	1992	32,046	3,075	26,100	1,611	579	49	623
	1997	33,130	2,973	26,787	2,088	605	53	612
	2002	32,201	2,957	24,412	2,724	1,309	204	544
Percentage of women	1987	36.8	20.0	29.8	82.2	34.5	56.3	33.5
	1992	39.0	22.5	31.4	81.0	34.2	69.9	38.1
	1997	39.8	22.8	30.5	79.8	37.4	79.4	40.2
	2002	41.2	24.1	29.4	77.4	47.2	71.8	42.5

Source: Based on Statistics Bureau, Ministry of Internal Affairs and Communications, *Employment Status Survey.*

We thus see that the number of nonregular workers in the labor force has increased considerably among both men and women. Corporations have been pressed to cut labor costs with the deepening recession, and the resulting impact, although affecting both men and women, has been greater on women.

Wages

Turning now to the gender gap in relation to wages, we see from table 1-8 that the wage gap is narrowing only for full-time workers (expressed as "ordinary workers" in the table): women made 55.3 percent of men's wages in 1980 whereas in 2004 they made 65.7 percent.

The gap in wages for full-time work has shrunk for the following reasons: (1) women attaining higher levels of education, (2) women staying longer at a single workplace, and (3) society no longer accepting discrimination against women. In spite of this narrowing of the

Table 1-8 Wages for ordinary workers and all workers by sex (1980–2004)

(1,000 yen; %)

Year	Ordinary workers			All workers, incl. part-time		
	Female	Male	Female/male	Female	Male	Female/male
1980	122.5	221.7	55.3	123.9	227.0	54.6
1981	130.5	235.3	55.5	130.6	240.4	54.3
1982	136.2	246.1	55.3	135.4	251.7	53.8
1983	141.2	254.4	55.5	139.4	261.3	53.3
1984	146.6	265.1	55.3	144.4	272.7	53.0
1985	153.6	274.0	56.1	148.5	280.5	52.9
1986	158.9	280.8	56.6	154.2	289.0	53.4
1987	164.8	286.1	57.6	159.6	297.4	53.7
1988	169.5	296.1	57.2	159.0	304.5	52.2
1989	176.7	310.0	57.0	164.1	316.4	51.9
1990	186.1	326.2	57.1	156.5	306.4	51.1
1991	195.7	340.6	57.5	165.0	320.1	51.5
1992	203.6	345.6	58.9	171.0	327.9	52.1
1993	207.5	349.4	59.4	173.8	332.9	52.2
1994	213.7	357.1	59.8	177.8	340.4	52.2
1995	217.5	361.3	60.2	180.2	345.9	52.1
1996	221.3	366.1	60.4	182.9	349.6	52.3
1997	225.3	371.8	60.6	185.0	353.8	52.3
1998	226.8	367.9	61.6	185.1	352.0	52.6
1999	230.7	367.2	62.8	180.2	349.4	51.6
2000	235.1	370.3	63.5	181.3	353.1	51.4
2001	237.1	373.5	63.5	181.1	350.4	51.7
2002	238.8	367.7	64.9	180.1	346.0	52.1
2003	239.4	368.6	64.9	180.0	346.5	51.9
2004	241.7	367.7	65.7	175.9	342.8	51.3

Notes: 1. Figures for "wages" are contractual cash earnings (scheduled cash earnings + nonscheduled cash earnings).
　　　　 2. "Ordinary workers" refers to regular workers to whom general scheduled working hours are applied.
　　　　 3. Figures for "ordinary workers" for 1980 and 1981 are for business establishments with ten regular workers or more, and figures for other years are for establishments with five regular workers or more. Figures for "all workers, incl. part-time" are for establishments with thirty regular workers or more through 1989 statistics and for establishments with five regular workers or more for statistics in and after 1990.

Sources: Based on Ministry of Health, Labor, and Welfare, *Basic Survey on Wage Structure* and *Maitsuki kinrō tōkei yōran* (Monthly statistics on employment).

wage gap, however, women still make only 65.7 percent of men's wages, highlighting the fact that this is still a serious problem in Japan.

In contrast, if we look at wages for all workers, including part-time workers, women's wages have declined slightly from 54.6 percent of men's in 1980 to 51.3 percent in 2004. Since the wage gap for full-time workers has shrunk, this slight decline is probably the result of the wage gap for part-time workers.

Looking at table 1-9, we can compare hourly wages for full-time and part-time female workers. According to the table, hourly wages for part-time female workers were 70.9 percent of those for full-time female workers in 1989, and declined overall to stand at 65.7 percent in 2004. In other words, the gap between female part-time workers and female full-time workers has widened, a trend seen for male part-time and male full-time workers, as well; part-time workers overall are at an increasing disadvantage in terms of hourly wages compared with full-time workers.

It is noteworthy, however, that the gender disparity for part-time workers has shrunk considerably, from women receiving 74.8 percent compared with men in 1989 to 89.3 percent in 2004. The gender gap is definitely closing both for part-time workers, as shown in table 1-9, and for full-time workers, as in table 1-8. This is a positive development. The problem, though, is that both male and female part-time workers are at a disadvantage in terms of wages compared with full-time workers.

Years at one company

Next, let's look at length of service—the number of years a person works at one company. Figure 1-6 depicts the difference between men and women in this regard. Looking at the most recent comparison, we find that female full-time workers are at the same company for 9 years while female part-time workers are there for 5.1 years. Male full-time workers, on the other hand, are employed at the same place for 13.4 years; compared with men, female full-time workers give 4.4 fewer years of service at a single company. This tells us that women change or quit their jobs more frequently than men do.

Table 1-9 Hourly scheduled cash earnings of ordinary workers and part-time workers by sex, and the wage gap (1989–2004)

(Yen; %)

Year	Female		Male		Wage gap			
	Ordinary workers	Part-Time workers	Ordinary workers	Part-Time workers	Female part-time/ male part-time	Female part-time/ female ordinary	Male part-time/ male ordinary	Female part-time/ male ordinary
1989	934	662	1,542	885	74.8	70.9	57.4	42.9
1990	989	712	1,632	944	75.4	72.0	57.8	43.6
1991	1,072	770	1,756	1,023	75.3	71.8	58.3	43.8
1992	1,127	809	1,812	1,053	76.8	71.8	58.1	44.6
1993	1,187	832	1,904	1,046	79.5	70.1	54.9	43.7
1994	1,201	848	1,915	1,037	81.8	70.6	54.2	44.3
1995	1,213	854	1,919	1,061	80.5	70.4	55.3	44.5
1996	1,255	870	1,976	1,071	81.2	69.3	54.2	44.0
1997	1,281	871	2,006	1,037	84.0	68.0	51.7	43.4
1998	1,295	886	2,002	1,040	85.2	68.4	51.9	44.3
1999	1,318	887	2,016	1,025	86.5	67.3	50.8	44.0
2000	1,329	889	2,005	1,026	86.6	66.9	51.2	44.3
2001	1,340	890	2,028	1,029	86.5	66.4	50.7	43.9
2002	1,372	891	2,025	991	89.9	64.9	48.9	44.0
2003	1,359	893	2,009	1,003	89.0	65.7	49.9	44.5
2004	1,376	904	1,999	1,012	89.3	65.7	50.6	45.2

Note: Figures for the hourly scheduled cash earnings for ordinary workers are calculated by dividing the monthly scheduled cash earnings by the actual number of scheduled hours worked in the month.

Source: Based on Ministry of Health, Labor, and Welfare, *Basic Survey on Wage Structure*.

Of particular importance is the fact that, while female part-time workers give 3.9 fewer years of service to a single company than female full-time workers do, their time at one company is increasing at a faster pace than that of female full-time workers. We noted earlier that the number of nonregular workers, especially women, is rapidly increasing in the labor market in Japan, and this means that the length of service of nonregular workers is increasing. More and more female part-time workers are becoming "core part-time employees," or in other words, workers who have duties and responsibilities at the workplace that are virtually the same as those of full-time employees, but who have less job security and less favorable terms of employment.

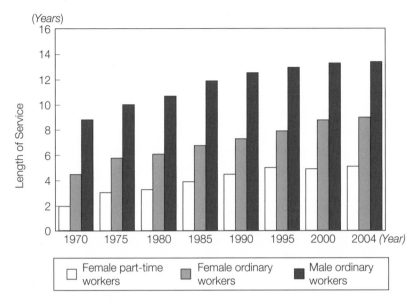

Fig. 1-6 Average length of service by sex and employment type (1970–2004)

Note: The figures for part-time workers in 1975 are for the manufacturing industry only, as data for all industries are not available.

Source: Based on Ministry of Health, Labor, and Welfare, *Basic Survey on Wage Structure*.

Career tracking

Many Japanese corporations use a two-track personnel system, with important differences between the management track (*sōgōshoku*) and the clerical track (*ippanshoku*). Management-track employees are candidates to become executives in the future. They perform key duties in the workplace and are given responsibilities where they must exercise judgment. In contrast, clerical-track employees perform support or routine work and have very limited opportunity for future promotion. In addition, management-track positions can include transfers requiring a move to a different part of the country.

Some companies also have a quasi-management track (*junsōgōshoku*) and a specialized track (*senmonshoku*). The quasi-management track is a management-track position that has some characteristics of clerical work; the key duties performed and the conditions for transfers are somewhat more limited than those of management-track jobs. On the specialized track, employees are engaged in specialized work, and they are much less likely to be considered for an executive position in the future than management-track employees.

Figure 1-7 gives the percentage of male and female new university graduates hired in fiscal 2003 and 2006 for positions in these four tracks—management, quasi-management, specialized, and clerical. Looking at the management track, we see that the percentage of companies that hired both men and women was somewhat greater than the percentage of companies that said they hired only men. It is safe to assume, though, that even if both men and women were hired in this category, the number of men hired considerably exceeded the number of women hired. The management track is still predominantly male.

On the other hand, 30 to 42 percent of companies said they hired both men and women for the clerical track, while 52 to 64 percent indicated that they hired only women for these positions—very few companies said that they hired only men for clerical-track positions. Here too, even if a company indicated that it hired both men and women, we can assume that mainly women were hired. Clerical-track, support positions are largely held by women.

The quasi-management and specialized tracks lie midway between the management and clerical tracks in terms of work content, as in terms of the percentages of men and women hired for these tracks. For this reason, our discussion will focus on the management and the clerical tracks, which lie on the two opposite ends of the spectrum in terms of male-female distribution.

Why are women hired for the majority of clerical-track positions and men for the majority of management-track positions? We can cite several reasons. First, a division of labor based on gender remains strong in the Japanese consciousness: both management and labor believe that men are focused on a career outside the home while women work in order to supplement the household budget so that support positions are most suitable for them.

Second is the nature of the modern corporation, which has a range of duties that must be performed. Some jobs are complicated

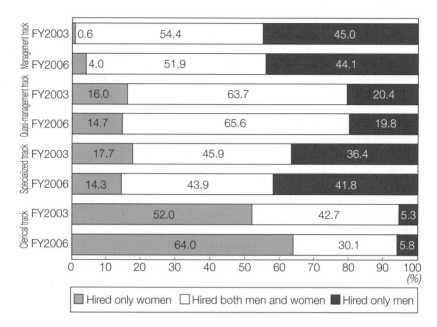

Fig. 1-7 Hiring of new university graduates by career track (FY2003 and FY2006)

Note: "Management track" are jobs in which employees engage in planning; the jobs include nationwide transfer. "Quasi-management track" are positions in which employees perform duties equivalent to planning; the positions do not involve transfers that require a change of address, but do include transfers within a limited area. "Specialized track" are jobs in which employees engage in specialized work. "Clerical track" are positions in which employees perform routine work; the positions do not include transfers that require a change of address.

Source: Based on Ministry of Health, Labor, and Welfare, *Josei koyō kanri kihon chōsa* (Basic survey of employment management of women).

and require sophisticated skills, while others can be done following comparatively simple procedures; some jobs carry considerable responsibility and some do not. Having such a variety of jobs and duties that must be carried out, corporations will be most efficient if they can assign and transfer workers as necessary, and it is the two-track system that makes possible such an efficient deployment of human resources.

A third factor is the difference in the academic courses and majors that men and women select at school, as will be considered in more detail later. Men tend to take courses that will help them in corporate settings while women do not focus so strongly on courses that will come in handy in company work. Moreover, a higher percentage of men than women attend university. These gender differences in educational attainment also contribute to the gender gap in management-track and clerical-track positions.

The method of managing human resources based on career tracking took root three to four decades ago at Japanese companies, particularly at large corporations. The problem is that women were placed in clerical-track positions while management-track positions were taken by men. At the time, this was a rational management method for corporations, but the gender disparity in personnel placement to which it gave rise is no longer appropriate in today's world of gender equality—having many women in clerical-track positions has become a sign of discrimination. Although not a deliberate policy of out-and-out discrimination, it can be interpreted as an invisible, indirect form of discrimination.

The Equal Employment Opportunity Law (EEOL) was introduced in 1985 more than two decades ago to ban discrimination against women, and has been strengthened since. It seeks to eliminate gender discrimination in such areas as recruitment, placement, promotion, and wages.

In Japan, however, laws may be strict, but the actual observance and enforcement be lax. The EEOL is no exception, and there is a need for the law to be enforced and penalties to be applied more rigorously. At the same time, sentiment in favor of ending discrimination against women is spreading in Japanese society, and, as we saw in figure 1-7, career tracking is losing its hold, albeit gradually, as times change.

In regard to the issue, I have a modest proposal: how about more men choosing the clerical track? Japanese men have become a symbol of overwork, and most of these suffering individuals are in management-track positions. Wouldn't it be a positive development if men sought out a more moderate work life and took clerical-track positions? Actually, the number of such men, although still small, is growing. We need not be concerned that there would be no one to fill the management-track positions left vacant since many women having a high level of education, sophisticated skills, and a good work ethic are now available. Needless to say, such women will need societal support for a good work-life balance, measures so that they can both work and have a home life.

I should note that what I have just proposed has the potential to exacerbate disparities among women. Until now, most women have been engaged in clerical-level work even if they were employed full-time. If we include part-time workers as well, it is clear that very few women have had management-track positions. As a result, no great gap has appeared between women who are career-oriented and those who are not. However, any increase in the number of women in management-track positions might very well result in a gap among women.

The Gender Gap and Lifestyle

Time use

Table 1-10 shows how men and women spend their time; it details time use for two-income married couples, married couples where the wife is a full-time homemaker, and working singles.* For all married couples, it is assumed that the man, or husband, is working. Obviously, in couples where both spouses are working, the woman is also employed, whereas in couples where the wife is a full-time homemaker, the woman is not engaged in paid work.

Time spent on "physiological needs" includes time spent sleeping, engaging in personal grooming, having meals, enjoying rest and relaxation, and receiving medical examinations and treatment. Time spent on work for pay or profit includes commuting time to and from work or school and time spent engaged in work or schoolwork. Time spent on housework refers to housework, provision of nursing care and childcare, etc. Leisure time refers to time spent on such activities as transportation, TV watching, newspaper reading, hobbies, and volunteer work. These definitions are as common sense would dictate.

* Note that "singles" (*mikonsha*) refers to "singles who have never married," as in the surveys cited in this book.

Table 1-10 Daily time use by two-income married couples, one-income married couples in which only the husband works, and never-married working persons (2001)

(Hours.minutes)

	Both husband and wife are working			
	Weekdays		Sundays	
	Wife	Husband	Wife	Husband
Population age 15 or over (1,000 persons)	8,246	8,259	8,476	8,505
Time spent on physiological needs	10.48	10.49	12.17	12.43
Time spent on work for pay or profit	6.14	9.44	1.29	2.19
Time spent on housework	3.54	0.16	4.45	1.08
Leisure time	3.04	3.15	5.27	7.49

	Husband is working and wife is not working			
	Weekdays		Sundays	
	Wife	Husband	Wife	Husband
Population age 15 or over (1,000 persons)	9,331	9,319	9,465	9,466
Time spent on physiological needs	11.33	11.00	12.28	12.55
Time spent on work for pay or profit	0.05	9.25	0.03	2.18
Time spent on housework	7.19	0.18	5.48	1.15
Leisure time	5.04	3.17	5.41	7.31

	Never-married working persons			
	Weekdays		Sundays	
	Female	Male	Female	Male
Population age 15 or over (1,000 persons)	8,013	10,196	8,145	10,365
Time spent on physiological needs	11.26	10.52	13.10	12.33
Time spent on work for pay or profit	8.12	9.08	2.47	2.59
Time spent on housework	0.44	0.13	1.28	0.39
Leisure time	3.37	3.46	6.35	7.49

Source: Based on Statistics Bureau, Ministry of Internal Affairs and Communications, *2001 Survey on Time Use and Leisure Activities*.

In two-income households, where both spouses are working, the greatest difference between the spouses on weekdays is the time spent on work for pay or profit: 9 hours and 44 minutes a day for the husband versus 6 hours and 14 minutes for the wife. In other words, the husband works 3 hours and 30 minutes longer than his wife. In contrast, the wife spends that amount more on housework. Although these couples are described as "two income," the husband commits himself to longer hours of paid work while the wife devotes herself to longer hours of housework. It is evident that the traditional sex roles of the husband working outside the home while the wife is responsible for housework and childrearing is still alive and well even in two-income couples.

The time spent by full-time homemakers on housework is long at about 7 hours a day on weekdays, but this is natural given the definition of full-time homemaker. What is interesting, though, is leisure time: full-time homemakers have 2 hours more leisure time a day on weekdays than their husbands. Although full-time homemakers spend much time on housework, they are also blessed with free time that they can use any way they wish. We cannot call this a "free ride," but we can say that these women have extra time.

The total time spent by two-income couples on housework on a weekday is a combined 4 hours and 10 minutes compared with 7 hours and 37 minutes for a full-time homemaker and her working husband—thus two-income couples spend only about half the time on housework as one-income couples. We can interpret this differential in two ways. First, we could suppose that two-income couples have a somewhat poorer quality of life because they are neglecting the housework. Or, we could decide that two-income couples are efficient in their housework and so complete it in a short time. Second, perhaps full-time homemakers are doing a very thorough job of the housework so that one-income couples have a higher quality of life. Or perhaps the full-time homemakers are performing the housework in a time-consuming way. The question of which interpretation applies likely depends on how a couple tackles the housework and on the personalities of the husband and wife.

When we turn to singles, we see virtually no difference between men and women in time use. For example, men work only slightly longer than women, with men spending 9 hours and 8 minutes on work for pay or profit, and women 8 hours and 12 minutes. There is also virtually no difference in their amount of leisure time. It is noteworthy that the amount of time spent on housework is short for both men and women, and that the difference between men and women is only about 30 minutes, with men devoting a mere 13 minutes a day to housework. Since they are single, no doubt the volume of housework is relatively small, and single persons also eat out and purchase ready-made food more often.

Favorite pastimes

Table 1-11 lists the top ten pastimes for men and women in Japan. We see that the Japanese spend the most time on reading, reflecting the importance placed on self-cultivation. Of course, without knowing what is being read, we cannot say for sure how edifying it actually is. The next most popular hobbies are singing karaoke and viewing films.

We also find certain marked differences according to gender. Activities significantly more popular among women than men (a difference of at least 5 percentage points) are reading, viewing films, gardening, viewing art, and cooking and baking as a hobby. In contrast, men show a preference for playing home video games, watching sports, and playing *pachinko* slot machines. As a man, I hate to say it, but it does seem that women enjoy more refined hobbies and amusements than men do.

Unpaid work

Unpaid work refers to work for which the worker gains no wages or other form of monetary compensation. An example is housework performed in one's own home. If, however, someone outside your family does your cooking, cleaning, or laundering and is paid compensation for such services, then this housework becomes paid work. In this way, there are paid and unpaid forms even of housework.

One form of unpaid work that tends to be overlooked is volunteer work and other civic participation. Until about a decade ago,

Table 1-11 Participation rate by sex and pastime (2001)

(%)

Pastime	Total	Female	Male
Reading as a hobby	46.2	56.2	43.8
Singing karaoke	45.2	52.0	47.8
Viewing films (excl. TV and videos, etc.)	37.5	50.7	36.3
Other	31.6	32.2	33.9
Gardening	31.6	36.6	23.6
Playing home video games (incl. use of portable game machines)	28.1	24.2	39.3
Watching sports (excl. sports on TV, etc.)	21.4	19.1	26.1
Playing *pachinko* slot machines	21.3	10.5	32.6
Viewing art (excl. art on TV, etc.)	21.1	27.4	16.9
Cooking and baking as a hobby	16.4	34.6	5.6

Note: "Participation rate" is the percentage of persons who engaged in the pastime during the one-year period from October 20, 2000, through October 19, 2001.

Source: Based on Statistics Bureau, Ministry of Internal Affairs and Communications, *2001 Survey on Time Use and Leisure Activities*.

such activities were listed under leisure time in Japanese government statistics. Today, however, they are listed under unpaid labor. The related statistics are not presented here, but women spend 30 to 60 minutes more on unpaid work than men do.

What, speaking in terms of economics, is the monetary value of unpaid work in Japan? In 2001, such work was estimated at 129 trillion yen, which would amount to approximately 25.5 percent of the nation's gross domestic product (GDP). Thus unpaid work has quite a high monetary value—if housework and various volunteer activities were purchased on the market, the nation's GDP would increase by more than a quarter.

In fact, housework, childcare, and nursing care are gradually starting to become for-pay services now. Although they used to be performed by full-time homemakers, mothers, and daughters-in-law, they are now more and more frequently being obtained through restaurants, daycare services, and nursing homes, or, in other words, they are increasingly being outsourced. This change can be seen as promoting the trend to think in terms of the market value of services that were unpaid work a decade ago.

Let's look further at the gender gap in regard to unpaid work. In figure 1-8, we see that in 2001 women performed about 1.89 million yen worth of unpaid work per capita annually while men performed about 430,000 yen worth. Women thus performed about 4.3 times worth of unpaid work as men. However, looking at this over time, we note that the gap has narrowed considerably as women performed about 9 times worth of unpaid work as men two decades earlier in 1981.

There are several reasons for this narrowing. First, women have decreased the amount of time they spend on unpaid work, while

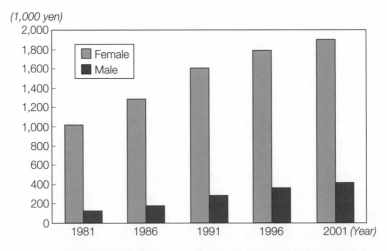

Fig. 1-8 Annual per capita monetary value of unpaid work by sex (1981–2001)

Sources: The above figure is based on the following: For 1981–96: Economic Planning Agency, *Anata no kaji no nedan wa ikura desu ka?* (How much is your housework worth?) (1997) and *Monetary Valuation of Unpaid Work in 1996* (1998). For 2001: Hamada K., "Mushō rōdō to shotoku bunpai: shūnyū kaisō betsu no mushō rōdō no kahei hyōka" (Unpaid labor and income distribution: Monetary valuation of unpaid labor by income bracket), *Kikan kakei keizai kenkyū* (Quarterly journal of the Institute for Research on Household Economics) 69 (Winter 2006): 56–69.

men have slightly increased the time they spend. Second, the gender gap in the base wage used to calculate the monetary value has narrowed slightly. That having been said, the monetary value of women's unpaid work in 1981 was slightly over 1 million yen while that of men's was around 100,000 yen. Twenty years later, women's unpaid work was worth around 1.9 million yen while men's was worth around 400,000 yen. In absolute figures, then, the increase in the monetary value of women's unpaid work has been greater than that of men's, and the gender gap has actually widened.

Household income and consumption

The question of how much money a household makes and spends is a critical issue in economics. What gaps are to be found in this regard between men and women? Since household finances take many forms we will not analyze them as a single entity here. In particular the case of two-income households is complicated, as the household income changes depending on whether the wife works full- or part-time. If we add full-time homemakers into the mix, the question becomes even more complex. These matters will be left for in-depth discussion later in this book and here we will consider only unmarried persons, a group where we can focus on the disparity between men and women. There is also value in drawing a gender comparison using this group because unmarried persons are forced to support themselves.

Tables 1-12 and 1-13 show the gender disparity in average monthly income and expenditures for unmarried persons in actual figures, as well as giving data for women as a percentage of men's for ease of comparison. Let's first look at monthly income. In the younger generation under the age of thirty, the disparity between unmarried men and women is not that large, standing at only about 40,000 yen a month. The gap expands, however, as the age group becomes higher, reaching 140,000 yen, for example, for people in their fifties. Men's wages increase with age at a higher rate than for women, due to a variety of reasons, and the gender gap thus widens. This is also true for women's income as a percentage of men's.

Table 1-12 Average monthly income of unmarried worker households by sex and age group, and the gender disparity in income (2004)

(Yen)

	Under age 30		30–39		40–49		50–59		60–69	
	Female	Male	Female	Male	Female	Male	Female	Male	Female	Male
Income	228,054	269,282	290,746	366,291	323,772	427,373	252,749	395,220	219,012	305,787
(Male = 100)	85	—	79	—	76	—	64	—	72	—
Disposable income	195,902	231,851	244,508	309,125	267,664	355,160	215,576	323,741	198,758	279,775
(Male = 100)	84	—	79	—	75	—	67	—	71	—

Source: Based on Statistics Bureau, Ministry of Internal Affairs and Communications, *National Survey of Family Income and Expenditure, 2004*.

Table 1-13 Average monthly expenditures of unmarried worker households by sex and age group, and the gender disparity in expenditures (2004)

(Yen)

	Under age 30		30–39		40–49		50–59		60–69	
	Female	Male	Female	Male	Female	Male	Female	Male	Female	Male
Expenditures	205,584	216,336	274,172	288,687	268,339	311,078	241,596	263,612	205,139	258,895
(Male = 100)	95	—	95	—	86	—	92	—	79	—
Living expenditures	173,432	178,904	227,934	231,520	212,231	238,865	204,423	192,132	184,885	232,883
(Male = 100)	97	—	98	—	89	—	106	—	79	—
Non-living expenditures	32,152	37,431	46,238	57,167	56,109	72,213	37,173	71,480	20,253	26,012
(Male = 100)	86	—	81	—	78	—	52	—	78	—

Source: Based on Statistics Bureau, Ministry of Internal Affairs and Communications, *National Survey of Family Income and Expenditure, 2004*.

Turning to living expenditures, there is virtually no gender disparity in the younger generation under age thirty, with the difference in expenditures between men and women at only 5,000 yen or so a month. Non-living expenditures, such as taxes and social insurance, also differ by about the same amount. Thus, there is not much disparity in the standard of living between young unmarried men and women. This changes as age increases, however. In the fifties age bracket, for example, women's living expenditures are higher than men's. This reflects gender differences in types of expenditure: women spend more on such things as clothes, footwear, medical care, and furniture than men do, resulting in higher living expenditures. The gender gap in non-living expenditures also increases with age, but it is men who spend more.

In the case of unmarried people, therefore, it is clear that the income gap expands with age so that the gap in standard of living widens as well. It is markedly more difficult for unmarried women to make ends meet than for their male counterparts.

Next, let's compare the income gap and lifestyle challenges of single-mother households and single-father households. Table 1-14 shows the annual income for these two types of families. While the actual number of single-mother and single-father households did not change very much from 1998 to 2003 (see table 1-15), there remains a vast difference in income between them. In 2002, the average income for single-mother households was 2.12 million yen but this figure was 3.90 million yen for single-father households, or nearly twice as much. This markedly low income of single-mother households can be attributed to the restrictions childrearing places on the working hours of single mothers on top of the lower incomes seen for women.

In table 1-15, we see that the areas single-parent households find challenging differ greatly by gender. For example, 43.7 percent of single-mother households reported having tight household budgets in fiscal 2003 versus 31.5 percent of single-father households, reflecting the income gap shown in table 1-14. Single mothers have difficulty with housing, as well. This too reflects economic ability. On the other hand, only 1.1 percent of women reported having trouble with housework, in contrast to over one-third of single fathers. This category probably includes childrearing, as well. To sum up, single-mother households face financial difficulties, whereas single-father households are hard pressed by housework and childrearing.

Table 1-14 Annual income for single-mother and single-father households (FY1997 and FY2002)

(Persons; million yen)

		Single-mother households		Single-father households	
		FY1997	FY2002	FY1997	FY2002
Average no. of household members		3.16	3.36	3.45	3.97
Average no. of working household members		1.05	0.88	1.11	0.97
Average income		2.29	2.12	4.22	3.90
Distribution	Of which, earned income	—	1.62	—	3.20
	First quartile	1.18	1.13	2.51	2.33
	Second quartile (median)	1.94	1.83	4.05	3.62
	Third quartile	2.91	2.76	5.78	5.13
Average income per household member		0.73	0.63	1.22	0.98
Average income per working person		2.18	2.42	3.80	4.02

Note: There is no FY1997 data for salaries and wages.

Source: Based on Ministry of Health, Labor, and Welfare, *Heisei 15 nendo zenkoku boshi setai tō chōsa* (National survey on single-mother and other households, FY2003).

Table 1-15 Challenges of single-mother and single-father households (FY1998 and FY2003)

(1,000 households; %)

	Fiscal year	No. of house-holds	Challenge, by percentage of households						
			Total (%)	House-hold budget	Work	Housing	Health	House-work	Other
Single-mother households	1998	711.9	100.0	37.9	22.4	18.5	12.6	1.8	6.8
	2003	975.9	100.0	43.7	22.5	17.4	10.0	1.1	5.2
Single-father households	1998	111.4	100.0	19.7	11.4	12.6	15.6	34.1	6.6
	2003	121.3	100.0	31.5	14.2	5.5	8.7	34.6	5.5

Source: Based on Ministry of Health, Labor, and Welfare, *Heisei 15 nendo zenkoku boshi setai tō chōsa* (National survey on single-mother and other households, FY2003).

The Gender Gap and Education

Turning now to education, what differences are there between men and women as to the highest educational level reached? Figure 1-9 traces these trends over the past half century.

First, we observe that about the same percentages of boys and girls go on to high school after compulsory education; in other words, the figures for boys and girls have risen in parallel. Moreover, until around 1975 (the end of the period of high economic growth in Japan), the percentage of children going on to high school

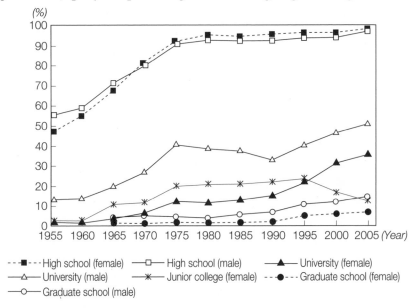

Fig. 1-9 Education continuance rate by sex and type of school (1955–2005)

Source: Based on Ministry of Education, Culture, Sports, Science, and Technology, *Gakkō kihon chōsa* (Basic survey on schools).

rose dramatically and, after passing the 90 percent mark, has continued to register slight growth. Today essentially all children—98 percent—continue on to high school.

Second, looking at four-year colleges and universities, we see that around 13 to 15 percent of men and 2 to 3 percent of women went to university in 1955. A university education was thus something that only a fraction of men and virtually no women received; it was a symbol of being a member of the elite in those days.

From around 1965, however, the percentage of men attending university started to increase dramatically, reaching 40 percent around 1975. The percentage of women going on to higher education also rose considerably—although not as rapidly as for men—to pass the 10 percent mark around 1975. The key reason for this sudden jump in university attendance for both males and females was the substantial rise in household income during the period of Japan's economic miracle. Of course, natural aptitude, academic ability, and personal effort are important, but household finances are also crucial for a child's college education: it becomes easier for children to attend university as households become more affluent. These statistics hint of the many young people who had to abandon their hopes of continuing education because of their families' straitened financial circumstances before the period of high economic growth.

We should note here that the percentage of men attending four-year colleges or universities dropped slightly after 1975, falling to about 33 percent around 1990, while that for women during the period showed no downward trend, but rather stayed at about the same level. In fact, between 1985 and 1990, the percentage of women continuing on to university increased somewhat. These respective changes reflect the fact that women who had the ability and desire to attend university had become able to do so, thanks to the solid financial situation of their parents.

The 1990s saw a second increase in Japanese going on to university that continued for a decade and a half. In 2005, about 50 percent of men and 37 percent of women went to university. Nowadays, university attendance is limited less and less by home finances so that children can advance to university almost regardless of their aptitude and desire for higher education. This is also revealed in the poor academic ability among university students today.

A third trend is the rise and then fall in the number of women attending junior college. In Japan virtually no men attend junior college, so that these schools can be considered a special institution of higher education for women. Often these institutions are attended by women who may want to attend a four-year university, but have compromised on their dreams and settled for junior college. Perhaps the woman's parents have financial limitations. Or maybe she is not very career-oriented and does not have any particular drive to attend a four-year school. If she is interested in specializing in subjects popular among women, such as home economics and early childhood education, then attending a junior college might be the best option.

In the 1970s the percentage of women advancing to junior college jumped dramatically and then increased more slowly after that. Since 1995, however, it has dropped as women who used to attend junior colleges have shifted to four-year schools. In 2005, altogether more than 50 percent of women advanced to either a junior college or a four-year school. In other words, the percentage of women advancing to higher education, including both junior colleges and four-year schools, is higher than that for men. We should not conclude, though, that women have a greater drive for higher education than men. After all, the percentage of men going on to four-year colleges or universities is still quite high.

Fourth, we can note that the percentage of Japanese going on to graduate school has seen a steady increase over the past two decades, with about 15 percent of men and 8 percent of women going on to graduate school in 2005. At play here is the high rate of advancement to master's programs in science and technology, and the recent popularity of specialized programs such as business schools and law schools. Comparing men and women, the rate of women advancing to graduate school is still about half that of men, meaning that women are in quite the minority.

To summarize, we see that almost all Japanese attend high school, with no disparity between the sexes. Today there is also no gender gap in university attendance although, as we have seen, a considerable percentage of women go to junior college, rather than a four-year school, and the proportion of women continuing on to graduate school is markedly lower than that of men. In terms of higher education, therefore, we have now entered an age where there is little difference between men and women in terms of quantity, but unfortunately the same cannot be said of the quality of education received.

Chapter Two

Women and Social Class

I n our study of the new inequality among women in Japan, the first issue I want to look at is women's social class, or women's status. Specific variables associated with inequality include income, assets, standard of living, education, occupation, employment status, marriage, and children; but class—or a household's overall livelihood and social standing—can be considered as encompassing all of these. Therefore, before examining inequality among women in relation to each of those individual variables, we will analyze class or status in relation to women to gain an overview.

Let's take a moment to look at the difference between the two terms "class" and "status" (referred to as "stratum" [pl. "strata"] in academic circles). One way of distinguishing the two terms is to look at the difference between Marxist theory, which uses the term "class," and non-Marxist thought, which prefers the term "status." Marxist theory sees these figuratively, vis-à-vis relations between ruler and ruled or exploiter and exploited, as in such terms as "capitalist class" and "working class." In contrast, non-Marxist theory does not focus on class conflict, but looks at differences between groups that share common characteristics. Even with their preferred term of "status," though, non-Marxist scholars recognize that there are privileged (high status) groups and underprivileged (low status) groups so the non-Marxist concept of status does not ignore antagonism or tensions between the different status groups. As you might expect, the concept of status also involves measuring how much more privileged those of high status are than those of low status, and considering policies to narrow the gap between the two. That having been said, I have used "class" and "status" essentially interchangeably in this book.

The issue of women and social class/status presents us with a very complex problem: should we derive a woman's class/status based on the woman herself or based on the household of which the woman is a part? If we focus on the woman herself, no particular problem in assigning class arises if she is unmarried. If we focus on the household, the woman might have a husband, and she herself may or may not be engaged in paid employment. The question then arises of on whom the household's status should be based: should we focus on the husband or the wife or both? Rather complex issues arise, therefore, when we focus on the household in assigning class. In this chapter, we will first wrestle with this issue: how should a woman's social class be determined?

Once we have considered that issue, we will look at the impact the social class of parents has on that of a daughter. We also will look at the social class that a daughter joins when she marries and creates a household of her own. Of course, the question of what social class men join when they marry is also intriguing, but it cannot be denied that marriage has a much greater impact on the social class of women. As captured in the Japanese phrase tama no koshi ("she married into money" [literally, "bejeweled palanquin"]), a woman's social class can change depending on the man she marries. This is particularly true in cases where the wife does not work. Recently there have been cases where men, too, change their status through marriage, as we can see in the new Japanese phrase gyaku tama no koshi ("he married into money" [literally, "reverse bejeweled palanquin"]).

Determining a Woman's Social Class

In cases where the husband is the sole breadwinner and the wife is a full-time homemaker, the analysis of the wife's social class is not particularly difficult. It would be quite natural to derive the status of the household based solely upon the husband's education, occupation, and income. The margin of error would also be minimal. Even in this kind of household, though, we should not ignore the wife's level of education.

Today, however, many wives are employed outside the home. This presents rather complex issues: How should we derive the social class of the wife herself in this case? How should we handle the relationship between her social class and that of her husband? We must also take into consideration the point made by feminist theorists that no analysis of a woman's social class should ignore the woman herself.

This matter is also related to the question of whether social class should be derived based on the individual or on the household, or, in other words, whether individuals (men and women) or households (couples) should be regarded as the smallest unit of society. If individuals are the base unit, individualism is emphasized, whereas the priority shifts to families or couples if households are considered the smallest social unit. Opinion remains divided about which approach is best, but we must resolve this question because, in reality, some wives are gainfully employed and some are not, depending on the couple. Let's look at the ways sociologists have tackled this issue.

Past approaches

Japanese sociologists have used various methods to determine women's social class. Let me give a brief overview.

First, there is the approach developed by Naoi (1990), which features the following three models:

1. Borrowed status model: This model derives social class based on the education level, occupation, and income of the

husband and on the assets the couple shares. Basically, the
wife's class is derived from the husband.

2. Independent status model: This model derives social class
   based on the education level, occupation, and income of the
   wife and on the assets the couple shares.
3. Shared status model: This model derives social class based on
   the average education level, occupation, and income of both the
   husband and the wife and on the assets the couple shares.

With the borrowed status model, the husband represents the
household. Even if one wants to focus on the social class of the woman
herself, this approach derives her class completely from her husband's
status. Feminist thinking disapproves of this model. There may be
little ground for criticism of this model if the wife does not work, but
there are problems in cases where the wife works, and particularly in
cases where the wife's social status is higher than the husband's.

The independent status model works well in the case of
unmarried women. This model takes into consideration only the
woman in the case of couples, however, so male chauvinistic thinking would likely criticize it. Our interest is in women's social class,
though, so using the wife's status is logical. However, the model cannot be applied to the case of full-time homemakers.

The third, shared status model uses the average of the couple
to represent the household's social class, so this approach should
draw little criticism. This model is particularly effective in the case
of two-income couples, but raises the question of whether the wife's
occupation and income should be rendered as zero in the case of full-
time homemakers. In response to this problem, Akagawa (2000)
introduces a model that gives an occupational prestige score to full-
time homemaking.

Building on Naoi's three models, Akagawa adds the following:

4. Dominant status model: This model compares the education level, occupation, and income of the husband and the
   wife and assigns social class based on the spouse ranking
   higher in these variables. Since, in this model, the spouse
   with the higher employment status rather than simply the

husband represents the household, it does not give priority to the male.

Akagawa then attempts to explain the class identification of married women using these four models. (He limits his discussion to married women because including divorced and other unmarried women in the sample complicates the matter, as explained above.) Positing five social classes—upper, upper-middle, lower-middle, upper-lower, and lower-lower—Akagawa looks at variables for married women's self-reported social class, as listed in table 2-1. He conducts a regression analysis for each of the four models to determine which one best explains women's self-reported class identification.

Of the four models, the independent status model was the least effective in explaining married women's self-reported class identification; in Japan today the wife's status cannot be used to explain her class identification. This matches what our intuition would tell us. The other three models were about equal in explanatory power. In all four models, income was the variable that exerted the greatest influence on class identification. We can conclude from this that income determines social class in Japan.

Table 2-1 Models to explain married women's class identification

1. Borrowed Status Model
    Variables: Husband's education level, income, and occupational prestige
2. Independent Status Model
    Variables: Wife's education level, income, and occupational prestige
3. Shared Status Model
    Variables: Average education level (average of the number of years of education of the husband and the wife), couple's income, and average occupational prestige (average of the occupational prestige scores of the husband and the wife)
4. Dominant Status Model
    Variables: Wife's or husband's education level, income, and occupational prestige, whichever spouse's are higher

Note: In all four models, the occupational prestige score for full-time homemaking (43.1) was used in the case of nonworking wives.

Source: Akagawa (2000, 51).

Up to this point, the sample has been composed of all types of married women, including full-time homemakers and full-time and part-time working women. If we limit the sample to married women who have full-time work and therefore a comparatively high income, however, the dominant status model is the most effective in explaining the class identification results, followed by the borrowed status model, the shared status model, and the independent status model, in that order. Although this sample is composed of married women who enjoy a higher income than other women (e.g., full-time homemakers and part-time workers) and are no doubt quite independent minded, the independent status model was surprisingly ineffective in explaining the results.

In other words, although feminist critics want a woman's social class derived based on the woman herself, the independent status model (the model that looks at the woman's own level of education, occupation, and income) in fact is very poor at explaining class identification even when the sample is limited to married women with full-time work. In Japan very few married women are highly educated and career-oriented; most married women with full-time work are unfortunately only supplementing their husband's income. The husband's status is thus more important than the wife's in explaining class identification. This can be said even more categorically if the sample is composed of married women who do part-time work or are full-time homemakers: in Japan it is still the husband—the male—who determines a household's social class.

Who is dominant: the husband or the wife?

Shirahase (2005) adopts a different nomenclature from Akagawa in looking at the social class of women. In her terms, the borrowed status model becomes the traditional approach; the independent status model, the individual approach; and the dominant status model, the dominance approach. She eliminates the shared status model. In addition, she divides the traditional approach into (1) female-dominant families, (2) homogamous families, and (3) male-dominant families.

The traditional approach is founded on the idea that class should be based on the family, rather than on one individual, the husband or the wife. It is called "traditional" because, in the days when most wives were full-time homemakers, the husband was the head of the household in the vast majority of cases and it was assumed as a matter of course that his status determined the family's social class. As I have already mentioned, feminists have voiced strong criticism of this approach.

In Shirahase's division of the traditional approach into subcategories, she fails to clearly distinguish female- and male-dominant families from cases of female or male dominance under the dominance approach. Her argument is, therefore, not very persuasive. In the traditional approach, the husband is automatically assumed to be the head of the household in most cases, while in the dominance approach the householder is determined based on the spouse that has greater influence on the social class of the family. (This corresponds to the dominant status model in Akagawa's study.) Since it is not clear what the characteristics are of a female-dominant family under Shirahase's traditional approach, it is ambiguous what the difference is between the female-dominant family under the traditional approach and the case where the female is dominant under the dominance approach.

What is interesting about Shirahase's work, however, is the percentage of families in the three categories she creates within the traditional approach. Under these, a family is determined to be female-dominant, homogamous, or male-dominant based on three variables: (1) working or not working, (2) working full-time or part-time, and (3) differences in social status. In table 2-2, we can see Shirahase's distribution of family types in Japan for all married households and for two-income households. It tells us that male-dominant families are in the vast majority, although significantly less so for households where the wife also works. Second, the percentages of female-dominant and homogamous families are not so different for married households in total and for two-income households alone.

Next, let's compare the situation in Japan with that in Europe as summarized in table 2-3. (Due to the lack of data for work hours in Europe, the variable of full-time or part-time employment has

Table 2-2 Distribution of family types in Japan

(%)

	All married	Two-income
Female-dominant	7.8	13.0
Homogamous	7.2	12.8
Male-dominant	85.1	74.2
Total	100.0	100.0
n (sample size)	2,290	1,221

Source: Shirahase (2000, 145, table 7-2).

Table 2-3 Distribution of family types in Japan and Europe

(%)

	Family type	Employment status only	Incl. work hours
Japan (*n* = 1,076)	Female-dominant Homogamous Male-dominant	11.1 9.8 79.2	6.2 7.3 86.5
Britain (*n* = 1,058)	Female-dominant Homogamous Male-dominant	18.7 11.7 69.6	6.2 7.3 86.5
France (*n* = 16,246)	Female-dominant Homogamous Male-dominant	22.4 17.6 60.0	
West Germany (*n* = 4,600)	Female-dominant Homogamous Male-dominant	11.1 7.6 81.3	
Hungary (*n* = 11,726)	Female-dominant Homogamous Male-dominant	32.9 24.3 42.8	
Sweden (*n* = 1,676)	Female-dominant Homogamous Male-dominant	19.2 20.9 59.9	

Note: To ensure maximum comparability between the data from Europe's Comparative Analysis of Social Mobility in Industrial Nations (CASMIN) and the Japanese data, the table employs figures from the *1985 shakai kaisō to shakai idō zenkoku chōsa* (*SSM chōsa*) (1985 National survey of social stratification and social mobility [SSM survey]). British figures are from the *1983 British General Election Survey*, not CASMIN.

Source: Shirahase (2000, 146, table 7-3).

not been applied.) We see that West Germany has a low percentage of female-dominant households at 11.1 percent, the same as in Japan, followed by Britain at 18.7 percent, Sweden at 19.2 percent, and France at 22.4 percent. Hungary comes in rather high at 32.9 percent, but this figure reflects a unique characteristic of that socialist country at the time of the survey: Hungarian women were self-employed farmers whereas men were employees of large-scale, state-run farms.

Summarizing what we have learned so far, female-dominant families only make up around a tenth of families in Japan. Although European countries do have a higher percentage of female-dominant families than Japan, male-dominant families are still in the majority. In addition, homogamous families constitute about 20 percent of families in France and Sweden, a rather high percentage. In the world's industrialized countries, therefore, even today most families are male-dominant and female-dominant families still are in the minority, trends that are more pronounced in Japan.

A final question to consider is exactly what factors women (i.e., wives) use to decide their social class. Shirahase (2005) has made some interesting findings in this regard, as shown in tables 2-4 and 2-5. In table 2-4, we can see the level of importance wives place on eleven different factors in identifying their own social class while table 2-5 divides these by family type: male-dominant, homogamous, or female-dominant.

We observe in table 2-4 that the most important factor by far is general affluence, which is cited by more than 40 percent of wives. The next most important factor is the husband's income, with figures ranging from 23 to 30 percent. In third place are the household's assets at about 10 percent. Surprisingly, the wife's own income was ranked low, at less than 10 percent, reflecting the fact that a wife's income is generally lower than her husband's. The remaining factors, including the wife's and husband's occupation and education level, carry very little weight in wives' assessment of their own social class.

Table 2-4 Factors in the class identification of wives

(%)

	All married	Nonworking	Working
Own income	7.1	3.4	5.5
Husband's income	23.0	30.3	23.7
Own education level	3.9	3.2	4.4
Husband's education level	0.4	0.7	0.3
Own occupation	4.4	1.6	4.7
Own social contribution activities	2.2	1.8	1.8
Husband's occupation	4.2	4.8	4.9
Own family background	1.6	1.1	0.8
Husband's family background	1.0	2.1	0.5
Assets	9.8	10.6	10.1
General affluence	42.5	40.6	43.2

Note: Based on *1985 SSM chōsa* (1985 SSM survey).
Source: Shirahase (2005, 44, table 2-5).

Table 2-5 Factors in the class identification of wives by family type

(%)

	Male-dominant	Homogamous	Female-dominant
Own income	3.6	5.4	10.9
Husband's income	27.2	21.5	20.0
Own education level	4.0	1.1	6.4
Husband's education level	0.5	0.0	0.9
Own occupation	3.0	8.6	0.9
Own social contribution activities	1.9	3.2	0.9
Husband's occupation	5.0	6.5	2.7
Own family background	1.1	1.1	0.0
Husband's family background	1.4	0.0	0.9
Assets	10.1	11.8	10.0
General affluence	42.1	40.9	46.4

Note: Based on *1985 SSM chōsa* (1985 SSM survey).
Source: Shirahase (2005, 44, table 2-6).

Although the wife's and husband's occupation and education level thus appear to be very minor factors, it would be a mistake to take that at face value. After all, if the husband has an advanced education and a good occupation, this almost certainly will have a positive impact on his income and the household's general affluence. We should regard education and occupation as important background factors.

Turning to table 2-5, we see that its findings are similar to those presented in table 2-4, namely, that general affluence and the husband's income are the key factors. It is clear that great importance is placed on a household's financial situation in Japan. We should note, however, that wives in male-dominant families placed only slightly more importance on the husband's income (27.2 percent) than wives in female-dominant families (20.0 percent) did.

Based on these two tables, we can safely conclude that finances (general affluence and husband's income) are the major factor for women in identifying their social class. From a woman's perspective, class in Japanese society is determined by financial position. It would be foolhardy, however, to ignore the indirect influence of education.

An interesting question here is whether men use different factors in class identification than their wives. Akagawa (2000) has made an excellent analysis of this. According to his findings, husbands also view finances—including general affluence, lifestyle satisfaction, and income—as the major factor, so there is little difference between husbands and wives in this regard. Since both husbands and wives place the priority on finances in determining their social class, we can conclude that class in Japanese society overall is decided by a household's financial situation.

The Impact of Class Background on a Woman's Life

Son or daughter?

A key interest in sociology is how the social class of parents affects the education, occupation, income, and overall social class of their children. Do the vast majority of children from upper-class families stay in the upper class? Are the chances low that a lower-class child can break out of the lower class? Social class is measured using such discrete variables as education, occupation, and income, and it is generally considered a composite of them. In other words, social class is a collective term defined by these variables. Sometimes, however, an individual variable of education, occupation, or income is used to represent social class.

By focusing on an individual variable, we can ask: If the parents have a high level of education, will the children also? What is the relationship between the occupations of parents and children? Between their incomes? In the analyses to date of parent-child social class, the principal focus has been on the relationship between father and son; the main concern has been to examine how a father's education, occupation, income, and class influence those of his son.

There are various reasons why such questions of social mobility have traditionally been discussed in terms of father and son. The father's education, occupation, and income were an obvious area of interest because fathers were the chief wage earners. Similarly, sons were of interest because they also were the wage earners. Even though there were of course many cases where the mother worked, her income was generally lower than her husband's so it was quite natural to derive the family's class based on the husband. In the children's generation as well, the husband continued to be the breadwinner of the family even if the wife also worked, as she generally worked part-time for lower wages.

The times have changed, however; women are better educated now, and more of them are working than in the past. As a result, interest is growing in the situation of daughters, with sociologists increasingly looking at how the social class of the parents affects a woman's education, occupation, income, and social class. Such questions are particularly relevant for our examination in this book of the differentials among women.

The education of daughters

First, let's look at the impact of parental social class on the educational attainment of daughters. Factors in advanced education include natural ability and personal effort as well as the family's financial means, but, as already mentioned, before the period of rapid economic growth, parental financial status was the deciding factor in Japan. Only the sons of middle-class and upper-class families were able to go on to higher education. It is important to note that it was only the son, the male, who received such education with women's education lagging quite far behind.

Thanks to Japan's economic miracle, however, families became more affluent, and it became possible for daughters also to go on to higher education. In figure 2-1, we can see the impact of the father's occupation on a daughter's attending high school by birth cohort (the group of people born during a particular period). In 2008, the cohort born between 1936 and 1945 was aged 63–72, the one born between 1946 and 1960 was 48–62, and the one born between 1961 and 1974 was 34–47. In this case, the family's social class is represented by the father's occupation. We observe here a dramatic rise in high school attendance by girls raised in families of a lower social class, including agricultural, self-employed blue-collar, employed blue-collar, and self-employed white-collar families. The percentage of females raised in families of a higher social class (employed

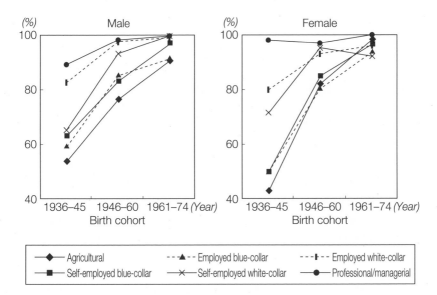

Fig. 2-1 Percentage of children continuing on to high school by father's occupational class

Note: Based on *SSM chōsa* (SSM survey) data for each year.
Source: Ojima and Kondō (2000, 33, fig. 2-2).

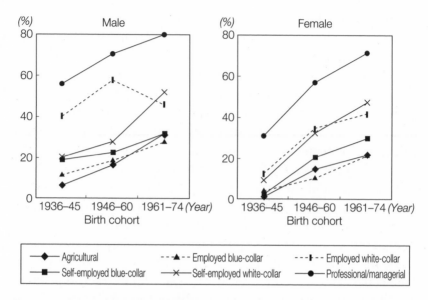

Fig. 2-2 Percentage of children continuing on to higher education by father's occupation

Note: Based on *SSM chōsa* (SSM survey) data for each year.
Source: Ojima and Kondō (2000, 35, fig. 2-4).

white-collar and professional/managerial families) who went on to high school was already high even in the oldest cohort.

Figure 2-2 shows the same issue in relation to university education (including junior college). In the oldest cohort, the percentage of girls from the lower social class families who went on to university was very small at less than 20 percent. This was also true for daughters of employed white-collar workers. Only girls raised in professional/managerial families had a fairly high rate of university attendance at somewhat under 40 percent. What is noteworthy here is that the percentage of females going on to higher education increases across all class categories as age decreases. We can see from this that an improved financial situation made it possible for parents to send their daughters on for higher education.

More importantly, we see that parental class has a major impact on the percentage of women who advance to higher education even in the youngest cohort born from 1961 to 1974. For example, only a little over 20 percent of girls raised in agricultural and employed blue-collar families go on for higher education, whereas the figure is over 70 percent for those raised in professional/managerial families. That is a huge disparity. Whether or not a girl can go on to higher education depends greatly upon what social class she has been born into. If her parents are of a lower social class, it will be hard for a girl to receive a higher education even if she has a strong desire to do so. Although we of course cannot discount the girl's own abilities and efforts, it is evident that family income and social class are a stronger constraint on the education of daughters than of sons.

Figure 2-3 expresses this a little more clearly. It shows how differentials in a family's circumstances (i.e., standard of living) influence the rate of university attendance for women; family circumstances are represented by a relative ranking of standard of liv-

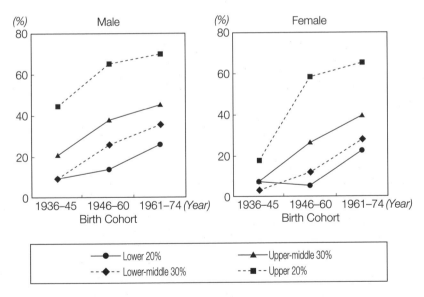

Fig. 2-3 Percentage of children continuing on to higher education by family financial circumstances

Note: Based on *SSM chōsa* (SSM survey) data for each year.
Source: Ojima and Kondō (2000, 36, fig. 2-5).

ing, with 20 percent of families at the upper range, 30 percent at the upper-middle, 30 percent at the lower-middle, and 20 percent at the lower. What is clear from this figure is that daughters from families with the highest standard of living also have the highest rate of advancement to university and that the percentage going on to higher education steadily falls as the family's circumstances decline to the upper-middle, the lower-middle, and the lower range. We can also observe that daughters of families in the upper 20 percent boast quite a high rate of higher education, showing again the impact of the family's financial situation on whether or not a daughter can attend university. In fact, only the daughters of families with a standard of living in the upper 20 percent have a university entrance rate of over 50 percent.

Today in the early years of the twenty-first century, it seems that this gap may be shrinking slightly if we look at the young generation who are in their twenties: parental finances have improved and, even more importantly, girls have a stronger desire to continue their education. However, we must also note a countervailing force, that is, the significant tightening of household finances in the post-bubble downturn that has plagued Japan since the 1990s. This is expected to limit the number of girls who go on to university, although we must wait a little longer for data to know the exact influence of such competing factors.

To summarize, the level of education that women attain—particularly the question of higher education—is greatly influenced by social class, as seen in the major impact exerted by the father's occupation, the family's overall finances, and the like. Moreover, social class has a greater impact on the education of girls than on that of boys. Thinking of the future, parents have a much stronger resolve to send their sons to university—even if it means some hardship—than in the case of their daughters.

We should also keep in mind that junior colleges, rather than four-year universities, have long been the mainstream in women's higher education, as was discussed in chapter 1. In other words, in tight times, women have often had to make do with junior college, giving up dreams of going to a four-year university. Although this is not as true as it was a generation ago, parental finances still have a slightly stronger influence on higher education for girls than for boys.

Occupation and social class of daughters

Having looked at parental social class and education, let's turn to the impact of family background on women's occupational choice and social class. To what degree does the father's occupation affect that of a daughter? I would like to refer here to the excellent work on this issue by Hashimoto (2001 and 2003). As a Marxist, Hashimoto defines occupation in terms of class and focuses on class society, including intergenerational class mobility.

Hashimoto looks at the mobility of parent and child in four social classes that he defines somewhat differently from the usual occupational categories, such as professional/managerial employees, white-collar employees, and agricultural workers:

1. Capitalist class: Employers, managers, the self-employed, and family workers at corporations or organizations with five or more employees.
2. New middle class: Male clerical employees and male and female professional/managerial employees.
3. Working class: Female clerical employees and male and female employees other than professional/managerial employees.
4. Old middle class: Employers, managers, the self-employed, and family workers at corporations or organizations with fewer than five employees.

Let's look at some of the strengths and weaknesses of these occupation-based class categories. First, we note the strong Marxist flavor in Hashimoto's usage of such terms as "capitalist class" and "working class." Second, as Hashimoto himself admits, the categories are almost too broad because of their focus on workers, and the "old middle class" is a rather vague classification as it includes self-employed workers and agricultural workers. Third, in his scheme, employees of corporations with five or more employees would belong to the new middle class when they are young, but then some of them would become employers or managers of those same corporations as they moved up the company ranks with age. It is ambiguous how we should handle people who belong to the new middle class in their younger years, but to the capitalist class in their older years.

Keeping in mind the imprecise nature of the categories, let's look at the relationship between the social class of fathers and daughters in table 2-6, which shows class mobility based on the father's social class (represented by main occupation) and the daughter's social class (represented by current occupation). The figures that lie on the diagonal from the top left corner of the table to the bottom right corner are cases where the father and daughter are in the same class. The table shows us, then, that 23.6 percent, or less than one-fourth, of fathers and daughters are both in the capitalist class. This is a low figure. The percentage of fathers and daughters who are both in the new middle class is 19.0 percent, which is even lower. Thus we can conclude that it is hard for daughters of the two upper classes to remain in their father's social class. Similarly, we note that the percentage of women moving up from the lower categories to the higher ones is very low, in the range of 5 to 10 percent. In other words, the upward mobility rate is very low.

In contrast, a very high percentage, 70.2 percent, of daughters of working-class fathers are still in that class, indicating that there is little changing of classes among the working class, a highly significant finding. A much lower figure, 31.6 percent, is seen for the

Table 2-6 Intergenerational class mobility of women (1995)

(Cases)

Father's class (main occupation)	Daughter's class (current occupation)				
	Capitalist class	New middle class	Working class	Old middle class	Total
Capitalist class	30 (23.6)	8 (6.3)	61 (48.0)	28 (22.0)	127 (100.0)
New middle class	17 (5.6)	58 (19.0)	186 (60.8)	45 (14.7)	306 (100.0)
Working class	18 (5.1)	36 (10.1)	250 (70.2)	52 (14.6)	356 (100.0)
Old middle class	38 (5.4)	60 (8.5)	386 (54.5)	224 (31.6)	708 (100.0)
Total	103 (6.9)	162 (10.8)	883 (59.0)	349 (23.3)	1,497 (100.0)

Notes: 1. Figures in parentheses are percentages.
2. Based on *1995 SSM chōsa* (1995 SSM survey) data.
Source: Hashimoto (2001, 183, table 6-1).

old middle class, but 54.5 percent of women born in the old middle class have moved to the working class. Thus, we see that the mobility rate is quite high within the two lower classes.

How does this compare with the data for fathers and sons? Although I have not included a table for men, 38.6 percent of sons born in the capitalist class have stayed in that class, and the figure for the new middle class is 52.8 percent—percentages much higher than those for women. And, as already noted, the percentage of women who end up in the working class is high. Overall, therefore, women's class mobility is somewhat higher than that of men. In other words, more daughters than sons move to a class different from that of their fathers. Taken in the positive sense, this can be interpreted to mean that daughters can freely move to a different social class from that of their family of origin. Taken in the negative sense, it implies that daughters are forced out to a different class because the oldest son inherits the father's status and daughters are cut off from the intergenerational inheritance. In families with no sons, on the other hand, the daughter's class does not seem to be defined by the parents' class. It is not clear which interpretation is correct, but it likely depends on how one views society.

Looking more closely at the social status of women, we find that only 6.9 percent of women are in the capitalist class, signifying that a very small percentage is in the upper class, while the figure for men is rather high at 10.6 percent. Since the total percentage of women in either the new or old middle class is 34.1 percent, we can say that one in three women are in the middle class. What is surprising is the high percentage—59.0 percent—of women in the working class, meaning that the vast majority of women are in the lower class; the corresponding figure for men is 37.2 percent. This comparison makes it evident how extraordinarily high the figure for women is.

Why do so many women have low status? First of all, full-time homemakers are not included in this analysis. If they were incorporated and assigned the status of their husbands, the percentage of women in the working class would not be as high. Second, as has already been mentioned, daughters rarely inherit their father's occupation due to competition with male siblings and so end up in a lower class. And a third reason why a high percentage of women in Japan end up in a lower class is because of their lower educational attainment and their overall attitude toward work, which is quite different from that of men.

Women's Social Class

Looking at the social class of present-day Japanese women from various angles, we have seen that there are many different criteria and methods for defining and evaluating class. Because there are various approaches, it is not easy to reach a conclusion about class. Should social class be derived from occupation, in line with the Marxist theory of class, or from living conditions and lifestyle? Rather than trying to synthesize the results of various methods, we will simply look at the question using a few different criteria.

In table 2-7, we can see social class in terms of employment. First, what is the distribution of occupations among Japanese women overall? A very low 5.8 percent of women do professional/managerial work. Thus, very few women belong to the upper class.

Table 2-7 Employment status of women by education level (age 35–54)

	Professional/managerial	Regular employed white-collar	Regular employed blue-collar	Self-employed white-collar	Self-employed blue-collar	Part-time employed white-collar	Part-time employed blue-collar	Non-working	n	%
University	16.5	11.0	0.0	24.8	0.9	13.8	0.0	36.7	109	8.0
Junior college	12.0	14.2	1.1	15.8	3.3	14.2	4.4	35.0	183	13.4
High school	4.0	14.8	5.7	14.5	5.6	15.3	12.6	27.6	826	60.4
Junior high school	2.4	7.2	13.6	7.2	13.2	11.2	23.6	25.6	250	18.3
Total (%)	5.8	13.0	6.1	13.9	6.3	13.5	12.5	28.9	1,368	100.0

Note: Includes spouseless women.

Source: Based on *1995 SSM chōsa* (1995 SSM survey) data.

If we add to that regular employed white-collar (13.0 percent) and self-employed white-collar (13.9 percent) women, the figure rises to 32.7 percent. However, since most regular employed white-collar and self-employed white-collar workers are considered to be part of the middle class, it is safe to say that no more than 10 percent of all women are in the upper class.

Blue-collar and part-time employed white-collar women make up the remaining 38.4 percent, and these can be considered to belong to the middle or lower class. In other words, if we divide working Japanese women into social classes based on the occupational categories just considered, we find a handful of women in the upper class and many in the middle and lower class. At issue in this analysis by occupation is the impact of full-time homemakers, who are categorized under the 28.9 percent of nonworking women. Almost all full-time homemakers derive their class from their husband, so we cannot determine here the social class of a nonworking woman. Thus, it would be more accurate to say that we are looking here only at the social class of women who are gainfully employed.

Table 2-7 also shows employment in terms of educational attainment. The higher the educational level, the higher the percentage of women in professional/managerial jobs. On the other hand, the lower the educational level, the higher the percentage of blue-collar workers. Turning to white-collar (mainly clerical) workers, a category that lies between the first two, we see that junior college and high school graduates make up a higher percentage than do university or junior high school graduates.

Let's look now at the unique classifications created by Miura (2005), a marketing analyst who has conducted studies of work and class. His research is based on a self-assessment questionnaire survey in which he asked women to identify the class (upper, middle, or lower) to which they thought they belonged. Thus, it looks at class in a somewhat different way from the objective class categories used so far in this book. In Miura's survey, on average about 10 to 15 percent of women identified themselves as upper class, a rather low figure. In fact, the percentage of women who identified themselves as being in the lower class was higher overall than the percentage who chose the middle class. According to Miura, who created the term "underclass society" (*karyū shakai*), the majority of Japanese women identify themselves as lower class, a finding that does not differ greatly from those of Hara and Seiyama (1999) and Hashimoto (2001).

Applying his background as a marketing analyst, Miura has created catchy names for class categories mainly for young women, as shown in figure 2-4. Since Miura does not indicate the exact percentage of women in each of these five categories, we will not discuss here into which categories the majority of Japanese women fit.

1. *Oyome-kei* (homemaker group): These women aspire to be full-time homemakers and to marry a man who seems likely to join the upper class. They are daughters of middle- and upper-class families. Many of them have graduated from a junior college or four-year university.

2. *Mirionēze-kei* ("career woman" group): These women have graduated from four-year universities and are very career-oriented. Their husbands also have high incomes.

3. *Kamayatsu-onna-kei* ("artistic career" group): These women learned a trade at junior college or vocational school, and they work in that profession (e.g., hairdressing, patisserie, fashion design). They are not concerned with upward mobility and are indifferent about marriage, as well.

4. *Gyaru-kei* (mobile, "young married" group): Many of these women have graduated from high school or vocational school or have dropped out of high school. Many of them work in the service industry, sales, social welfare, or early childhood education. They are very marriage-oriented.

5. *OL-kei* ("office lady" group): These are women other than those in the above four categories. Their educational backgrounds, occupations, and views on marriage vary. Miura estimates that the vast majority of women fall under the *OL-kei* category, which I think is probably correct.

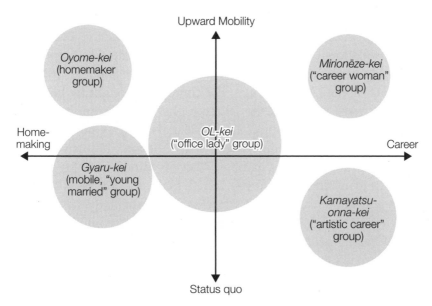

Fig. 2-4 Miura's categories of women

Notes: 1. Coined by Miura, the term *Kamayatsu-onna* refers to young women who adhere to an increasingly popular fashion trend that is modeled after somewhat slovenly middle-aged Japanese rock star Monsieur Kamayatsu. *Kamayatsu-onna* are relaxed, like to do things their own way, and aim to keep things simple and easy. These women have learned a trade and are not interested in becoming full-time homemakers. (See Miura A., *Kamayatsu-onna no jidai* [The era of *Kamayatsu-onna*]. [Tokyo: Makino, 2005].)

2. The English translation of this chart was prepared based largely on Yasumoto S. 2006. "The Impact of the 'Korean Wave' on Japan" (paper presented at the 16th Biennial Conference of the Asian Studies Association of Australia, Wollongong, http://coombs.anu.edu.au/SpecialProj/ASAA/biennial-conference/2006/

Source: Miura (2005, 42, fig. 2-1).

The Impact of Class Background on Marriage

One final point of interest regarding social class is the role of class background in choosing a marriage partner. Marriage is discussed in detail in a different chapter so we will focus here exclusively on this one question.

Before doing that, though, let me give a simple list of the criteria people might use in selecting a marriage partner: (1) education, (2) occupation, (3) income, (4) family background (i.e., class background), (5) personal appearance, (6) personality, and (7) living with parents or not. A decade ago, the conditions sought by Japanese women were known as the "three highs"—high education, high income, and physical height. In Tachibanaki (1997a), however, marriage is described in somewhat pessimistic and impulsive terms, including "Marriage is a gamble," "Love is blind," and "My partner isn't quite my dream come true, but I'll make do." Relations between men and women are endlessly fascinating, particularly the question of whether to seek the ideal marriage partner or to compromise.

What are people actually basing their marriage decisions on? A brief overview is in order: (1) Marriages between men and women with the same level of education (educational homogamy) are increasing. The same can be said of occupation. (2) Family background (class background) was important about a decade ago, but its influence has decreased substantially. (3) Women emphasize a man's income while men value a woman's personal appearance. (4) Both men and women place considerable emphasis on personality. (5) Women have different criteria and conditions for a marriage partner than men do because they have the option of being full-time homemakers.

Let's look more closely at the impact of class, the focus of this chapter, on marriage by considering the data in table 2-8, which shows the class background of each spouse by marriage cohort. Figures on the diagonal from the top left of a marriage cohort to the bottom right of that cohort show the percentage of marriages where the parents of each member of the couple are of the same class background. From the figures we see that the percentage of marriages where the parents on both sides are of the same class decreases as the marriage cohort becomes younger; more and more young people in Japan are marrying partners from a different class background.

In particular, class homogamy (marriages between children of similar family backgrounds) of people from farming families has dropped considerably. This reflects the great decline in the number of agricultural workers. A similar decrease in class homogamy is

Table 2-8 Class background of husband and wife by marriage cohort

(%)

Wife's class background	Married 1932–59	Professional/managerial	Clerical/sales	Self-employed	Agricultural	Skilled blue-collar	Unskilled blue-collar	Total	(n)
		Husband's class background							
	Professional/managerial	36.6	7.3	13.0	36.6	3.3	3.3	100.0	(123)
	Clerical/sales	21.6	18.9	14.9	35.1	9.5	0.0	100.0	(74)
	Self-employed	15.3	5.6	25.0	40.3	6.5	7.3	100.0	(124)
	Agricultural	7.9	6.1	10.7	68.8	2.6	3.8	100.0	(494)
	Skilled blue-collar	10.3	5.1	25.6	43.6	10.3	5.1	100.0	(39)
	Unskilled blue-collar	0.0	12.9	32.3	45.2	0.0	9.7	100.0	(31)
	Married 1960–74	Professional/managerial	Clerical/sales	Self-employed	Agricultural	Skilled blue-collar	Unskilled blue-collar	Total	(n)
	Professional/managerial	32.9	14.5	16.2	27.4	7.3	1.7	100.0	(234)
	Clerical/sales	16.5	21.6	13.1	34.1	10.2	4.5	100.0	(176)
	Self-employed	18.1	8.4	26.9	34.5	6.3	5.9	100.0	(238)
	Agricultural	10.4	10.9	11.4	56.3	5.1	6.0	100.0	(588)
	Skilled blue-collar	8.0	14.3	20.5	37.5	15.2	4.5	100.0	(112)
	Unskilled blue-collar	9.5	12.2	17.6	37.8	8.1	14.9	100.0	(74)
	Married 1975–95	Professional/managerial	Clerical/sales	Self-employed	Agricultural	Skilled blue-collar	Unskilled blue-collar	Total	(n)
	Professional/managerial	26.6	17.3	11.0	30.8	8.0	6.3	100.0	(237)
	Clerical/sales	19.8	18.6	10.8	34.7	12.0	4.2	100.0	(167)
	Self-employed	25.0	6.8	21.2	31.8	8.3	6.8	100.0	(132)
	Agricultural	14.2	14.5	7.8	48.4	8.6	6.5	100.0	(372)
	Skilled blue-collar	16.8	16.0	12.0	31.2	12.8	11.2	100.0	(125)
	Unskilled blue-collar	9.9	13.2	17.6	29.7	7.7	22.0	100.0	(91)

Notes: 1. Figures in parentheses are number of cases in sample.
2. Compiled from *1985 SSM chōsa* (1985 SSM survey) and *1995 SSM chōsa* (1995 SSM survey).

Source: Shirahase (2005, 69, table 3-4).

occurring among people from professional/managerial families. In contrast, marriages between children of unskilled workers are on the increase. Putting it all together, this means that class homogamy in classes that are comparatively well off is on the decline while that in classes that are not so well off is on the rise.

Shirahase, however, points out that we cannot conclude that class homogamy has declined as much as the figures might indicate given the changes in Japan's industrial structure and other external conditions over the sixty or so years since the end of World War II— the decline of agriculture, the growth of industry and services, and the increase of white-collar work. Nonetheless, it seems reasonable to say there has been no increase in class homogamy and that it has, at the very least, declined somewhat.

Chapter Three

Disparities in Education

While almost all children finish compulsory education, some continue on to high school, junior college, university, and graduate school. In this chapter, we will look at the level of education that women attain in Japan, analyzing the inequalities or differentials that arise among highly educated women and those who end their studies at an earlier stage.

Before focusing specifically on women's education, however, we should take a look at more general issues, such as why a person seeks education and the conditions surrounding that education. Since there are issues common to both men and women and issues unique to women, we will start with an overview of matters common to both genders.

Women can be classified into highly educated and lesser educated at the end of their school education, and some very interesting issues arise due to the impact of this division on women's subsequent employment and lifestyle, as we will note later in this chapter. We will also see that while it is generally true that a highly educated woman is one who has graduated from junior college or university and a lesser-educated woman is someone who has graduated from junior high or high school, that distinction must be modified somewhat depending on the historical period.

Education "Supply and Demand"

The economic concept of supply and demand offers one tool for looking at the level of education people receive. A basic idea in my specialty of economics is that commodity price and transaction volume are determined at the point where supply and demand meet in the market. We can consider the desire for education to be education "demand" and the acceptance of students and provision of education by schools and other educational institutions to constitute education "supply." It is important to know how these two are formed, and Oshio (2002) offers a solid discussion of the economics of education.

As I said, economic theory states that transactions take place at the point where supply and demand intersect. What determines this point in the case of education? Let's look at the real-life case of a school entrance exam as an example. Taking the number of school applicants as demand and the student-body capacity as supply, we know that competition will arise if the number of applicants exceeds capacity. Since in Japan student admittance is usually decided based on an entrance exam, the number of students who pass the exam is the point where supply and demand meet. Some of those who pass the entrance exam may decide not to attend, but nevertheless it is easy to see that the number of students admitted is where supply and demand intersect.

We can take this same principle for one school and apply it nationally: the total number of people who want to attend high school or university is demand, and the total number of people who can be admitted constitutes supply. In this way, education level or the percentage of students seeking further education can be analyzed in terms of the relationship between supply and demand.

Education demand

Let's start our discussion of education demand by specifying some of the possible motives people have in seeking education: (1) education brings a good occupation and increased earning power; (2) studying at school is useful for networking with others; (3) education refines general knowledge, scholarship, and character; (4) the pursuit of education enables one to keep up with others who continue their schooling or to postpone entry into the work force; and (5) education serves as an advantage when seeking a marriage partner. We can further divide these five reasons into two broad categories, with reasons 1 and 2 being related to occupation or income and reasons 3 through 5 being unrelated to occupation or income. We will be using these two broad categories in our analysis.

In the case of women, however, it is somewhat difficult to divide the reasons for seeking education into these two categories. For example, reason 5—that education is advantageous for marriage— is indeed a motive unrelated to the occupation or income of the woman herself; however, if she should desire a marriage partner with a high income, she would be more likely to marry such a man if she were highly educated herself. This means that reason 5 can also be interpreted as being a motive related to occupation or income. In our discussion here, however, we are limiting ourselves to the motives of the woman herself, so we will keep reason 5 under the "unrelated" category.

Now let's look more closely at this category of motives related to occupation or income. Generally speaking, the harder the occupation is to perform and the greater the skills required, the more advanced will be the education requisite to obtaining a job in that area and the higher the wages such a job can command. A simple example would be doctors. Doctors in Japan must study at a university faculty of medicine for a minimum of six years, after which they face internships and other training. As everyone knows, though, doctors have a high income. In this way, it is commonly accepted that a high level of education is required to achieve motives related to occupation or income.

In economics, this is explained using the theories of human capital and of screening. The human capital argument states that a person's productivity is increased by education and training, and since a highly productive person usually contributes more to his or her corporation or organization, that person receives high wages. The screening theory, on the other hand, states that employers select applicants who have a high level of education or who possess particular credentials because these people have convincing evidence that they are competent; these people are in an advantageous position for promotion as well. These two lines of thinking are well established in the world of economics, and they both speak of the potential for people with a high level of education, training, and credentials to make a high income. Where the two theories differ is that the human capital argument states that education increases productivity, while the screening argument focuses only on the acquisition of education itself and does not look into whether it actually increases productivity.

These two theories thus explain education demand in terms of future occupation or income, but there are other motives for seeking a higher education. Deepening one's general education and knowledge is a noble aim, and the desire to meet a good marriage partner is very human and not to be despised. There is no need for economists to try to explain all such motives in some comprehensive theory.

Of greater significance from the perspective of economics are the factors blocking the fulfillment of education demand. People want to have a certain level of education or to attend a certain school, but not everyone is able to achieve such goals. What factors prevent them from doing so? We can cite the following three categories:

1. Economic reasons, including school fees
2. Innate ability and academic achievement
3. Personal effort

Looking at economic reasons, everyone knows that educating a child costs money. Compulsory education is not so expensive, but if one's child goes on to high school, junior college, university, and graduate school, the tuition is hefty. If the child attends a private school rather than a public school for elementary and junior high school as well, tuition and other expenses add up to a much larger sum. Since it is the child's parents who cover the school fees, their economic situation plays quite an important role in determining a child's education.

One economic factor often overlooked is the forgone earnings that arise when a child chooses to go on to higher education. If we

compare a person who gets a job right after high school with someone who continues on to a four-year university, we see that the student who goes on to university gives up four years of earnings that
he or she would have made going to work right after high school.
Those earnings are called forgone earnings. This is considered
an expense for the university student that must be deducted from
future earned income. The remainder is the university attendee's
net income.

More importantly, if a child does not go on to university, his
or her parents are relieved of the burden of paying university fees.
Indeed, if the parents are in financial straits, the child can help
them out with the income earned over those four years. And if
there is a family business, whether in agriculture, commerce, or
industry, that business will also benefit if children join it right after
high school. This last case is often seen in developing countries,
and in Japan too before World War II and for a time afterward,
children were raised with the expectation that they would join the
family business. Not very many children have done so since Japan's
economic miracle and period of high economic growth, however.
Instead, they have gone to work as paid employees at factories,
offices, or retail businesses.

In the early postwar period, Japan was still poor. Some parents
did not have the financial resources to be able to cover tuition, and
this hampered their children's ambitions for higher education. Students had to abandon their dreams of going on to higher education,
and some children even sent their parents a portion of their hard-
earned income. We should also note that this situation was especially true for girls. In contrast, quite a few low-income families did
everything they could to provide their sons with a higher education.
Since males were seen as the breadwinner, there was little motivation in those days to educate women for future earning power or
future professional status.

I would like to turn now to the second and third factors blocking the fulfillment of education demand, namely, innate ability/aca-
demic achievement and personal effort. If innate ability is distributed
according to a certain probability (normal distribution, for example),

that distribution can be assumed to remain more or less constant in every era. In other words, even though ability might skip a generation from grandparent to grandchild, the distribution will be about the same across the generations for the Japanese people overall. Thus, the numbers of those of outstanding innate ability and those of inferior ability do not fluctuate much from generation to generation.

The case of academic achievement is different, however. Even if the distribution of innate ability does not change from generation to generation, the average academic achievement of the new generation can increase from that of the previous generation if the children study assiduously or if teaching methods improve. Of course, if children stop studying or teaching quality declines, it is also possible for average academic achievement to drop. This means that the distribution of academic achievement changes from generation to generation even though the distribution of natural ability does not.

Turning to personal effort, our interest here is not in the increase or decrease in academic achievement per se, but in who is putting forth effort. Earlier we said that incentives for education related to future occupation or income were greater for males than for females in Japan in the early postwar period. If this is the case, it is highly likely that boys persevered more at their studies. Parents, too, might have sent their sons to cram schools or hired private tutors for them, but rarely did so for their daughters. We can say that every home and school was committed to improving the scholastic record of boys but was less concerned about that of girls, resulting in a differing level of response from the two genders. This is one hypothesis to explain why a higher percentage of males than females went on to higher education.

Let's return to our discussion of the distribution of innate ability and look at another aspect of it, namely, the popular belief in a gender difference in aptitude. One common assumption is that males are good at the natural and social sciences and mathematics, while females are good at languages, the humanities, and the arts. In figure 3-1 we see that in Japan undergraduate men are in fact concentrated in the natural and social sciences and engineering while women tend to major in the humanities and home economics, giving some credence to this commonly held belief.

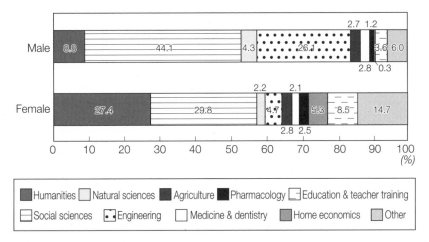

Fig. 3-1 University students by major field of study

Source: Based on Ministry of Education, Culture, Sports, Science, and Technology, *Heisei 16 nendo gakkō kihon chōsa* (Basic survey on schools, FY2004).

Since I am not a specialist in education, I cannot easily judge whether there is any such gender difference in aptitude. A generation or so ago, junior high and high school boys showed interest in mathematics and the natural and social sciences, and their exam grades were also generally higher in these areas than those of girls. On the other hand, girls showed interest in Japanese, English, art, and music, and their scores were high in these areas. These facts were thought to indicate an innate gender differential.

Recently, however, various studies have called into question such assumptions. For instance, the Organization for Economic Cooperation and Development (OECD) has been conducting an ongoing comparative study of academic achievement in the industrialized nations, the so-called PISA (Program for International Student Assessment) survey.

Table 3-1 shows the 2003 PISA scores for academic achievement in four areas: reading literacy, mathematical literacy, scientific literacy, and problem solving. The results for Japan would seem at first glance to support the common stereotype: girls are 22 points higher in reading literacy than boys, suggesting that girls are good

Table 3-1 OECD Program for International Student Assessment (PISA): 2003 survey results

(Score points)

		Reading literacy	Mathematical literacy	Scientific literacy	Problem solving
Japan	Male	487	538	550	546
	Female	509	530	546	548
	Difference	+22 (significant)	-8 (not significant)	-4 (not significant)	+2 (not significant)
Japan mean		498 (rank: 14)	534 (rank: 6)	548 (rank: 2)	547 (rank: 4)
OECD mean		494	500	500	500
OECD	Male	477	506	503	499
	Female	511	494	497	501
	Difference	+34 (significant)	-12 (significant)	-6 (significant)	+2 (not significant)

Source: Based on OECD, *OECD Program for International Student Assessment (PISA), 2003.*

at language, while boys are a few points higher in mathematical and scientific literacy.

A closer look, however, reveals that although boys do indeed have slightly higher math and science scores, that difference is not statistically significant—there is in fact no meaningful gap in the math and science scores between boys and girls. Therefore, the common belief that boys are innately better at mathematics and science than girls is proved wrong here.

Moreover, this is true not only of Japan, but of the OECD overall. Since student assessments in industrialized nations show that the gap between boys and girls is not so large, we must discard the idea that men predominate in science and engineering at university or in occupational choice because they are vastly superior in math and science. We must, instead, consider why men favor science and engineering even though there is no gender difference in ability.

There is, however, a significant difference in achievement between boys and girls in reading literacy, both in Japan and in the OECD countries. Girls are strong in language, have a good understanding of the written word, and excel in communication skills, no doubt one reason why women tend to major in language and the humanities at university. So perhaps, on the contrary, we should postulate that men gravitate toward math and science not because of any natural talent in those areas but because, compared with women, they lack ability in language and the humanities; they drift into mathematics and science at university and find work in those fields because they are unsuited to other fields.

Ironically, this very superiority of women in the humanities puts them at a disadvantage in the job market; there are steady employment opportunities for students specializing in scientific fields, such as the natural sciences, engineering, agriculture, or medicine, but not many corporate job offers for those majoring in the liberal arts, such as literature and sociology. In this area at least, science-oriented men are clearly at an advantage over humanities-oriented women.

The social sciences occupy an intermediate position between the sciences and the humanities, although leaning toward the liberal arts. For some reason, fields such as law, economics, and business management have not been very popular among women in Japan, even though there is quite a large number of corporate and government jobs for majors in these fields. Thus we can say that men have been at an advantage in the social sciences as well.

Education supply

Education supply can be viewed here as the number of schools available from high school through university, as well as the number of applicants such schools choose to admit. More particularly, high schools are divided into general education, commercial, and technical tracks and universities into law, engineering, medicine, and other faculties, so that education supply also varies by track and faculty.

Although economics tells us that supply and demand will each adjust to a point of equilibrium, this adjustment between supply and demand is rather slow in the case of education. The supply side is particularly slow to adjust, as it takes funds and time to build schools and find teachers. For this reason, demand is apt to exceed supply, giving rise to quotas. In the case of education, Japanese schools limit admission based on rigorous entrance exams. Of course, the opposite situation may also prevail, of school places exceeding the number of applicants.

In addition, there are three other factors to keep in mind here. First, the above supply situation applies only to high schools and above. In compulsory education (elementary and junior high schools), measures are taken so that supply matches demand—having demand determine supply is a unique characteristic of compulsory education. Second, the position of public and private schools is quite different. The disparity in tuition costs affects demand, while, on the supply side, private schools face a tighter management situation because they are not funded by tax revenues. Third, Japan has both coed and single-sex schools, and this complicates the supply and demand situation. This is particularly important in discussing the education of women.

Women's Education in Terms of Supply and Demand

Continuing to apply the economic tools of supply and demand, let's look at how the education of women in Japan has changed in the postwar period. How have motives for seeking higher education changed and the importance of education costs, innate ability, and personal effort evolved? And what new disparities among women have emerged?

It will be easier to identify such changes in women's education if we divide the postwar years into five periods. The first four periods follow Ojima and Kondō (2000) and Ojima (2003); period V, the final period, is my addition.

> Period I: Generation born between 1935 and 1945
> Period II: Generation born between 1946 and 1960
> Period III: Generation born between 1961 and 1974
> Period IV: Generation born between 1975 and 1985
> Period V: Generation born in or after 1986

Generational differences

The period I generation entered high school prior to Japan's economic miracle, and the number of girls going on to high school and university was much lower than that for boys—less than 10 percent of the women in that generation continued on to junior college or university. Such a low rate for women was due to the overall lack of affluence, as also seen in the fact that only about 20 percent of men went on to university at that time. As explained earlier, families did not have the luxury of allowing forgone earnings, and in some cases, children even needed to work to help out their parents financially.

When less than 10 percent of women go on to higher education (junior college or university), only a very small group of elite women stands alongside the more than 90 percent of women who ended their studies relatively early. There is, therefore, a very large education gap among women in that generation, those aged sixty-five or over today.

What was the effect of this great disparity in education? Lacking academic credentials, very few women became leaders in society and women executives, managers, attorneys, doctors, and university professors were rare. Indeed, elite women of this generation are often introduced as the "first woman ever to hold such-and-such a post." Most women thus fell into the low-income bracket as they did not have the education to acquire good jobs even if they did work.

The period II generation, however, grew up right at the height of Japan's rapid economic growth. Household incomes rose dramatically, easing the financial constraints of period I and opening the way for a marked increase in the percentage of women going on to high school and higher education. It is during this period that the gender gap in high school attendance vanished, with more than 90 percent of both boys and girls continuing on to high school for virtually universal high school attendance by the end of the period. The percentage of women going on to higher education also rose, topping 30 percent at the end of the period, but we should note that the increase in women entering junior college was more than twice that in women enrolling at university, making junior college the main form of higher education for women then.

Period II thus saw the start of a closing of the education gap among women. Highly educated women constituted an elite in period I, but with the increase in the number of women going on to higher education, this was no longer the case in period II. Considering that over half of the women going on to higher education went to junior college, though, those who attended four-year universities could still be called something of an elite.

It is particularly noteworthy that few women of this generation were gainfully employed throughout their lives even if they did go on to junior college or university. Most women only worked until marriage or until they had their first child, after which they became homemakers. Even highly educated women showed a strong inclination toward being full-time homemakers in those days.

Some career-oriented women did continue to work after marriage and childbirth, though. More than in the corporate world, where it was customary for women to resign at marriage or childbirth, female civil servants and teachers kept their jobs. The public service and education sectors had measures, however imperfect, to support women in balancing work and childrearing responsibilities as well as an absence of gender discrimination in working conditions. Such women made up only a very small fraction of all women, however.

Then in period III, the percentages of men and women going on to high school, junior college, or university leveled off. The major factor in such stagnation would seem to be the end of dramatic increases in family incomes as the period of high economic growth drew to a close.

Ojima (2003) also points to deliberate policies adopted at the time to hold down the number of students going on to higher education. Some 40 percent of men and more than 30 percent of women were enrolling in higher education, and this was thought to be too high. The percentage of men going on to university even declined, albeit slightly, during this period. The restraint policies owed much to the drop in national and local government tax revenues due to the sluggish economy, which meant that the public sector had to cut its expenditures on education. In other words, higher education supply stopped growing or even contracted.

Another important factor was that during this period, people started to reconsider the value of a university education. From before the war through the early postwar period, university graduates were few in number, giving them a prominent position in society; university graduates were the elite class in Japan. As the number of university graduates increased, however, their elite status was diminished and, not surprisingly, society started to question the meaning of a university education. The slight drop in attendance at higher education among men, i.e., those who would be the family breadwinner throughout their lives, reflects such questioning. To the extent that women had a smaller presence in higher education than men, they were not so affected by this reassessment of higher education, and the percentage of women going on to higher education showed no decline during that period.

What about the education gap among women during this period? It continued largely unchanged in period III, with a substantial differential existing between highly educated and lesser educated women. Two key reasons for this were (1) many families still lacked the financial resources to provide higher education for their daughters and (2) women at that time on the whole did not yet feel a strong drive to go on to university. Save for a few exceptions, women were not yet strongly motivated by thoughts of future income or career.

During period IV, however, a watershed event occurred in women's education: women attending four-year universities came for the first time to outnumber those attending junior college. The total percentage of women going on to either university or junior college did not rise; rather, the percentage of women going to university rose and the percentage going to junior college fell. In other words, women who in the past would have gone to junior college had switched to the four-year university group.

Why did the percentage of women going on to four-year universities increase to over 30 percent? A variety of reasons can be cited. First was the economy. Although not on a par with the time of Japan's economic miracle, economic growth was stable. Even a slight rise in household incomes meant that parental finances would not keep their daughters from attending a university.

A second factor is that the birthrate started to decline during this period. With the decrease in the number of children per household, it became possible for each child to have more education. Analysts in both education and economics have found a correlation between the number of children per family and the level of education those children receive, so we can say that the decrease in the number of children opened the way for more daughters to continue on to university. For further details, see Tachibanaki and Kimura (2008).

Another factor in more women going to university was the societal reevaluation of women's lives that occurred during this period: more and more people argued that women should be independent and not subordinate to men. Feminist thought was on the rise, resulting in a questioning of traditional gender roles. More and more women thought about having their own career, for which they needed a college diploma. As a result, many more women went on to four-year universities. In other words, we see in period IV a dramatic increase among women in interest in higher education related to occupation or income, noteworthy as a sign of the changing times.

In this period, we can also see a change in the nature of the education gap among women. Instead of there being a very small minority of highly educated women, women came to be more evenly divided into the highly educated and the lesser educated as more and more women attended university. Although female university graduates by no means made up the majority of women, there had come to be a considerable number of them present in Japanese society.

The present generation

In the present generation of period V, the percentage of women going on to junior college or university has surpassed that of men. It must be added, however, that a fair number of these women attend junior college, so there are still more men than women going on to four-year universities.

This period, the generation born in or after 1986, is characterized by two major changes in women's education: (1) the shift from single-sex to coed education and (2) the increasing presence of women at prestigious and difficult-to-enter academic institutions. The two changes are interrelated since women seeking admission at elite coed schools naturally enough exerted pressure on girls' high schools and women's universities to become coeducational.

The first major change in women's education, the trend toward coeducation, is occurring at both the high school and university level. For example, public high schools in the Kita-Kantō and Tōhoku regions, traditionally single-sex, are increasingly going coeducational, as are private high schools nationwide.

Women's universities that have started admitting men include, in the Kansai region alone, Ōtemae University (which was Ōtemae University for Women until coeducation in 2000), Kobe Yamate University (2002), Tezukayama Gakuin University (2003), Kyoto Tachibana University (which was Kyoto Tachibana Women's University until coeducation in 2005), and Osaka Ōtani University (which was Ōtani Women's University until coeducation in 2006). (There were never any male-only universities in Japan.)

If we look at the number of students at women's universities as a percentage of all female university students, we can determine the extent to which female students are shifting from women's universities to coed institutions. We see that in 1985 women enrolled at women's universities made up 17 percent of all female university students, but by 2004 that figure had dropped to 13 percent. This marked decrease of 4 percentage points can be attributed both to the impact of coeducation at women's universities and the shift of women from women's universities to traditionally coed institutions.

Next, let's look more closely at the second major change in women's education in period V, women's increasing presence at elite universities, by examining the record at the top university in Japan, the University of Tokyo. As seen in table 3-2, women made up a mere 5.6 percent of students entering the University of Tokyo in 1977. By 1987, they had increased to 10 percent, with a sharp increase to nearly 20 percent in the early years of the twenty-first century. We can thus see a dramatic rise in the number of women matriculating at the university from the late twentieth century to the early years of the twenty-first.

We can take the class matriculating in 2003, namely, students born around 1985, as representative of this rise. Coeducation at women's universities also commenced fully at around this time. In other words, female university students born around 1985 shifted

Table 3-2 Female students at the University of Tokyo

(A) Women as a percentage of matriculating students by year *(%)*

1977	1987	2001	2003	2006
5.6	10.0	17.5	18.3	20.1

(B) Women as a percentage of matriculating students by major (2006) *(%)*

Liberal Arts I	Liberal Arts II	Liberal Arts III	Natural Sciences I	Natural Sciences II	Natural Sciences III
20.8	17.2	39.3	6.3	24.8	12.2

Note: Most students who enter the University of Tokyo in the Liberal Arts I program enter the Faculty of Law; Liberal Arts II, the Faculty of Economics; Liberal Arts III, the Faculty of Letters or the Faculty of Education; Natural Sciences I, the Faculty of Science or the Faculty of Engineering; Natural Sciences II, the Faculty of Science, the Faculty of Pharmaceutical Sciences, or the Faculty of Agriculture; and Natural Sciences III, the Faculty of Medicine.

Source: Based on University of Tokyo website (http://www.u-tokyo.ac.jp/index_e.html).

from women's universities to coed universities and started to matriculate at prestigious, highly selective schools in considerable numbers, marking the start of a new period, period V.

How significant was this shift of female students to coed and elite schools? At women's universities, the major fields of study were literature, the humanities, home economics, music, and other arts. Women did not study with future work in mind; rather the main educational aim was to impart general knowledge and better prepare them for life as homemakers. There were, of course, exceptions, with some women's universities also teaching the natural sciences, pharmaceutical sciences, and other subjects useful for finding work. The trend toward coeducation, however, was clearly motivated by the need to provide women with an education more suitable for future jobs, as university administrations came to recognize that many female students now planned to work after graduation.

Why did women start to matriculate in larger numbers at prestigious schools like the University of Tokyo? We can cite multiple reasons, starting with the desire, discussed above, of more and more women to major in academic areas that would help them in their job search after graduation. They therefore started turning toward national and public universities, which offered majors affording good employment opportunities but unavailable at private schools, such as science, engineering, agriculture, medicine, law, and economics.

A second reason is that Japan has long put great emphasis on an individual's educational background. In such a "credentials society," a high school graduate is better than a junior high graduate, a university graduate is better than a high school graduate, and so on. And of course, the more prestigious one's alma mater, the better. Thus, more and more women thought that it would be advantageous for their post-graduation job search and later promotions to matriculate at as elite a university as possible. This is a key motivation for men, too, leading to Japan's university—and high school—entrance exam "hell." Given society's placing such a strong value on academic credentials, we cannot criticize career-minded women for striving to enter a prestigious school.

Discrimination against women is an indisputable fact of life in many areas of Japanese society, and women try to overcome those barriers by obtaining the highest qualifications possible, for example, majoring in law and becoming a lawyer or acquiring special skills in science and engineering. Another form of qualification is the cachet of graduating from a prestigious, highly selective school, and often women focus more than men on being admitted to as good a university as possible.

A more indirect reason why women started to aim at entering prestigious universities is that girls came to do as well as boys in terms of academic record in junior high and high school. Earlier in this chapter, we noted that girls scored higher in reading literacy than boys and were equivalent in mathematical and scientific literacy. It is easy to imagine girls starting to realize, as their marks in school drew even with those of boys, that they could get into good schools if they studied hard.

A fourth factor is changing attitudes in the home toward education. In eras when families had many children and males were to be the breadwinners, it was natural for parents to be more committed to their sons' education. They did not think very much about sending their daughters to a good university. However, with the decrease in the number of children per family, financial affluence increased. As the idea took root that women also should work, many parents became interested in sending their daughters to prestigious junior high and high schools and then on to elite universities. Tokyo's three elite girls' high schools—Futaba, Joshi Gakuin, and Ōin, known as the *Joshi-gosanke*—reflect this development.

Let's now consider how the above changes in period V have influenced education differentials among women. In period IV, two increasingly equal-sized groups were formed as more and more women attended university. There was thus an education gap between the highly educated (composed of junior college and university graduates) and the lesser educated (the more numerous high school graduates). To this dual structure, we must add the new feature of period V, namely, the notable number of women graduating from prestigious universities, which in the past had been almost exclusively the reserve of males. This means the emergence of a three-tiered structure: one tier composed of the few female graduates of elite universities, another tier comprising "average" highly educated women graduating from non-elite universities and junior colleges, and the final tier of high school graduates.

Only a few years have passed since women started receiving degrees from prestigious universities in such numbers, so they have not yet taken up prominent positions in core sectors of society. We must assume, though, that in the future these women will become mid-level and senior leaders. We can easily foresee that women will come to make up a sizeable number of the executives, managers, professionals, senior bureaucrats, academics, attorneys, doctors, and politicians in Japan—in other words, leaders in a wide range of sectors. There is a good chance that some of the positions monopolized by highly educated men in the past will be taken by these ultra-educated women.

There are several conditions, however, that must be fulfilled for women to replace men in these positions, conditions closely linked to the future course of Japan. First, women's participation in leadership will depend on whether it becomes customary in this country for women to continue to work after marriage and childbirth. Up to now, a considerable number of women, even among the highly educated, have given up their careers when they married or had a child. If that practice continues, the number of female leaders will not increase as much as might be expected. This will depend on the kind of life women want to lead, the amount of childcare and other assistance society offers to career-minded women, and the attitude men and husbands adopt.

A second important consideration is how Japan addresses the problem of discrimination against women. Discrimination against women exists in hiring and promotion in every field, but it is particularly severe at the level where ultra-educated women will be competing. One good example is the post of top executive at a major corporation. As long as the glass ceiling remains in place, ultra-educated, career-minded women will likely still be unable to assume top leadership positions.

Third, will Japan continue to put such great emphasis on academic background? While the ultra-educated female population is clearly set to increase, if society ceases to think that graduates of highly selective universities are decisively better than others, then ultra-educated women will lose their advantage and find the competition drastically harder.

Will Japan continue to stress academic credentials?

I would now like to give my personal opinion about whether Japan will continue to emphasize academic credentials. In many sectors of society today, graduates of the elite universities have a definite advantage, but I predict that this will gradually decrease in the future. I base this assessment on several factors.

First, corporations and government are starting to adopt employee evaluation methods that focus on ability and performance, which is likely to reduce the tremendous emphasis placed on academic background. Indeed, graduates of prestigious schools no longer make up the majority of corporate presidents and officers as they did in the past, and graduates of a wide variety of universities are now becoming company executives. In the national government as well, graduates of the University of Tokyo Faculty of Law no longer have a monopoly on the vice minister and bureau director-general positions as they did in the past.

No doubt one's alma mater will continue to play a major role for new graduates seeking jobs, however, as they do not yet have work experience on which to be evaluated. In such a case, corporations tend to use academic achievement as the main selection criterion, and the national government also currently bases its hiring mainly on academic examinations. Under such a hiring policy, people who have passed the most rigorous university entrance exams will have the advantage.

While graduates of prestigious and difficult-to-enter universities will likely continue to be at an advantage in being hired, as they have proven themselves to be high achievers, subsequent promotion will be based on work performance, leadership skills, ability to cooperate with others, and other evaluation criteria. I estimate, therefore, that academic background will play considerably less of a role as a criterion. Highly educated people will be able to benefit from their educational background in their first job search, but education will not have that much significance as they gain work experience. Overall, the influence of educational background will decrease.

However, the above estimate is focused on promotions in corporations and government, and there are many other sectors where education will remain significant. Indeed, there is a chance that educational background will become even more important for professionals, such as engineers, academics, attorneys, accountants, doctors, and pharmacists. By educational background, I am speaking here of professional skills more than school name—to have high-level, specialized skills in these areas requires training and brainpower. I estimate, therefore, that there will be no decline in the importance placed on academic background in the professions. On the contrary, it may even increase. Since more and more women are entering professional fields, there will be no decline in the emphasis placed on academic credentials for women. Consequently, for women working in these professions, there is continuing value in graduating from a prestigious university.

One issue that arises here is how to prove that these elite universities really do have superior records in research and education and that their graduates actually are superior to those educated at other schools. Further, are their graduates superior because of the outstanding education offered at prestigious universities or simply because they were gifted enough to enter such universities to begin with?

Proving this is beyond my scope of expertise, but it seems reasonable to take a hybrid of the two theories, rather than taking either one alone. That is, attending a prestigious university helps to improve a student's innate abilities and productivity to some degree, being admitted to an elite school is proof that the student can work hard toward a goal, and, above all, graduating from such a school gives the student confidence.

From this, we can glimpse the raison d'être of Japan's "credentials society" and see the sense in women striving to enter an elite university. With the ongoing importance of educational background in the professions, women will continue to seek a high-level education and the gap between the highly educated and the lesser educated will continue to expand.

The Widening Education Gaps among Women

Thus far, we have traced the changing conditions of the education of women in Japan, theorizing that women will increasingly come to fall into one of two groups in a dual-track system: one group composed of the very small number of elite university graduates plus the considerable number of graduates of "average" women's universities, and junior colleges; and the other group composed of the majority, the women who finish their education with junior high or high school. From the description of the present generation, it is clear that there are three groups today: (1) the ultra-educated, (2) the highly educated, and (3) the lesser educated. This then represents the dawn of a tripolar differential in women's education. Let's look at each of the three groups in more detail.

The ultra-educated

This group is composed of women graduating from prestigious universities. Although the men as well as the women who attend such schools tend to be placed on the fast track in Japan, management policies at corporations and government offices, as mentioned earlier, are shifting to promotions based on ability and work performance. One's alma mater will still be important in finding a first job, but it is my belief that the importance placed on educational background will diminish overall. Educational qualifications will remain important, however, in regard to the professions, and more and more talented women are likely to enter these fields.

To look more closely at the question of women entering the professions, let's turn again to table 3-2. The second half of this table gives statistics for women as a percentage of matriculating students at the University of Tokyo by field of study. We see that, as could be expected, women are concentrated in the fields of letters and education (Liberal Arts III), making up nearly 40 percent of majors. Women account for slightly less than 25 percent of majors in science, pharmaceutical sciences, and agriculture (Natural Sciences II); about 20 percent of majors in law (Liberal Arts I); and about 12 percent of majors in medicine (Natural Sciences III). These figures are generally higher than those in science and engineering (Natural Sciences I) and economics (Liberal Arts II).

Thus, the more popular fields train professionals (doctors, pharmacists, and lawyers) and include the acquisition of credentials. In contrast, engineering and economics are not so popular among women, showing perhaps that women are not very interested in working at corporations. At any rate, these University of Tokyo figures are one piece of evidence that women are targeting the professions.

Why are the professions a good fit for ultra-educated women? Or, conversely, why are men suited for managerial roles? Let's examine these questions more closely.

First, to find a generalist position at a corporation or government office and succeed in being promoted requires both taxing work and long hours. Once an employee has risen to an executive or managerial position, the work is unrelenting. For those in the professions, however, the work hours are comparatively flexible and the work itself is not that harsh. From this perspective, men are suited to managerial work because they have more physical strength while women are more suited to the professions.

Second, women's favoring of the professions could be considered a wise choice from the perspective of work-life balance as well, since it is easier as a professional to control one's work volume and work hours while raising children. For example, staff personnel can take childcare leave more easily than line personnel because it causes less interruption in the workplace. Line positions also require long overtime hours for promotion, interfering with childrearing.

These two points are likely to invite feminist criticism that it is incorrect to say only men are suited to managerial positions, that many women aspire to be managers, and that the active cooperation of husbands in childcare is to be expected in a gender-equal society. My response to such a critique is that I am not precluding women from becoming managers but rather respect the freedom of all to decide what kind of life they want. I agree that the active cooperation of husbands is required; however, the reality in Japan is that men are still forced to overwork and, as a result, not much cooperation can be expected from them. Indeed, eliminating male overwork in this country is also an important public policy objective.

On a personal note, I prefer doing work that I enjoy at a pace I set myself and the professions are perfect for this. At the risk of repeating myself, I would like to say again that each person is free to become a manager or to assume whatever other position he or she chooses to pursue.

The highly educated

The highly educated group is made up of graduates of non-elite universities, women's universities, and junior colleges. As women of ability and academic achievement, they can be expected to take up leadership and middle-echelon positions. One or two decades ago, when few women were able to acquire higher education, they were the elite class. For better or worse, many of them became full-time homemakers when they married or had their first child, raising the question of whether their talents and potential were being fully utilized.

Needless to say, it is each woman's prerogative to work or be a stay-at-home wife and mother, so we cannot judge the matter based solely from the view of human resources. However, in period V, one in two women are attending junior college or university. With so many women receiving higher education, it would seem only reasonable to raise the bar and increase as much as possible the presence of women as fully contributing members of the work force.

Highly educated women have many options in choice of occupation and in whether to work full- or part-time. They can aspire to be managers or become rank-and-file employees at corporations, whichever they prefer. They can become teachers or civil servants, be self-employed, or enter other occupations, depending on the abilities and desires of the woman herself as well as the jobs offered by society. In general, though, since Japan is a postindustrial society, most highly educated women will have white-collar or service jobs. Much can be expected of the contribution of women as core workers in these areas, particularly in view of the looming labor shortage with the decline in Japan's birthrate.

The lesser educated

Junior high or high school graduates comprise this category. Actually very few women end their education at graduation from junior high school these days so most of the women in this category are high school graduates. Of the three categories of ultra-educated, highly educated, and lesser educated, the last group represents the largest challenge for society. Let's look at why that should be so.

First, most women in this category can only find low-level jobs, working in clerical, blue-collar, or service-industry positions. Since they have not attended junior college or university, very few of them can obtain better-paying, high-level jobs. They fall into the low-income bracket at the bottom of today's increasingly unequal society.

A second factor in their disadvantageous position is the division of workers into regular staff and nonregular staff at Japanese companies, which is another aspect of our unequal society, as I will discuss in a later chapter. Many nonregular staff members, including part-time and dispatched workers, are junior high or high school graduates; more importantly, most nonregular staff are female. Thus lesser-educated women have unstable as well as poorly paid jobs. It would be rash to assume, however, that all nonregular staff members have simply stumbled into this status; some women select this option intentionally for various reasons.

Finally, we should not overlook the role of the education provided today by Japanese high schools, where the majority of students enroll in the general education track. Education in this track clusters around five main subjects—Japanese, mathematics, English, science, and social studies. Students do not focus on subjects likely to be directly applicable to an occupation, and classes in agriculture, industrial arts, business, healthcare, or social work are rare. In other words, the general education track concentrates on subjects needed for university entrance exams. While this is good for students going on to university, those who go to work immediately after high school do not acquire the skills they need. As a result, their only option after graduation is to find jobs as unskilled workers.

There is no problem per se in teaching students core academic courses, such as Japanese and mathematics. More than the subjects taught, the problem lies in the teaching philosophy of instructors and the lack of career counseling for students. Although teachers in the general education track are diligent in providing the kind of education that prepares students for university, they are much less so in providing career counseling and job placement services for students who have realized that they are not suited to academics and have abandoned the idea of going to university in favor of finding a job. This problem is especially prevalent at high schools—both public and private—registering weaker scores on Japan's standardized scholastic aptitude test.

In Tachibanaki (2004a), I looked into what type of person ends up becoming a freeter (a floating part-time worker) and found that most had attended or dropped out of general education programs at high schools having low test scores. This suggests a problem with the education being offered in this track. A change in course is clearly called for, with teachers in these programs rethinking their teaching philosophy and comprehensive career counseling being made available to students. Or perhaps a framework could be established for general education graduates who have no marketable skills to raise their skill level through vocational training offered by the public sector, allowing them to seek out better employment.

What other measures could be taken? One thing I would very much like to see is for students entering high school to give serious consideration to going to a vocational high school that would give them skills helpful later in finding a job, rather than pursuing the general education track with some vague notion of going on to university. As long as Japan remains a "credentials society," however, it is natural for parents and students alike to set their hearts on the track leading to university; it will not be easy to nudge some away from the academic track to the vocational track.

As mentioned earlier, though, I forecast that Japan will place less emphasis on academic credentials in the future. Although society in general does not yet realize this, people are starting to notice that those around them with university degrees are not enjoying all that much of an advantage. The amount of faith placed in academic background is bound to decrease, albeit gradually, as more and more people realize that acquiring practical skills—rather than an advanced education—will enable them to earn a high income. Thus, the signs are good that more and more priority will be given to vocational education.

In this regard, it is crucial that society and corporations offer appropriately favorable wages and working conditions to those who are not highly educated but who are highly skilled. In other words, promotions and wages should be decided based on worker productivity and not solely on educational background.

Chapter Four

Marriage and Divorce

The lament is frequently heard in Japan these days that women no longer want to marry and have children, but is that really so? This chapter will look into why people decide to marry, how they choose a marriage partner, and how those marriages fare.

The rise in the divorce rate also receives much comment. Until two or three decades ago, few Japanese couples divorced even if they were unhappy in their marriages. This reality is reflected in the following sayings and comments: "A child cements a marriage." "Divorce might hurt my reputation." "I will have a hard time making ends meet if I get divorced." The Japanese divorce rate is in fact rising today, though, so we need to investigate why this has occurred.

Why People Marry

Do Japanese young people want to marry?

In chapter 1, we briefly looked at the percentage of Japanese that marry and the percentage that remain single throughout their lives. Since more than 90 percent of men and women marry, we can call Japan a "marrying society." It is true that the divorce rate has risen, but we must remember that many divorced people remarry. Surveying all Japanese, we find that the overwhelming majority of people of an appropriate age for marriage are in fact married, be it a first marriage or a remarriage. Why, then, the common belief that more and more people never marry?

Let's look at the facts. Table 4-1 traces changes in the desire of singles* (age 18–34) to marry at some point in their lives. We see that in periodic surveys from 1982 to 2005, men responding that they did not intend ever to marry increased threefold from 2.3 percent to 7.1 percent, while the percentage of women so responding rose only slightly from 4.1 percent to 5.6 percent. According to the data, then, it would be more accurate to say that it is men, not women, who no longer want to marry.

This is also clear from changes in the other response, "intend to marry someday." The figure for men dropped 9 percentage points, from 95.9 percent in 1982 to 87.0 percent in 2005, but the figure for women fell only 4 percentage points from 94.2 to 90.0 percent. In fact, therefore, the desire never to marry has risen more among men than among women.

In analyzing these statistics, however, we must determine whether that is an active or passive lack of intent. Namely, did such respondents never have any interest in marriage, or were they interested in marriage in the early years but then gave up on it after failing to find a marriage partner?

---

* Note that "singles" (*mikonsha*) refers to "singles who have never married," as in the surveys cited in this book.

Table 4-1 Desire of never-married persons to marry by survey

Male (%)

	8th Survey (1982)	9th Survey (1987)	10th Survey (1992)	11th Survey (1997)	12th Survey (2002)	13th Survey (2005)
Intend to marry someday	95.9	91.8	90.0	85.9	87.0	87.0
Do not intend ever to marry	2.3	4.5	4.9	6.3	5.4	7.1
Not known	1.8	3.7	5.1	7.8	7.7	5.9
Total (age 18–34)	100.0	100.0	100.0	100.0	100.0	100.0
n	2,732	3,299	4,215	3,982	3,897	3,139

Female (%)

	8th Survey (1982)	9th Survey (1987)	10th Survey (1992)	11th Survey (1997)	12th Survey (2002)	13th Survey (2005)
Intend to marry someday	94.2	92.9	90.2	89.1	88.3	90.0
Do not intend ever to marry	4.1	4.6	5.2	4.9	5.0	5.6
Not known	1.7	2.5	4.6	6.0	6.7	4.3
Total (age 18–34)	100.0	100.0	100.0	100.0	100.0	100.0
n	2,110	2,605	3,647	3,612	3,494	3,064

Question: Taking a lifelong perspective, which best describes your desire to marry?
   1. Intend to marry someday   2. Do not intend ever to marry
Note: Subjects are never-married persons aged 18–34.
Source: National Institute of Population and Social Security Research (2007, vol. II, 13, table 1-1).

Of course, among those actively rejecting marriage may be those who do so because they decided from the start that, for some reason or other, they would not be able to find a marriage partner. Similarly, among those more passively rejecting marriage, the degree of passive intent varies depending on how hard they have searched for a marriage partner and on how much they have held out for their ideal in a mate. These few examples show us that neither active rejection nor passive rejection can be considered as purely one or the other.

The categories of active and passive rejection are somewhat imprecise, but figure 4-1 will help us distinguish the two. This figure shows the degree to which men and women are holding out for Mr. or Ms. Right, and in every survey women have indicated that they "will wait for an ideal partner" at a rate that is 5 percentage points

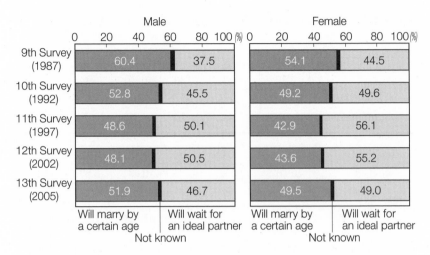

Fig. 4-1 Views on marriage (marriage age/ideal partner) by survey

Question: Taking a lifelong perspective, which best describes your intent to marry?
1. Will marry by a certain age   2. Will wait for an ideal partner

Note: Subjects are never-married persons aged 18–34 who have indicated that they intend to marry someday.

Source: National Institute of Population and Social Security Research (2007, vol. II, 16, fig. 1-1).

higher on average than men. Although this difference between men and women is not so large, we can say that women are somewhat more particular about finding an ideal mate.

Table 4-2 shows this even more clearly by presenting views on marriage by gender and age group, essentially taking the information in figure 4-1 and recasting it by age group. Looking at the 25–34 age groups, we find that a significantly higher percentage of women than men in these older age brackets are waiting for an ideal partner—for example, 65.5 percent of women ages 30–34. We can observe a strong trend among men to marry even if they have to compromise on their partner, whereas women show greater reluctance to compromise the older they become.

Let's look at why women tend to hold out for Mr. Right as they get older. Most single women work so they have some kind of income. However, as we have already seen, the majority of single women want to marry if they can. This means that women are

Table 4-2 Views on marriage (marriage age/ideal partner) by age group

13th Survey (2005)   *(%)*

Age at time of survey	Male				Female			
	Total (*n*)	Will marry by a certain age	Will wait for an ideal partner	Not known	Total (*n*)	Will marry by a certain age	Will wait for an ideal partner	Not known
Total (age 18–34)	100.0 (2,732)	51.9	46.7	1.3	100.0 (2,759)	49.5	49.0	1.4
18–19	100.0 (373)	52.3	46.1	1.6	100.0 (484)	50.6	48.1	1.2
20–24	100.0 (899)	52.8	46.3	0.9	100.0 (1,086)	54.9	43.8	1.3
25–29	100.0 (902)	54.9	43.6	1.6	100.0 (766)	50.4	47.9	1.7
30–34	100.0 (558)	45.5	53.0	1.4	100.0 (423)	33.1	65.5	1.4

Question: Taking a lifelong perspective, which best describes your intent to marry?
    1. Will marry by a certain age   2. Will wait for an ideal partner

Note: Subjects are never-married persons aged 18–34 who have indicated that they intend to marry someday.

Source: Based on National Institute of Population and Social Security Research (2007, vol. II, 17, table 1-6).

looking for a marriage partner regardless of whether they intend to become full-time homemakers or to continue working outside the home after they marry. Naturally, some women are successful in their search for a partner and others are not. For those who have not found a partner relatively early, the choice between marriage and work then looms as a more serious matter. In some cases, women may start to think that they may not be able to marry. Such women try to obtain some kind of economic security so that they can make it on their own if they end up remaining single and never marrying. They may make an active decision to work in their current position for the rest of their lives. If they do not have regular employment, they may look for full-time work or work that would offer them long-term employment.

Women in their thirties who have in this way gained confidence in their financial future then start to think that it would be okay not to marry if they do not find a good marriage partner. In other words, conditions that allow one to wait for an ideal marriage partner come into place for women in their thirties, but such is not the case for men, whose economic and other conditions seldom improve markedly when they are in their late twenties or early thirties. For this reason, the percentage of men who insist on waiting for an ideal partner does not increase with age.

Another reason why women in their thirties are particular about a marriage partner or start thinking that it would be okay never to marry is that often women start to have confidence in their own professional abilities around this age. They start to focus more and more on their career and feel more passion for their job than for marriage. Rather than marrying and having their time taken up with caring for their husband's needs, or having to interrupt their career because of childrearing responsibilities, they choose the path of dedicating themselves to their own career.

What are the Japanese looking for in marriage?

We can learn much about marriage in Japan by examining people's motives for marrying. Figure 4-2 shows the chief merits of marriage as cited by male and female respondents. By far the greatest motivations for both men and women are (1) to "have emotional support" and (2) to "have one's own children and family." This shows that the Japanese get married with the hope of finding psychological comfort and building a family.

The next most frequently cited advantages to marriage were (1) to "live with a person one loves," (2) to "gain social credibility," and (3) to "meet expectations of parents and society." These, however, carry only about half the importance of the first two above. Looking now at the difference between men's and women's responses, we find that men place considerable importance on gaining social credibility while women value living with a person they love: men have a drive to settle down while women value emotion.

Turning to changes over time, we see one noteworthy development: the percentage of people citing "have one's own children and family" as a merit of marriage has increased dramatically for both men and women since 1987, rising from 20 to 33 percent for men

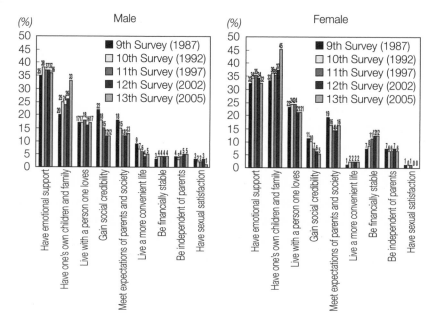

Fig. 4-2 The merits of marriage by survey

Note: The above bar graphs show the percentage of never-married subjects aged 18–34 who regard each item (up to two choices) as a main merit of marriage.

Source: National Institute of Population and Social Security Research (2007, vol. II, 28, fig. 2-5).

and from 33 to 45 percent for women and becoming the number-one benefit in marriage cited by women in 2005.

Why has having one's own children and family risen dramatically in recent years as a reason to marry? We need to examine why this trend is pronounced among women, in particular, because it would seem at first glance to be in contradiction to the fact that Japan's birthrate is on the decline today.

Also, the response of being financially stable has increased for women from 7 to 12 percent, despite the decline of the traditional idea that men are the breadwinners and a woman's place is in the home. How should we interpret this increase in the percentage of women seeking financial stability in marriage?

Regarding the first point, the number of so-called shotgun weddings is on the rise in Japan. More and more couples are marrying after a child is conceived or born. Such changing attitudes might well have an impact on this response.

As for being financially stable, it is true that the traditional view of a woman's place being in the home has steadily fallen out of favor. However, a new trend toward full-time homemaking has also emerged among women since the 1990s. These new full-time homemakers are women who marry men with comparatively high incomes and do not work themselves. Does this mean that talk of the changing gender roles was just that—talk—and women do not actually have a very strong desire to work? Is the marked rise in women in the labor force in recent years simply a reflection of the increase in part-time working wives who took up jobs to compensate for the decrease in their husbands' incomes with the economic downturn from the 1990s into the new century?

In these days of economic instability, it is natural that women would look to marriage to be financially comfortable and have their own children and family. It is curious, though, that women cite having children and a family as the number-one reason to marry, and yet the birthrate is in fact declining. There appears to be a contradiction here: women want children, but are actually having fewer of them. We will be addressing this seemingly contradictory survey finding in the next chapter.

The marriage partner: ideal and reality

What do people seek in a marriage partner? What kind of person do people hope to marry? Let's try to answer these questions.

Table 4-3 presents the attributes that Japanese singles are looking for in a marriage partner. This table is from the National Institute of Population and Social Security Research's *Shusshō dōkō kihon chōsa* (Japanese national fertility survey), which I will be citing frequently in this chapter. The 2005 survey report, however, did not include this question so the data given in the table is slightly old, from 1997.

Nonetheless, based on table 4-3, we can see how people looking for a marriage partner rank such attributes as physical appearance, character, educational background, economic stability, occupation, common hobbies, and coresidence with parents. As you might

Table 4-3 Attributes desired in a marriage partner by level of priority

Male   *(%)*

Attribute	Total	(Sub-total) High priority + priority	High priority	Priority	Low priority	Not known	(Subtotal) High priority + priority
		11th Survey (1997)					10th Survey
Educational background	100	23.5	2.2	21.3	74.3	2.2	29.8
Occupation	100	35.8	3.0	32.8	61.8	2.4	39.5
Economic stability	100	30.8	2.8	28.0	66.8	2.5	26.7
Character	100	95.2	82.9	12.3	2.6	2.2	94.1
Physical appearance	100	74.0	19.6	54.3	23.3	2.7	79.6
Understanding re work responsibilities	100	88.3	42.5	45.7	9.5	2.2	—
Cooperation with housework	100	86.8	34.9	51.9	10.7	2.5	—
Common hobbies	100	70.4	22.0	48.5	27.3	2.3	—
Coresidence with parents	100	58.9	15.5	43.4	38.8	2.3	—

Female   *(%)*

Attribute	Total	(Sub-total) High priority + priority	High priority	Priority	Low priority	Not known	(Subtotal) High priority + priority
		11th Survey (1997)					10th Survey
Educational background	100	49.7	7.7	42.0	49.2	1.1	54.6
Occupation	100	77.9	21.8	56.1	20.9	1.3	78.0
Economic stability	100	90.9	33.5	57.4	8.0	1.1	88.7
Character	100	97.8	92.2	5.6	1.0	1.1	97.3
Physical appearance	100	67.3	12.8	54.5	31.4	1.3	67.7
Understanding re work responsibilities	100	88.4	46.5	41.9	10.3	1.3	—
Cooperation with housework	100	89.8	43.6	46.2	8.8	1.4	—
Common hobbies	100	78.9	30.4	48.5	19.9	1.2	—
Coresidence with parents	100	78.8	34.0	44.9	19.8	1.4	—

Question: When deciding on a marriage partner, to what degree do you put priority on the following attributes?
    1. High priority   2. Priority   3. Low priority

Note: Subjects are never-married persons aged 18–34 who have indicated that they intend to marry someday. Total number of subjects is 3,420 males and 3,218 females. "Coresidence with parents" means residence with the male's parents.

Source: National Institute of Population and Social Security Research, *Heisei 9 nen dai 11 kai shusshō dōkō kihon chōsa, dai II hōkokusho: dokushin seinensō no kekkonkan to kazokukan* (Eleventh Japanese national fertility survey, 1997, volume II: Attitudes toward marriage and family among unmarried Japanese youth) (1999), 64, table 8-1.

expect, preferences vary widely from person to person. More importantly, one's level of interest in a person inevitably changes depending on the level of these attributes that one possesses oneself.

Social psychologists such as Suzuki Hirohisa, who contributed a chapter to *Kekkon* (Marriage) (Yoshikawa et al. 1995), have some interesting insights on this issue. They cite two theories on marriage: one of complementarity and one of similarity. The theory of complementarity states that a couple that has different attributes has a good marriage because the partners complement each other. In contrast, the theory of similarity claims that sharing generally similar social views and attributes creates a good marriage.

As I see it, the theory of complementarity means that a person without financial security looks for someone who has that; a weak-willed person is attracted to a strong-willed person; a short person seeks a tall person; a person who is not intelligent wants one who is. The theory of similarity claims the opposite—the more physically attractive a man or woman is, the more he or she looks for that trait in a marriage partner; the more brilliant a person is, the more he or she looks for intelligence in a partner. It is clear that people will vary on whether they want their marriage partner to be opposite or similar to them and on which attributes they particularly want in a mate.

Social psychologists maintain that most people place the highest priority on physical attraction and appearance. However, cultural anthropologists such as Minoura Yasuko, who also wrote a chapter in *Kekkon*, maintain that men instinctually look to a woman's physical appearance while women stress a man's income and occupation. Today, though, more and more women have careers of their own so this preference cited by cultural anthropologists may be changing somewhat, and the social psychologist view that people particularly value physical attraction and appearance may be more persuasive. Statistics from 1983, while a little dated, indicate that personality and love are ranked at the top by both men and women, though, so perhaps it is physical attraction plus personality that people value.

A decade or so ago, women's ideal for a husband was popularly believed to be one who possessed the "three highs"—a high level of education, a high salary, and physical height. Recently, the term "three Cs" has come into vogue. Proposed by Ogura (2003), the three Cs stand for "comfortable," "communicative," and "cooperative." That is, a woman's ideal man is one who offers a financially comfortable lifestyle, who shares similar values and is emotionally communicative, and who is cooperative in housework and childcare. With the "three highs," the focus was on appearance and income, whereas with the "three Cs" the emphasis is on being able to enjoy living with one's partner. Both show, however, the importance of financial security, so we can conclude that women are concerned about a man's income whatever the era.

Unfortunately, economists have little to contribute to the discussion of what people look for in a marriage partner. Economics can only say that, of the many attributes sought in a marriage partner, income is of prime importance, followed by educational background and occupation. The impact of finances and economic stability on marriage is discussed in Tachibanaki (1997a) and Tachibanaki and Kimura (2008), so I will not discuss that topic here. Educational background and occupation are best studied by educators and sociologists, respectively.

Sociologists such as Ueno Chizuko, who also contributed to *Kekkon*, have conducted interesting analyses of educational background and occupation, as we can see in table 4-4, which looks at homogamy (homogeneity in marriage partners) in education for arranged and love (i.e., nonarranged) marriages. What is surprising about this table is that the vast majority of love marriages are between people with the same educational background. Unsurprisingly, there is an even higher rate of educational homogamy for arranged marriages. Such results would seem to confirm the theory of like seeking like in marriage.

In figure 4-3 we can see what changes have occurred in educational homogamy during the period from 1992 to 2005. We observe that educational homogamy overall decreased from 51.9 to 44.1 percent, while upward marriages for the wife (where the husband's level of education is higher than that of the wife) increased from 31.7 percent to 35.1 percent. Incidentally, in 2005 downward marriages (where the husband's level of education is lower than that of

Table 4-4 Degree of educational homogamy by type of marriage

Type of marriage	Husband's education level	Wife's Education Level			
		Junior high school graduate	High school graduate	Junior college or college of technology graduate	University graduate
Total	Junior high school graduate	2.45	0.52	0.13	0.03
	High school graduate	0.62	1.51	0.48	0.19
	Junior college or college of technology graduate	0.20	0.93	3.53	0.79
	University graduate	0.10	0.87	2.66	4.16
Arranged marriage	Junior high school graduate	2.23	0.52	0.05	—
	High school graduate	0.54	1.61	0.45	0.17
	Junior college or college of technology graduate	0.13	1.11	3.00	1.24
	University graduate	0.04	0.83	3.31	4.75
Love marriage	Junior high school graduate	2.65	0.53	0.18	0.05
	High school graduate	0.69	1.45	0.48	0.20
	Junior college or college of technology graduate	0.25	0.83	3.72	0.58
	University graduate	0.15	0.87	2.29	3.78

Sources: Based on Ministry of Health, Labor, and Welfare, *Shōwa 57 nen dai 8 ji shussanryoku chōsa* (Eighth national fertility survey, 1982), quoted in Yuzawa Y., *Zusetsu gendai Nihon no kazoku mondai* (The family in modern Japan [with charts and diagrams]) (Tokyo: Japan Broadcast Publishing, 1987), 63, fig. 30-2.

the wife) accounted for 20.9 percent of marriages, the smallest of the three categories, and that percentage showed very little change.

In Japan, marriages where the husband and wife have the same level of education plus marriages where the wife marries up together account for approximately 80 percent of all marriages. This reflects the fact that, on average, men still have a higher level of education than women in Japan. In our survey of trends in women's education, we noted that women have enjoyed a greater rise in educational

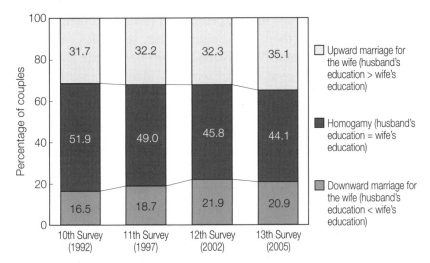

Fig. 4-3 Educational pairing in marriage

Source: National Institute of Population and Social Security Research (2007, vol. I, 21, fig. 1-4).

level than men have. In principle, this would imply that the percentage of educational homogamy should rise and that of wives marrying up should decline. The survey results—educational homogamy decreasing and women marrying up increasing—suggest then that individual couples are no longer demonstrating a strong preference in regard to the education level of their marriage partner.

I see this as a desirable trend for Japan. In the previous chapter, I forecast a decline in the importance placed on academic background in Japan, and the fact that people are no longer showing a strong preference in regard to the educational level of their marriage partner can be interpreted as one sign of that. In two expressions of the same trend, then, Japanese are becoming less particular about the educational background of their spouse at the same time that society is placing less importance on academic résumé.

We have just looked at what people seek in a marriage mate, and now I would like to discuss briefly why the majority of people are successful in finding a marriage partner. For this discussion, I will borrow from what are known in economics as search theory and job matching theory. First, let's look at the matter from the perspective of search theory and the lowering of the so-called reservation wage. According to this theory, people will give up on their original demands and lower their expectations if they search for a marriage partner for a long time. "Reservation wage" here is the lower-limit wage, the lowest wage at which a worker will accept a job offer and start work. Just as people gradually lower their reservation wage as their job search lengthens, we can posit that people will lower their requirements in a marriage partner.

Second, if we apply job matching theory to matchmaking, the more frequently men and women meet, the more tolerant of each other's differences they will become, until they eventually marry. Third, social psychology says that if people are in frequent contact and spend long periods of time together, propinquity gradually takes over even if they did not feel any particular attraction to each other originally. This essentially takes what job matching theory tells us and casts it in psychological terms regarding marriage.

Recasting these theories in simpler terms, we end up with these oft-found sentiments: "Marriage is a gamble." "Love is blind." "My partner isn't quite my dream come true, but I'll make do." See Tachibanaki (1997a) for more information. In the end, these common expressions capture many people's road to matrimony.

Why People Do Not Marry

So far, we have looked at factors in marrying, but let's turn now to factors in not marrying. We will consider not only the less than one in ten young men and women who express no interest from the start in marrying, but also those who do want to marry but find their way blocked for some reason or other. And let's also examine the question by age group, since it is likely that there will be large differences between, say, eighteen-year-olds and thirty-year-olds.

Percentage who never marry

An excellent source for our study of this issue is *Wagakuni dokushinsō no kekkonkan to kazokukan* (Attitudes toward marriage and family among Japanese singles), which is a report on the 2005 *Shusshō dōkō kihon chōsa* (Japanese national fertility survey) conducted by the National Institute of Population and Social Security Research. In this survey, singles were offered eleven reasons for never having married and were asked to select up to three that applied to them.

These eleven reasons for remaining single are listed in table 4-5, where they are further divided into five categories. The categories are self-explanatory: "Little felt need for marriage" is composed of those who at present feel no strong desire to marry. "Competing interest" includes cases where people do not marry because they are more interested in other things. "No marriage partner" refers to cases where a person would like to marry but has not found a suitable marriage partner. "Obstacle to marriage" means a person would like to marry but cannot for some concrete reason.

The categories are not mutually exclusive. For instance, the first two might include cases where a woman is in a relationship with a man but is not yet seriously considering marriage; some people may fall into both the third and fourth ones as well.

Table 4-5 Reasons for remaining single

Reason	Category	
1. Am too young to marry	Little felt need for marriage	Reasons for not marrying
2. Do not feel the need to marry		
3. Want to concentrate on work/study	Competing interest	
4. Want to enjoy hobbies or other pastimes		
5. Do not want to lose the freedom and carefree life of a single person		
6. Have not been able to meet a suitable partner	No marriage partner	Reasons for being unable to marry
7. Am unable to have a good relationship with the opposite sex		
8. Do not have enough money for marriage	Obstacle to marriage	
9. Have no prospect for housing after marriage		
10. Lack parental/societal approval of the match		
11. Other	Other	

Question: Of the eleven items, which best describes why you have remained single? Please select up to three responses. (If you have decided on a marriage partner, please select "11. Other.")

Source: National Institute of Population and Social Security Research (2007, vol. II, 46, table 5-1).

We could also make two broad categories of "reasons for not marrying"—reasons 1 through 5—and "reasons for being unable to marry"—reasons 6 through 10. Of course, some respondents will select items under both "reasons for not marrying" and "reasons for being unable to marry" so the total of these two categories does not add up to 100 percent but exceeds it.

In table 4-6 these reasons for remaining unmarried are broken down by age group. If we look at the total figures for all ages, 18–34, we see that "reasons for not marrying" slightly exceed "reasons for being unable to marry" at about 55 versus 45 percent of responses for both men and women. How should we interpret this? If "unable to marry" made up the majority, policies could then be taken to promote marriage among young people. But since that is in the minority by a small margin, it would seem best to focus our attention on why young people are not more aggressively trying to marry.

Particularly interesting in this regard are the differences among the age groups. For the 18–19 age group, "reasons for not marrying" exceed "reasons for being unable to marry" by nearly twice as much, but it is natural for the desire for marriage to be low in this young age bracket. As the age rises, the gap between the two categories decreases, and in the 25–29 age group, "not marrying" and "unable to marry" are almost equal. Both the percentage of people wanting to marry and the percentage of people unable to marry increase. Then in the 30–34 age group, "unable to marry" for the first time exceeds "not marrying"—people want to marry but are unable to.

We observe that "no marriage partner" is very high in both the 25–29 and the 30–34 age groups, and that this is an especially serious problem for those in their thirties. People become increasingly unwilling to compromise regarding their marriage partner and opportunities for meeting the opposite sex also decrease.

Also noteworthy is the frequency of "obstacle to marriage" as a factor in not being able to marry. We can see from the figures that this affects men more than women, as 33.3 percent of men and

Table 4-6 Reasons for remaining single by gender and age group

(%)

Age	Category	13th Survey (2005)	
		Male	Female
Total	Not marrying	70.5	72.2
	No need	47.2	51.7
	Competing interest	58.1	61.2
	Unable to marry	60.1	60.3
	No partner	41.4	43.6
	Obstacle	30.1	22.7
Age 18–19	Not marrying	83.2	84.8
	No need	72.7	75.6
	Competing interest	61.1	68.4
	Unable to marry	48.6	52.1
	No partner	32.9	36.2
	Obstacle	20.4	20.7
Age 20–24	Not marrying	75.9	80.6
	No need	56.6	62.4
	Competing interest	63.5	67.4
	Unable to marry	56.1	61.5
	No partner	34.2	39.6
	Obstacle	32.1	27.4
Age 25–29	Not marrying	67.8	62.8
	No need	38.2	35.5
	Competing interest	57.2	56.0
	Unable to marry	64.8	62.5
	No partner	44.4	47.1
	Obstacle	33.3	23.0
Age 30–34	Not marrying	58.3	54.2
	No need	30.1	27.7
	Competing interest	49.3	47.4
	Unable to marry	66.4	62.9
	No partner	53.2	55.0
	Obstacle	28.2	13.5

Note: This table shows the percentage of never-married persons by gender and age group who chose a response in the category. If a respondent selected more than one item in a given category, the selected items were lumped together and counted as one.

Source: Based on National Institute of Population and Social Security Research (2007, vol. II, 47, table 5-2).

23.0 percent of women in the 25–29 age group, and 28.2 percent of men and 13.5 percent of women in the 30–34 age group, indicated this as a reason they were single. The underlying cause here is the hard financial times the younger generation has encountered with the recession over the past fifteen to twenty years in Japan. The economic downturn has had a severe impact particularly on young people. The numbers of young unemployed, NEETs (people Not currently engaged in Employment, Education, or Training), and freeters have risen, and young people have not been able to find regular employment even in their late twenties or after turning thirty. As the burden of being the breadwinner still largely falls on men, they feel more strongly the financial impediments to marriage.

Lack of a suitable marriage partner becomes more serious for men over thirty, but this has not attracted much popular attention beyond schemes, mainly in farming villages, to bring in brides from other Asian countries. There is, however, a nearly defiant attitude among Japanese women over the age of thirty in regard to their own inability to marry.

In *Makeinu no tōboe* (Howl of the loser dogs), an influential bestseller published in 2003, Sakai Junko looks at childless women age thirty or over who have never married. A decade or two ago such women were pitied as losers in the game of life, but this book argues that such women need not think disparagingly of themselves. Every now and then, though, Sakai writes something that makes one wonder if, after all, the dream of women is to get married and have children—there is a whiff of self-consolation when she points out how living alone is easier—but the book is excellent in its insightful portrayal of the complex mindset of single, childless women in their thirties or beyond, and it certainly touched a nerve among young women in Japan.

Ueno and Nobuta (2004) and others have also taken up the issue of single women over thirty, suggesting various strategies for them to live alone and saying there is no need to cling to the traditional bond of marriage. Ueno Chizuko is a well-known advocate of feminism in Japan, and Ueno and Ogura (2002) is a helpful reference with its very accessible presentation of feminism through a series of dialogues between these two women. It will be intriguing to see to what extent feminism spreads among Japanese women and through Japanese society in general.

Obstacles to marriage

What obstacles to marriage do Japanese face? In the 2005 survey, single men and women who had indicated that they intended to marry someday and were currently dating someone were asked to select one or two factors that were hindering their getting married within the next year. Figure 4-4 graphs the results.

Before examining the answers in detail, let's first look at how prevalent this issue is in Japan. In fact, 67.2 percent of men and 68.9 percent of women responded that there was some impediment to their getting married. Such high figures—nearly 70 percent for both genders—make you realize that marriage is not simple. While I do not advocate plunging into marriage trusting in love to solve all problems, perhaps we can devise measures to address the barriers to marriage if we know what they are.

According to figure 4-4, lack of funds for marriage is the most frequent obstacle to marriage for both men and women, towering far above the other items. Occupation or work issues constitute the second most frequently cited impediment, and these also reflect concerns about achieving a financially stable married life. Although not shown in this figure, twenty years ago the statistics for work and occupation concerns were 10 percent for men and 13 percent for women. The fact that these rose dramatically to 22 percent and 23 percent, respectively, in 2005 shows us how great the impact of the economic slump has been and substantiates our earlier discussion of the reasons why people find themselves unable to marry.

Interestingly, the third most frequently cited barrier to marriage differs between men and women: men specify housing for their married life (18 percent) whereas women report that parental consent (17 percent) is holding them back from marriage. The financial issue of where to live after getting married can be grouped together with the second most serious problem, insufficient income or lack of regular employment; both are proof that marriage places a heavy financial burden and responsibility on men.

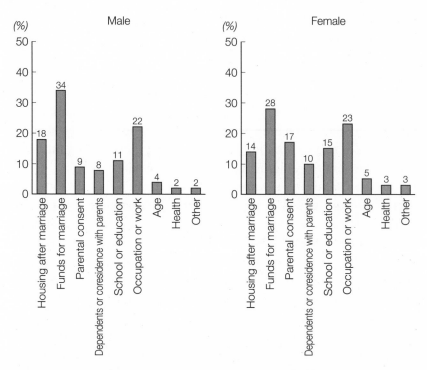

Fig. 4-4 Obstacles to marriage (13th Survey [2005])

Note: This figure shows the percentage of never-married persons who said the given factor was a major obstacle to their getting married. Respondents were permitted to indicate up to two items.

Source: Based on National Institute of Population and Social Security Research (2007, vol. II, 41, fig. 4-1).

On the other hand, the fact that women cite the problem of parental consent implies that the parents are being consulted or are expressing their views when a daughter marries. Evidently there are times that they do not approve of the marriage partner the daughter has chosen or that they have in mind someone else for her to marry. This raises the question of whether there are more cases of parent-child disagreement on this issue for daughters than for sons. (A mere 9 percent of men cited parental approval as a problem.) It seems that parents give more freedom to their sons than to their daughters in regard to marriage.

Why are Japanese parents lenient when their sons marry and yet interfering with their daughters? The answer lies in the realities of marriage in Japan. If both the husband and wife are employed, the wife will have an income as well and not be totally dependent financially on her husband. If the wife is a full-time homemaker, however, she is dependent on her husband's ability to make a living. A couple's lifestyle is heavily influenced by its income and assets, as is its degree of happiness. It is thus not altogether unnatural for parents to concern themselves with the income, occupation, education, and personality of their daughter's marriage partner, nor should they be unduly criticized for it.

At the same time, it is also true that when children have reached a marriageable age they are already adults and parents should not get heavily involved. Taking an active role in their children's education is a different matter, since the children are still young and are not financially independent, but marriage is the start of a child's second stage of life and so respecting a child's choice is important in the sense of ensuring his or her autonomy.

In addition, as we will discuss later, divorce is not something to be ashamed of in this day and age. If the couple reaches an impasse in their marriage, they have the option of divorce so there is no need to assume that a first marriage is of decisive importance.

I find it somewhat surprising that "funds for marriage" is the most frequently cited obstacle. "Funds for marriage" mainly refers to money to cover the wedding, the honeymoon, and starting life as a married couple. The last item, starting married life, is also related to "housing after marriage," another item in the survey. The reason young people cannot ready sufficient assets to marry is their low wages and income. The wages of young people in Japan have traditionally been kept low under the seniority-based wage system, and the situation has been worsened by the high unemployment rate among young people and their being unable to emerge from the status of NEET or freeter due to the recession over the past ten to fifteen years. Japan needs to raise the wages of its young people and secure full-time employment for them.

Marriage and the growing inequalities in society

The fact that a certain proportion of young people in Japan face a shortage of funds for marriage is related to the growing inequalities in society discussed in Tachibanaki (2006). We can assume that many times parents, if they are financially well-off, give their children the funds for marriage. You often hear of parents purchasing a condominium for their children to live in after they get married or readying a fancy bridal trousseau. Parents who are financially well-off can transfer their assets to their children as inheritance and gifts. This means that children of wealthy families at the upper end of society have no need to worry about having enough funds for marriage.

The story is different, however, for the children of those at the lower end of society. The children of poor families having few or no assets can expect no inheritance from their parents and little if any help in gathering together funds for marriage. Because of this, these young people must ready for marriage using their own money. As has already been pointed out, however, they cannot hope to build up such savings under the current employment and wage system in Japan. It is no wonder, therefore, that young people find themselves lacking money for marriage.

We can say that the times, with the great disparity between rich and poor in Japan today, have contributed to many young people lacking the funds to get married, but what is the proper response to this situation? I have several points to make in this regard.

First, even before this age of growing inequality, Japan had low-income families with few assets, and there was a long period before Japan became an affluent society, so people must have faced this obstacle before. To add some historical background to what is given in figure 4-4 here, roughly two decades ago, in 1987, 43 percent of men cited lack of funds as an obstacle to marriage, versus 34 percent in 2005—that is, the situation was more serious by almost 10 percentage points then. Incidentally, the second most frequently cited obstacle in 1987 was housing after marriage, at 17 percent. If we add that to the 43 percent for lack of marriage funds, the total is 60 percent: economic factors constituted a formidable barrier to marriage in 1987.

From this perspective, we can see that lack of marriage funds was a very prominent issue even in that era, which was known for its overall equality. Not very many Japanese were wealthy enough to secure marriage funds for their children even in 1987, in the era of stable growth that followed Japan's period of high economic expansion.

Second, we can note that two decades ago young people married even though marriage funds and housing after marriage were a problem and, moreover, they married at a young age. There was no trend of marrying later, as there is today. Couples could marry at a comparatively young age despite such economic factors, as they did not have elaborate wedding ceremonies or honeymoons and they lived in low-rent homes as newlyweds. True, the financial barrier was high, but the desire to get married was stronger so they lowered their standard of living to match their budgets and married.

Third, I find myself wondering why young people today can't follow the lead of these couples. For example, they could forgo an elaborate wedding ceremony and honeymoon. In fact, quite a few couples have started doing so, as seen in the new coinage *jimikon* or "modest wedding." Lavish weddings can be left to wealthy young people and their parents.

My fourth point in regard to money and marriage is to emphasize how crucial it is that young people be offered higher wages and that measures be taken to ensure that young people can obtain full-time jobs. The seniority-based wage system that keeps young people's wages low must be reviewed, and the minimum wage—the wage at which many young people work—must be raised substantially. New policies are needed to shift the host of part-timers, freeters, and other nonregular workers to positions as regular workers. For this, the public sector must make them more attractive to corporations by implementing vocational training for young people and raising their skill level. For details, refer to Tachibanaki (2002a, 2004a, and 2004b).

Choosing a Marriage Partner

What kinds of opportunities for interaction lead to marriage? More precisely, I want to look into where people meet and what kinds of relationships they have.

Where do people meet potential marriage partners?

Close to 90 percent of marriages in Japan are now nonarranged marriages, so-called love marriages. In contrast, arranged marriages, which constituted almost one out of every two marriages a few decades ago, have fallen to about 6 percent. Today, the vast majority of people marry after falling in love with their partner. Figure 4-5 traces the trends in love and arranged marriages from before World War II until the year 2005. Before the war, arranged marriages made up nearly 70 percent of all marriages. After the war, however, arranged marriages gradually declined in number and love marriages increased. By the late 1960s, there were more or less equal percentages of the two types of marriage, with each standing at about 46 percent. From that time until today, love marriages have continued to gain in popularity while arranged marriages have continued to decline.

As the terms are used here, arranged marriages are cases where the couple met through an arranged introduction (*miai*) or through a matrimonial agency. In contrast, love marriages include cases where the couple are childhood friends/neighbors or met at school, at work or through a job, through friends or siblings, in town or during a trip, through hobbies or personal enrichment classes, or through a part-time job.

I don't fully agree with how arranged and love marriages have been defined here. I will leave that discussion until later, however, and look at the statistics for the various abovementioned ways of meeting a marriage partner. Figure 4-6 captures that for us.

We see that "at work or through a job" and "through friends or siblings" together made up 60 percent in 2005, signifying that these two are the most common ways of meeting a marriage partner. The latter, "through friends or siblings," increased by about

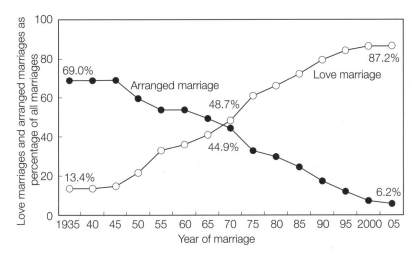

Fig. 4-5 Trends in love marriages and arranged marriages by year of marriage

Note: Subjects are first-marriage couples. This chart is based on data from the 7th Survey (for 1935–39 to 1970–74), the 8th Survey (for 1975–79), the 9th Survey (for 1980–84), the 10th Survey (for 1985–89), the 11th Survey (for 1990–94), the 12th Survey (for 1995–99), and the 13th Survey (for 2000–05).

Source: National Institute of Population and Social Security Research (2007, vol. I, 19, fig. 1-3).

10 percentage points from 1982; cases of people meeting at school also rose, from 6 to 11 percent. The remaining 15 percent or so is accounted for by "in town or during a trip," "through hobbies or personal enrichment classes," and "through a part-time job." These percentages correspond to what we might have observed in everyday life so they probably reflect the actual situation well enough.

Now, for my objections to the above definitions of arranged marriages (*miai kekkon*) and love marriages (*ren'ai kekkon*). It is hard to imagine that meeting "at work or through a job" or "through friends or siblings" and what is called here an "arranged introduction" differ all that much. In arranged introductions before the war and soon after it, there was an official matchmaker, with photographs and personal information being exchanged before a formal meeting where the candidates were introduced to each other. In earlier times, there were even cases where the two sets of parents decided on the

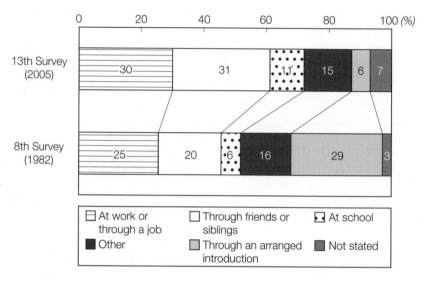

Fig. 4-6 How couples first met by survey

Note: The subjects are first-marriage couples who were married during the five years prior to each survey. "Other" is the total of "in town or during a trip," "through hobbies or personal enrichment classes," "through a part-time job," and "childhood friends/neighbors." Size of samples: 8th Survey: 1,298 13th Survey: 1,076

Source: Based on National Institute of Population and Social Security Research (2007, vol. I, 18, fig. 1-2).

marriage without their son and daughter ever meeting. These kinds of marriages can properly be called arranged marriages.

In arranged marriages in the postwar period, however, it has become common for the man and woman to build a relationship after the formal meeting where they are introduced. During that time, they at least develop feelings of mutual affection and decide that they would like to marry each other. And it is by no means uncommon for such introduced couples to decide not to marry if such feelings do not develop. It seems safe to assume then that such marriages are based on love, or at least affection, even if perhaps not as passionate a love as in the so-called love marriage.

Now let's take the case of meeting "through friends or siblings" as an example of how people in love marriages meet. While it is true that no photographs or personal information sheets are exchanged in advance as happens in arranged introductions, friends or siblings do provide an occasion for the man and woman to meet each other, and after the two are introduced it is common for them to start a relationship, as in arranged introductions. Thus the two cases are similar in both being means of introducing people.

The difference between the two is that an arranged introduction has marriage as its end goal from the start whereas meeting through friends or siblings is nothing more than a way for people to be introduced; the parties do not necessarily have marriage in mind. Since they are both ways for people to become acquainted, however, it seems strange to regard an arranged introduction as completely different from meeting through friends or siblings and to classify one as an arranged marriage and the other as a love marriage. It also seems to fly in the face of reality to see an arranged marriage as being devoid of affection and love, while a love marriage is seen as a love match. In this sense as well, the distinction between the two is fuzzy.

Since so-called arranged marriages have decreased to an insignificant percentage of marriages, it is now meaningless to divide marriages into love matches and arranged marriages. Figure 4-6 actually addresses the question of how people meet a marriage partner, and we should stop thinking in terms of "arranged marriage" and "love marriage."

Such meetings with the opposite sex lead to a relationship and, if all goes well, marriage. Let's briefly turn our attention, then, to relations with the opposite sex, the first step toward marriage.

Relations with the opposite sex

Figure 4-7 looks at single persons' relations with the opposite sex over the period from 1987 to 2005. The distinction here between "lover" and "friend" is not very clear so we will not dwell much on that aspect. What is truly surprising about this data, however, is that roughly half of these men and women reported that they were not in any relationship with the opposite sex. Moreover, such respondents have been rising over the period of these surveys. And if we subtract from that number those who claim not to be considering marriage (somewhat less than 10 percent), we can assume that over 40 percent of single people would like to have a friend or lover of the opposite sex.

Today relationships between men and women are freer, and there is more freedom in sexual behavior, as well. In this era, the fact that slightly over 40 percent of young people live a life where they have no relationship with the opposite sex and yet would like to have one draws a sad picture indeed. Of course, relationships with the opposite sex are not the only thing in life. There is the life of the mind, the world of the arts, sports and other leisure activities, and dedication to one's work, among others, so perhaps we should not be overly pessimistic about the situation. At any rate, it is a free world, so if young men and women are not relating much to the opposite sex it is the result of their own free choice and I will refrain from commenting further.

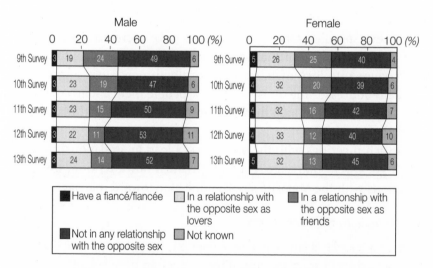

Fig. 4-7 Never-married persons' relations with the opposite sex by survey

Note: 1. Subjects are never-married persons aged 18–34.
2. "Have a fiancé/fiancée," "in a relationship with the opposite sex as lovers," and "in a relationship with the opposite sex as friends" are considered as "in a relationship with the opposite sex." The survey years are as follows: 9th Survey (1987), 10th Survey (1992), 11th Survey (1997), 12th Survey (2002), and 13th Survey (2005).

Source: National Institute of Population and Social Security Research (2007, vol. II, 31, fig. 3-1).

How Women View Marriage and Family

Since the subject of this book is inequalities among women, we should by no means neglect the views of women, and particularly married women, on marriage and family. Knowing the views of women—who play the major role in childbirth and childrearing—will also be valuable in predicting the future of marriage and the family in Japan.

In table 4-7 we can see the degree to which married women have agreed with various statements related to marriage and family. First, let's look at their perspectives on marriage itself. We see that nearly 40 percent of wives indicate they would not mind being single their whole life. Comparing this with the percentage of single women who want to marry (as we have already seen, that percentage stands at about 90 percent), we find, rather surprisingly, quite a strong affirmation of the single life.

Does this gap show a disillusionment with married life among women who have actually experienced it? Only 52 percent of married women say it is undesirable never to marry while single women still have high hopes for marriage. One is tempted to say that single women tend to see the world through rose-colored glasses while married women have had more of a taste of the harsh realities of life.

Interesting here is the high percentage—nearly 70 percent—of married women who feel that a man and woman should marry if they live together, versus the 24 percent approving of living together without getting married. According to the 2005 *Wagakuni dokushinsō no kekkonkan to kazokukan* (Attitudes toward marriage and family among Japanese singles) report by the National Institute of Population and Social Security Research, 7 to 8 percent of single women in Japan either are currently cohabitating with a male partner or have cohabitated with a partner in the past. That figure rises to around 10 percent for single women aged 25–34.

More importantly, cohabitation rates have doubled or tripled over the past twenty years. Unmarried couples living together are no longer a rarity, and we can expect this trend to continue in the

Table 4-7 Views of married women on marriage and family

(%)

	Agree	Totally agree	Some-what agree	Disagree	Totally disagree	Some-what disagree	Not stated	Total (n= 5,932)
1. It is not desirable to remain single for one's entire life.	52.2	12.1	40.1	39.8	8.6	31.2	8.1	100.0
2. Men and women should marry if they live together.	68.9	18.9	50.1	24.0	6.4	17.6	7.1	100.0
3. It is fine for unmarried men and women to have sexual relations if they love each other.	77.2	27.6	49.6	15.4	3.2	12.2	7.4	100.0
4. In any society, it is important that the two genders retain some of their distinguishing characteristics.	85.6	39.8	45.8	7.7	1.7	6.0	6.8	100.0
5. Even after getting married, one ought to have personal goals outside of one's marriage partner and family.	81.1	30.7	50.4	11.6	1.2	10.4	7.3	100.0
6. If married, it is natural to sacrifice half of one's individuality or lifestyle for the family.	40.4	5.6	34.8	52.5	14.0	38.5	7.1	100.0
7. Husbands should be the bread-winners and wives should take care of the home.	28.7	3.3	25.4	63.9	25.9	38.0	7.3	100.0
8. One ought to have children if one gets married.	71.2	19.4	51.8	20.9	7.6	13.3	7.9	100.0
9. It is best for the mother to stay at home and not to work at least when the children are young.	71.8	22.7	49.1	21.4	6.6	14.8	6.8	100.0
10. Once married, a couple should not get divorced just because of incompatibility.	51.0	12.7	38.2	41.2	12.1	29.1	7.9	100.0

Note: Subjects are women in first-marriage couples.

Source: National Institute of Population and Social Security Research (2007, vol. I, 60, table 7-1).

future as well. Why? First, as shown in table 4-7, we are in an age in which 24 percent of married women support cohabitation. In addition, nearly 80 percent approve of sexual relations before marriage. This figure, too, implies support for cohabitation. Second, it looks likely that the same legal rights granted to children born in wedlock will be given to those born out of wedlock. And third, other industrialized nations already have quite high rates of cohabitation.

Returning to the table, we can see signs of new ways of thinking about women's lives. Most significant in this regard is the fact that over 60 percent rejected the view that the role of husbands is to work and the role of wives is to take care of the home. Moreover, over 80 percent agreed that women should value their own lifestyle and personal goals even after getting married. This hints at a rejection of set gender roles and at an increased sense of independence and desire to work.

On the other hand, 70 percent of married women agreed that (1) "one ought to have children if one gets married" and (2) "it is best for the mother to be at home and not to work at least when the children are young." This appears to contradict the fact that slightly over 60 percent oppose the assignment of roles based on gender, as we just noted. How can this apparent contradiction be resolved?

It is true that women have gained more of a sense of independence with the postwar coeducation system, the movement to create a gender-equal society, and the rise of feminist thought. Looking at women's actual lives in Japan, however, we must recognize that it is women who inevitably must commit to the raising of children. This probably leads to women giving a high level of support, albeit possibly passive support, to the view that mothers of young children should be at home.

Another important factor in this regard was discussed in the chapter on education, namely, that the education that women receive puts them at a disadvantage compared with men in terms of employment outside the home and in terms of credentials and wages. As a result, it doesn't pay for women to work the same long hours as men do. Consequently it is still the wife who generally quits work to focus on raising children or who chooses to be a full-time homemaker from the start.

To summarize, a rather high percentage of married women espouse views that affirm marriage. They also have a strong desire, at least theoretically, to retain as much independence as possible after marriage. When it comes to actual marital life, however, about half of them are still willing to sacrifice themselves for their families. Therefore, many women commit to childrearing, and quite a number of women appear to support seemingly traditional gender roles, such as the idea that mothers of young children should be at home.

How might these views of women on marriage and family differ by age and education? Volume I of the National Institute of Population and Social Security Research's *Heisei 17 nen dai 13 kai shusshō dōkō kihon chōsa hōkokusho* (Report on the thirteenth Japanese national fertility survey, 2005) describes in detail such differences, but here we will only look at items where there is a particularly marked discrepancy by age.

Two items in particular showed markedly different responses according to the age of the respondent: cohabitation and premarital sexual relations. Figure 4-8 shows the percentage of married women who approve/disapprove of cohabitation and the percentage who approve/disapprove of premarital sex by the following three age groups: twenties, thirties, and forties. Let's look at cohabitation first. A total of 34.4 percent of married women in their twenties approve of cohabitation while only 17.9 percent of those in their forties condone it. From the fact that a high percentage of young women approve of cohabitation, we can predict that the number of people living together without marrying will increase in the future.

The same can be said of premarital sex. A total of 67.2 percent of married women in their forties condone it whereas it has the approval of 87.6 percent and 84.0 percent of those in their twenties and thirties, respectively. The vast majority of young women thus find nothing wrong with premarital sex, meaning that sexual liberation is widely supported by the younger generation.

This approval rate simply measures what women think, and the question of how sexually active single women actually are is another matter altogether. *Wagakuni dokushinsō no kekkonkan to kazokukan* does look into the question of sexual experience, and from this we know that a total of 58.2 percent of single men and 52.1 percent of single women age 18–34 report having had a sexual encounter with the opposite sex. We see a considerable gap, therefore, between the 80 percent-plus married women in their twenties and thirties approving of premarital sex, and the 50 percent-plus single women in this age group who are actually sexually experienced.

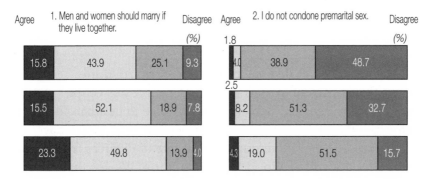

Fig. 4-8 Views of married women on marriage and family by birth decade

Notes: 1. Subjects are wives in first-marriage couples.
2. Top bar graphs: born in or after 1975 (age: 20s); middle bar graphs: born between 1965 and 1974 (age: 30s); bottom bar graphs: born between 1955 and 1964 (age: 40s). In each of the bar graphs, the percentage (%) of respondents who replied "totally agree," "somewhat agree," "somewhat disagree," and "totally disagree" are indicated in that order from left to right. "Totally agree" and "somewhat agree" together make up "agree," and "somewhat disagree" and "totally disagree" together constitute "disagree."
3. Born in or after 1975: *n*=2,522; born between 1965 and 1974: *n*=2,613; born between 1955 and 1964: *n*=797.

Source: Based on National Institute of Population and Social Security Research (2007, vol. I, 63, fig. 7-2).

This means that not all women who approve of premarital sex are actually engaging in it. Of course, this kind of gap between attitude and behavior, or between expectations and reality, arises in various areas of life—it is the difference between what a person thinks and what a person actually does. We noted earlier that a rather high percentage of singles are not in any relationship with the opposite sex, and this is surely a major factor at work here. In other words, many people are not in any relationship with the opposite sex themselves, but do approve of premarital sexual relations in theory.

Incidentally, *Wagakuni dokushinsō no kekkonkan to kazokukan* also found that 84.7 percent of single men and 82.4 percent of single women who are sexually active use contraception.

The Rising Divorce Rate

Finally, let's look at divorce, or the end of married life. Table 4-7 shows that 51 percent of married women believe that couples should not divorce whereas 41 percent deem divorce to be unavoidable in some cases. How frequently is divorce actually occurring today?

Figure 4-9 shows the number and rate of divorces from 1947, soon after the end of World War II, to 2004. We see that divorce has been steadily rising since the end of the war, except during two periods (1984–88 and 2003–04) and that the divorce rate today is three to four times higher than it was in 1947. Postwar Japan has indeed experienced a major increase in divorce.

How does Japan's divorce rate compare with that of other nations? In table 4-8, we see that Japan's 2004 divorce rate of 2.15 per 1,000 population is slightly lower than that of other industrialized countries. The rates in Russia and the United States are very high, at over 4 per 1,000 population; many of the countries with lower rates than Japan, such as France, Italy, and Brazil, are Catholic nations. If we shift our attention to Asian nations, we find that South Korea is quite a bit higher than Japan, at 3.05 per 1,000 population, while Thailand still has a low rate of divorce at 0.90. Overall, then, Japan's divorce rate is slightly lower than that of other industrialized countries, but that gap is narrowing.

Why has Japan's divorce rate risen? In chapter 1, we looked at the reasons cited for filing for divorce and found that the main reasons were incompatibility, violence and emotional abuse, infidelity, and refusal to provide money for living expenses. In the past, for whatever reasons, couples stayed together even if they had such problems in their marriage, but these days more and more people think it is better to leave the marriage than to suffer. For this reason, the divorce rate has increased.

Let me give some facts to back that up. Table 4-9 gives people's responses to the question of whether they approve of divorce if a couple cannot make their marriage work despite their best efforts to save it. In such a case, the vast majority of people approve of divorce.

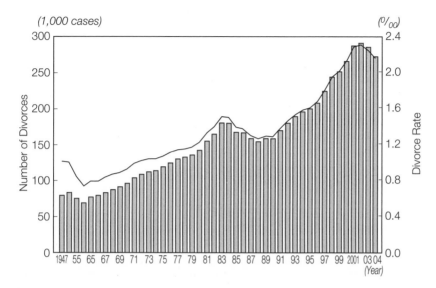

Fig. 4-9 Number of divorces and divorce rate (1947–2004)

Note: Divorce rate statistics are crude divorce rate figures.
Source: Based on Statistics and Information Department, Ministry of Health, Labor, and Welfare, *Vital Statistics of Japan*.

Table 4-8 International comparison of divorce rates (2004)

(⁰⁄₀₀)

Russia	5.30***	Sweden	2.39
United States	4.19*	Canada	2.32**
South Korea	3.05	Norway	2.30
Australia	2.85***	Japan	2.15
Britain	2.58**	France	1.90***
Finland	2.56	Thailand	0.90****
Hungary	2.51	Italy	0.69***
Germany	2.40***	Brazil	0.60

Note: Single asterisk (*): 1998; double asterisk (**): 2000; triple asterisk (***): 2001; quadruple asterisk (****): 1995.
Source: Based on National Institute of Population and Social Security Research, *Jinkō tōkei shiryōshū 2006* (Population statistics of Japan, 2006).

If the "somewhat approve" responses are included, the figure comes to 67.4 percent, meaning that roughly two-thirds of the respondents approve of divorce. It is clear that people support the idea of dissolving a marriage union, that they believe it better for a couple to divorce rather than continue in a failed marriage.

Now let's look at what people expect to gain from a divorce, as presented in table 4-10. A very large number of people expect that they will be able to relax mentally and enjoy free time if they divorce. It is also interesting that almost half of the respondents looked forward to being freed from having to see their spouse, whom they had grown to dislike. It seems that people's expectations are focused on being liberated from the "shackles" of matrimony.

Returning to table 4-9, we note that 11 percent responded either "disapprove" or "somewhat disapprove" and almost 22 percent were fence-sitters, choosing "hard to say." We should keep in mind then that not everyone approves of divorce.

Table 4-9 Do you approve of divorce if a couple is unable to make their marriage work despite their best efforts?

	(%)
Approve	40.9
Somewhat approve	26.5
Hard to say	21.5
Somewhat disapprove	5.1
Disapprove	5.9

Note: The survey sample was composed of men and women aged 30–69 living in Japan's three major metropolitan areas.

Source: Japan Institute of Life Insurance, *Raifu saikuru to seikatsu hoshō ni kansuru kenkyū* (Life cycle and life security) (2000), 19, table 1-8.

Table 4-10 What do you anticipate will improve by divorcing?

	(%)
Not having to see my spouse from whom I have become estranged	46.2
Being able to have my own free time	27.5
Being able to relax mentally	71.9
Being freed from the obligation to support dependent family members	7.1
Other	1.9

Source: Japan Institute of Life Insurance, *Raifu saikuru to seikatsu hoshō ni kansuru kenkyū* (Life cycle and life security) (2000), 19, table 1-9.

Why do some Japanese disapprove of divorce or sit on the fence about the issue? Table 4-11 lists perceived obstacles to divorce, and we can see that two factors are cited the most frequently by far—fear of losing one's economic footing and concern about one's children. Of the two, however, concern about the impact of divorce on the children is particularly high, hovering around 77 percent. Evidently the traditional thinking represented by the maxim "a child cements a marriage" (*ko wa kasugai*) is still strong and many hesitate to divorce for the sake of their children.

We also see in this table a considerable difference in the responses of men and women regarding the economic impact of divorce. Over 75 percent of women deemed covering daily living expenses an obstacle to divorce, versus 41 percent of men. This is a natural concern for full-time homemakers and for working women as well, considering the low wages women receive in Japan. The economic issue is even more serious for mothers, as they generally are awarded custody of the children in cases of divorce now and so must meet childcare expenses.

Finally, more men than women see "disgrace to parents and relatives" and "bad for reputation" as obstacles to divorcing. These statistics imply that men tend to be more bound by social norms, more indecisive, and more concerned about their reputation than women are.

Table 4-11 Obstacles to divorce

(%)

	Total	Male	Female
Hard to cover living expenses	58.0	41.0	75.4
Hard to balance work and childrearing	35.9	32.8	39.0
Bad influence on children	77.3	78.0	76.5
Disgrace to parents and relatives	7.0	7.9	6.1
Bad for reputation (in neighborhood and workplace)	13.0	16.7	9.3
Hard to divide up assets and property	10.0	9.0	11.1
Other	1.2	0.9	1.5

Source: Japan Institute of Life Insurance, *Raifu saikuru to seikatsu hoshō ni kansuru kenkyū* (Life cycle and life security) (2000), 20, table 1-10.

To summarize, various factors lead to divorce in Japan. In addition to incompatibility and differences in values and life goals, various types of problematic behavior by men are causes of divorce. Quite a high percentage of people approve of divorce, but we must also keep in mind that about one-third either disapprove or are unwilling to take a position on the issue. The main reasons why people sit on the fence are concerns about children and living expenses.

Divorce and Inequalities among Women

It is undeniable that the decision to divorce is one that couples make of their own volition, so that they themselves are responsible for handling any adverse fallout that may result. That said, it is also true that many divorces are due to the husband alone and that many women end up in dire financial straits after a divorce. According to Tachibanaki and Urakawa (2006), nearly half of all single-mother households are poor, and Japan needs to take steps to help these women.

If women who divorce face economic hardship and those who stay married are well-off financially, this represents a new type of inequality among women. Can anything be done to address this? Let me make a few proposals.

First, I would like to advise people to think long and hard before deciding on a divorce. In the past, many couples in Japan hesitated to take the step of divorce because they were concerned about the children or their own reputation. As we have seen here, however, the times are changing and the divorce rate is rising so I am afraid this proposal will have little effect.

Second, I would like to recommend that women continue to work after marriage and childbirth since they face various hardships if their marriage should end in divorce. This will be discussed in more detail in chapter 8, but if women continue to work, they can maintain their work skills and, if they do divorce, will not fall into poverty due to the sudden loss of income. If they stop working and later divorce, however, they will have trouble finding reemployment because their work skills will have deteriorated. To prevent this, they need to continue to work after marriage and childbirth, even though that poses its own challenges.

My third proposal is a plea to society and corporations to raise Japan's minimum wage. This is currently too low and should be increased by the amount necessary to ensure that a woman can earn a living wage. In the past, the thinking in Japan was that a married woman's part-time work was simply to supplement her husband's income. As a result, the minimum wage has been kept low. Today, however, the divorce rate has risen and poverty among single-mother households has started to become a serious problem. Japan needs to raise the minimum wage by a considerable margin to increase women's wages, among other reasons.

Fourth, Japan must strengthen childcare assistance so that single mothers can work the working hours stipulated by law or, if they so desire, work overtime hours. It has been hard for single mothers to work full working hours, and Japan should eliminate that barrier. We will discuss child-related policies in the next chapter so I will leave the topic here for now.

Chapter Five

Children and a Woman's Life

As noted in chapter 1, the birthrate in Japan is falling, and in this chapter we will look into this matter in more detail. Why is there a difference among the number of children that couples say they would ideally like to have, the number they plan to have, and the number they actually have?

To answer this question, we need to investigate the motivations behind the decision to have children as well as the factors that serve to inhibit couples from enlarging their families. Then we will be in a better position to consider policies that might be taken to alleviate the conditions acting to depress the birthrate in Japan.

And finally we will look at the impact of having—or not having—children on women's lives in terms of both macroeconomics and of social inequalities.

Japan's birthrate has been a key point of debate among economists. Kato (2001 and 2007) sees the declining birthrate as triggering a decline in Japan's economic growth because of the resultant shrinking of the labor force. Higuchi et al. (2006) is likewise representative of the mainstream view that regards the decreasing birthrate in negative terms. Akagawa (2004) and Harada and Suzuki (2005) disagree, however, insisting that the decline in the birthrate is no cause for worry. Personally, I think we have no choice but to accept the situation, as many people are choosing not to have a large number of children. That said, there are also many Japanese who want to have children, and policies should definitely be implemented to help them do so.

The Birthrate

Historical background

The final number of children a couple actually has is called the couple's completed fertility. How has this figure changed since 1940? Table 5-1 shows trends in completed fertility for couples married for 15–19 years and the distribution of the number of children per couple. This table tells us that the number of children per couple has been on a constant decline overall since 1940. Before World War

Table 5-1   Distribution of children per couple by survey (length of marriage: 15–19 years)

	None (%)	1 child (%)	2 children (%)	3 children (%)	4 children or more (%)	completed Fertility (children)	(±Standard Error)	(n)
1st Survey (1940)	—	—	—	—	—	4.27	—	—
2nd Survey (1952)	—	—	—	—	—	3.50	—	—
3rd Survey (1957)	—	—	—	—	—	3.60	—	—
4th Survey (1962)	—	—	—	—	—	2.83	—	—
5th Survey (1967)	—	—	—	—	—	2.65	—	—
6th Survey (1972)	—	—	—	—	—	2.20	—	—
7th Survey (1977)	3.0	11.0	57.0	23.8	5.1	2.19	(±0.023)	(1,427)
8th Survey (1982)	3.1	9.1	55.4	27.4	5.0	2.23	(±0.022)	(1,429)
9th Survey (1987)	2.7	9.6	57.8	25.9	3.9	2.19	(±0.019)	(1,755)
10th Survey (1992)	3.1	9.3	56.4	26.5	4.8	2.21	(±0.019)	(1,849)
11th Survey (1997)	3.7	9.8	53.6	27.9	5.0	2.21	(±0.023)	(1,334)
12th Survey (2002)	3.4	8.9	53.2	30.2	4.2	2.23	(±0.023)	(1,257)
13th Survey (2005)	5.6	11.7	56.0	22.4	4.3	2.09	(±0.027)	(1,078)

Note: Subjects are first-marriage couples who have been married for 15–19 years (excluding couples for whom the number of children is not known).

Source: Based on National Institute of Population and Social Security Research (2007, vol. I, 22, tables 2-1 and 2-2).

II, Japan had an explicit national policy of encouraging women to have children to boost the population; couples had four children on average. During the baby boom after the war, couples still had more than three children. From 1962, however, the number declined to between two and three on average, dropping around 1972 to 2.20. In 2005, it fell sharply to 2.09, but we should note that the number has not yet dropped below two.

What percentage of couples is remaining childless or settling for a single child? How many are having two, three, or four or more children? This table offers some useful information on such birthrate trends. First, childless couples were at 3 percent or so for a long time but rose sharply to 5.6 percent in 2005—a major cause in the decline in the completed fertility figure. Childless couples include both couples who intentionally have no children and those who want to have children but for whatever reason do not.

Second, we see that the percentage of couples with one child stood at around 9 percent for many years before suddenly moving to 11.7 percent in 2005—this also has contributed to the decreasing birthrate in recent years. The percentage of couples with two children has stayed between 50 and 60 percent with no substantial fluctuation while those with three children and those with four children or more have been on a slight decline overall for many years, yet another factor in the decline in the number of births.

Major influences on the birthrate

Next let's look at how the specific characteristics of each couple—area of residence, educational background, occupation—factor into the number of children they have. Since this information should also shed light on how childbirth affects disparities among women, and vice versa, we will look into it in some depth.

Table 5-2 presents completed fertility figures by the couple's current area of residence, the wife's level of education, and the occupation of each spouse. First, let's look at differences in birthrate by area of residence: nonurban areas (non-densely inhabited districts) have the highest rate at 2.19 children per couple, followed by small and medium-sized cities at 2.07, while the lowest birthrate—1.83 children

Table 5-2 Completed fertility by socioeconomic attribute (length of marriage: 15–19 years)

(1) Completed fertility by couple's current area of residence

Couple's current area of residence	13th Survey (2005)
Non-densely inhabited district	2.19 (39.5%)
Densely inhabited district (pop. under 2 million)	2.07 (48.7%)
Densely inhabited district (pop. 2 million or over)	1.83 (11.8%)

(2) Completed fertility by wife's level of education

Wife's level of education	13th Survey (2005)
Junior high school	2.20 (3.2%)
High school	2.15 (56.6%)
Junior college or college of technology	2.09 (25.0%)
University or higher	1.84 (14.1%)

(3) Completed fertility by husband's ccurrent occupation

Husband's current occupation	13th Survey (2005)
Agricultural/forestry/fishery	2.48 (2.1%)
Self-employed (non-agricultural)	2.18 (13.6%)
Professional/managerial	2.09 (37.6%)
Clerical/sales/service	2.03 (23.9%)
Manual labor	2.12 (10.3%)

(4) Completed fertility by wife's current occupation

Wife's current occupation	13th Survey (2005)
Agricultural/forestry/fishery	2.38 (1.5%)
Self-employed (non-agricultural)	2.11 (9.0%)
Professional/managerial	2.01 (9.4%)
Clerical/sales/service	1.91 (9.6%)
Manual labor	2.39 (7.9%)
Part-time/temporary	2.16 (32.7%)
Nonworking	1.98 (24.7%)

Notes: 1. Subjects are first-marriage couples. Percentage figures in parentheses are the percentages of all couples in the sample.
2. "High school" in table 2 includes those who have graduated from a specialized training college after high school. "Part-time/temporary" and "nonworking" are not included in table 3 because the samples were small.

Source: Based on National Institute of Population and Social Security Research (2007, vol. I, 24–25, table 2-4).

per couple—is found in major cities with a population of two million or over. Thus, there is a notable difference in the birthrate between urban and nonurban areas and, as Japanese are moving to the cities, the number of births can be expected to decline further.

Moving to the wife's education, we observe an inverse relationship between education and childbearing: the higher a woman's level of education, the fewer children she has. As we saw in chapter 3, Japanese women's level of education is rising so here too we can predict a continuing decline in the birthrate.

Let's take a look now at the husband's occupation. We see that men working in agriculture, forestry, and fishery have a rather high number of children, at 2.48, but since they make up only 2.1 percent of the total population as represented in this survey of married couples, this will not help the birthrate much. The occupational category with the next highest number of children is the self-employed at 2.18, but they also constitute a relatively low percentage of the population, 13.6 percent. The same is true of blue-collar workers (manual labor), who have a high number of children at 2.12, but make up only 10.3 percent of the population. On the other hand, white-collar workers, including the category of professional and managerial workers as well as that of clerical, sales, and service workers, have a relatively low birthrate, but roughly 60 percent of men work in these two occupational groupings. And since white-collar jobs are on the increase, this is another area exerting a downward pressure on the birthrate.

What about the wife's occupation? Two categories—part-time/ temporary and nonworking (full-time homemaker)—have been added to the occupational classifications used for men in the survey. As was the case for men, women involved in agriculture, forestry, and fishery have a rather high number of children at 2.38, but the percentage of women in this field is very small—1.5 percent— so the impact on the birthrate is also small. Similarly, female blue-collar workers (manual labor) have a surprisingly high number of children, at 2.39, but constitute no more than 8 percent of wives in the survey. Self-employed and white-collar wives (professional and managerial workers, and clerical, sales, and service workers) have from 1.91 to 2.11 children, a very average number; each of these categories accounts for only 9 percent or so of wives.

Two groups that do have a major impact on the birthrate are wives who are part-time and temporary workers and wives who are nonworking (full-time homemakers)—both have a rather high number of children and, more importantly, together they make up a high percentage of the population: 32.7 percent of wives are part-time and temporary workers while another 24.7 percent are nonworking. And that impact has two facets, namely, (1) women change from full-time to part-time and temporary employment or stop working altogether when they have children and (2) women being part-time and temporary workers or out of the labor force in itself has an impact on the number of children they have.

There is no way to know which of these two influences is stronger, but at the very minimum we can say that full-time homemakers and part-time and temporary workers in particular have a slightly higher number of births. If there is a societal consensus that increasing the number of births is desirable, then Japan should look to this group of full-time homemakers and wives engaged in part-time or temporary work, strictly avoiding, however, policies that would force women into these two forms of employment. Of course, every individual is free to decide his or her type of employment. Rather, as will be discussed at more length later, it is imperative that Japan become a society where women can bear and raise children while also working outside the home, and not be forced to choose between the two.

To summarize, in looking at the number of children couples have by area of residence, the wife's education, and the occupational categories of wives and husbands, we found evidence that Japan's birthrate is likely to continue to decline; trends serving to depress the birthrate include continuing urbanization, increased levels of female education, and the rise in the number of white-collar positions. The one exception, the only groups that are pushing the birthrate up, are nonworking women and wives engaged in part-time or temporary work. We need to stop ourselves from placing excessive pressure on them, however, as I have already mentioned.

Having children: the dream and the reality

Next, let's turn our attention to the discrepancies among the desired number of children, the planned number of children, and the actual number of children in Japanese families. How many children do couples consider to be the ideal number and how many do they actually have?

In figure 5-1 we can see the respective figures on family size classified by length of marriage. The desired number of children is from 2.30 to 2.56. If couples actually had this number of children, the current concerns about the declining birthrate would evaporate and the population would grow considerably. Under ideal circumstances, the Japanese would like to have many children.

However, ideal circumstances do not prevail and couples must adjust their expectations accordingly. As we can see in figure 5-1, the planned number of children is about 0.30 to 0.45 lower than

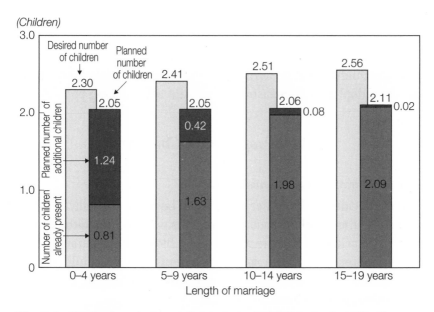

Fig. 5-1 Desired and planned number of children by length of marriage

Note: "Planned number of children" is the total of "number of children already present" and "planned number of additional children."

Source: National Institute of Population and Social Security Research (2007, vol. I, 35, fig. 4-1).

the ideal number, and the actual number of children in the family increases the longer the couple is married, as would be expected.

Additionally, we observe that there is virtually no difference between the planned and actual number of children for couples who have been married for 15–19 years, as is also true for couples married 10–14 years. Couples married at least ten years, therefore, have almost all achieved their planned family size. Moreover, their family size is around 2.0 children so it might seem that fears over the falling birthrate are exaggerated.

Such a rosy view comes with two large caveats, however. First, in the real world, not all marriages are long ones. One or the other spouse may die or the couple might decide to divorce. This means that not all couples have the two children they intend to have. Second, some women never marry and as of yet not many single women in Japan bear children, so their contribution to the nation's birthrate is near zero.

These two factors mean that the decline in the birthrate will remain a problem even if couples married for ten years or more have an average of two children each. It is unavoidable, therefore, that Japan's birthrate will turn into negative territory, that is, that not enough children will be born to maintain the population. Japan will need to adopt countermeasures to prevent a decreasing population.

Why People Have Children

Instinct, altruism, or economic transaction?

No one decides of his or her own will to be born. Basically children come into the world because their parents want a child, although we must also acknowledge the working of a biological imperative to reproduce. Since it is the choice of the parents to have a child, we can expect them to take financial responsibility for raising that child, and indeed most parents do just that.

It is both the duty and natural instinct of parents to take care of dependent babies, toddlers, and small children. We could say that children unilaterally receive economic benefits from their parents.

From the perspective of economics, therefore, childrearing can be seen as an act of altruism; if we define philanthropy as the unilateral provision of benefits without receiving compensation, parental care of children can be considered philanthropy.

It is also possible, however, to see childrearing not as an act of philanthropy, but as an economic transaction. This interpretation is supported by the following two phenomena.

First, after being raised by their parents, most people go on to have and raise their own children. Viewed from this perspective, childrearing is not a single act of extending economic benefit but continues in a line of giving and receiving from generation to generation.

Second, the common practice in countries around the world was for children to take care of the economic needs of their parents when they were elderly and could no longer work. Modern industrial societies, however, have public pension systems, and children no longer provide direct private support in many countries. Such pay-as-you-go public pension systems, where the present generation covers the previous generation's benefits, can be seen as parents being provided for by society overall—support that has traditionally been provided privately is now being provided on a societal level.

In this way, although people may not be consciously aware of it, childrearing is not simply an altruistic act but also is in some aspects an economic transaction.

Why do people have children? This economist would propose the following four concrete benefits of having children: children provide (1) the continuance of one's own genetic line, (2) children provide an outlet for affection and a reason for living, (3) a safety net for one's old age (a reason behind public support for the pension system), and (4) a source of labor, particularly in developing countries.

In terms of an economics of marriage or an economics of family, having and raising children is part of household production. Parents gain utility (satisfaction) by using the assets the household gains through this production activity: they enjoy the services gained through childrearing and the child's maturation—i.e., the children are providing a service to the parents. Children are like durable goods in this sense. Durable goods, such as motor vehicles and television sets, are goods that have a long durable life and provide service to the possessor. Refer to Tachibanaki and Kimura (2008) for more on an economic perspective on why people have children.

I imagine that some people will balk at this view of children as being equivalent to durable goods; they might well regard economics as a heartless business. However, it is not so long ago that in Japan families had children with the expectation of economic benefit. Children were a source of labor in farming and merchant families as they still are today in developing countries, where they make a large contribution to the family's income.

In the Japan of yesteryear, it was expected as a matter of course that children would take care of the financial needs of their elderly parents, serve as heirs, and see to the continuation of the family line. In the adoption system in Japan, children were in fact "goods" in an economic transaction to ensure succession and parental care in old age. Needless to say, parents provided, in turn, the service of rearing for both biological and adoptive children. Likening having children to purchasing durable consumer goods is similar to viewing having children as an economic transaction, where the children are to serve as successors, to take care of parents, or to work for the family as labor. Neither can be dismissed out of hand.

The first economist to take up the topic of why people have children was Thomas R. Malthus, in his famous *Essay on the Principle of Population*. In this essay, he postulated that whether a couple has children or not is greatly influenced by its economic circumstances, even more so than by the utility of having children. Let me recast his theory in more modern terms: Malthus looked at the high expenses involved in having children and said that the number of children a couple has depends on the amount of economic resources it possesses to cover food, clothing, and other needs. In other words, a poor couple does not have the extra resources to support having children, but a rich couple is able to do so. However, this theory is not borne out in reality. Today, the more affluent the country, the fewer children couples have, and the lower the country's level of development, the higher the number of children. In Japan as well, it is commonplace for the poor to have large families. It seems, then, that the financial circumstances of the couple are not so important and we must look to other factors.

"Quality children"

We can say that it is a natural human instinct to want children because children are cute and lovable. This is a much more persuasive argument than the one that claims people have children to perpetuate the family line, even if it might seem to put children on the same level as pets. If finances are a factor behind why parents have children, however, then it is possible to conduct an economic analysis of feeling children to be adorable. This is the claim of the Chicago School, a neoclassical school of thought within the academic community of economists centered on the University of Chicago. Readers are invited to consult Becker (1981) for more information, but the argument is that if the quality, rather than the quantity, of children is the important point—if parents desire "quality children"— then the parents' income becomes a major factor. Quality children can be defined as children who are good-looking, perform well in school, and can enter well-paying professions; children in this case are viewed as high-quality commodities.

Such a "high quality" child requires a considerable investment on the part of the parents in the child's food, clothing, health, education, etc. We can anticipate, therefore, that the interest of parents in the quality of children, rather than their quantity, will increase as their income rises. The theory of the members of the Chicago School, such as Gary S. Becker and Robert J. Willis, is that people's interest has in fact shifted to the quality of children, and this provides one explanation for why parental income and number of children are not positively related. While this theory has enhanced economic analysis of the issue of having children, it has not earned strong support in the United States, nor has it received much validation in Japan. I believe, however, that the idea of the quality of children can be useful in our analysis.

As has already been mentioned many times, Japan is struggling with a declining birthrate. We have considered various ways of analyzing the problem, but looking at it afresh from the perspective of the quality of children leads to a new insight: the impact of sky-rocketing school fees. If it is true that Japanese parents want quality children, they will invest a lot in education and will try to enroll their children at top-flight schools, to cultivate their children's aesthetic sensibilities through piano, painting, or voice lessons, and to develop their children's athletic skills so they might even be professional athletes in the future.

Such trends are often seen in Japan today, as reflected in such terms as *kyōiku mama* (pushy, education-minded mother), *ongaku mama* (music-oriented mother), or *supōtsu papa* (sports-obsessed father). It is a fact that childrearing expenses and school fees are quite high in Japan. Is the birthrate declining because of the high cost of raising children? If parents must spend a lot of money on children, they will have fewer children to ensure that they are of exceptional talent and quality.

What parents say

Let's look at how well the data confirm the possible motivations discussed above for having children. We will look at two questionnaire surveys for this; the first survey was conducted of married couples, and the second was of men and women separately.

Table 5-3 lists possible reasons for having children and the percentage of couples who chose it as a factor behind their decision to have children. The survey was of married couples who wanted to have one or more children. While the couples may have completed the questionnaire together in some cases, we can assume that many times either the husband or the wife completed it alone.

The most frequently cited reason for having children was "children add joy and richness to life," which, at 74.5 percent, towers above the others. We could say that in terms of the economic argument above, this reason corresponds to the increase in utility or satisfaction that having children brings. Obviously many find this reason compelling.

The next most popular reasons given were "it is natural for people to marry and have children" (56.4 percent) and "I want to

Table 5-3 Reasons for having children

	(Multiple answers permitted; %)
(n)	(5,488)
Children add joy and richness to life.	74.5
It is natural for people to marry and have children.	56.4
I want to have the child of the person I love.	32.8
Children bring stability to the marital relationship.	25.6
Children will be the mainstay of society in the future.	20.3
Children will help me in my old age.	17.9
My husband, parents, or others around me want children.	12.1
People around me will respect me if I have children.	5.7
Other	6.8

Source: Based on National Institute of Population and Social Security Research (2007, vol. I, 37, table 4-5).

have the child of the person I love" (32.8 percent). Both can be seen as instinctual. The first is entirely to be expected, as the biological imperative to reproduce is present in all animals. The second is a natural expression of human emotion: love develops between a man and woman, they marry, and they have children as a second expression of that love.

In fourth place was "children bring stability to the marital relationship," at 25.6 percent, which amounts to a recasting of the traditional Japanese saying that "a child cements a marriage." In other words, even if a rift develops between husband and wife, they will be reluctant to divorce if they have children.

Next, at 20.3 percent, was "children will be the mainstay of society in the future." This choice has much merit in terms of economics: children will be the work force of tomorrow and the drivers of economic development; their taxes and other payments will be the linchpin of the pension and other social insurance systems. We could say that this particular reason proves that children also are, so to speak, public assets.

The sixth most popular reason, "children will help me in my old age" (17.9 percent), was very important not so long ago. Since it was adult children who provided financial support to elderly parents or cared for them if they became sick or bedridden, it was natural to have children with that future objective in mind. Now the pension system has improved, however, and there is much more societal assistance in providing old-age care both at home and institutionally. As a result, the motivation of having children as insurance in old age has declined. This is proven by the low figure of 17.9 percent. For a more detailed discussion of these last two reasons, see Tachibanaki (2000 and 2002b).

The percentages for the remaining two reasons—"my husband, parents, or others around me want children" and "people around me will respect me if I have children"—are quite low. Family or societal pressure to have children has lost almost all meaning. Couples today are guided by their own desire for children rather than by concern about the views of others.

Next, let's look at the question from the woman's side in table 5-4, based on Fujita (2001). Respondents had eight options to choose from in the previous survey and eleven in this one. The options were quite similar, however, and the findings shown in the two surveys generally coincide. For example, the reasons most frequently cited were "I can enjoy watching the children grow up" and "I can have a lively home life." This is the same as in table 5-3. Moreover, wanting children's help in old age was very low here as well.

Where table 5-4 differs from table 5-3 is in being from the perspective of women alone and in highlighting the benefits that the parents themselves receive. As shown in such reasons as "I, too, can grow," "children make life worthwhile/more worthwhile," and "having children expands my network of friends, etc.," women see great emotional benefits from having children as well as the benefit of expanding one's range of social interaction. Women are conscious of the meaning of having children.

Another interesting point in this table is that overall a higher percentage of married women than single women[*] see benefits in having children. This is notable particularly in regard to the benefits that the

---

[*] Note that "singles" (*mikonsha*) refers to "singles who have never married," as in the other surveys cited in this book.

Table 5-4 Advantages of having children as reported by women in their thirties

(%)

		I can enjoy watching the children grow up.	I can have a lively home life.	I, too, can grow.	Children make life worthwhile/more worthwhile.	Children cement the marital bond.	Having children expands my network of friends, etc.	Having children will make my parents happy.	I can pass on my hopes to my children.	Having children reduces my concerns about old age.	I can rely on my children in an emergency.	Children can help me (with the housework, family business, etc.).
Overall	*n*=182	82.4	80.2	76.9	44.0	40.7	34.6	19.2	11.0	11.0	9.9	4.9
Never-married	*n*= 20	75.0	70.0	60.0	30.0	20.0	30.0	25.0	5.0	0.0	10.0	5.0
Married	*n*=154	82.5	79.9	82.5	45.5	37.0	44.8	18.8	5.2	9.7	11.7	11.7
Married: age 30–34	*n*= 65	90.8	81.5	83.1	47.7	46.2	49.2	26.2	9.2	15.4	15.4	13.8
Married: age 35–39	*n*= 89	76.4	78.7	82.0	43.8	30.3	41.6	13.5	2.2	5.6	9.0	10.1

Source: Based on Fujita (2001, 40, table 2-3).

woman herself receives, such as the opportunity to grow as a person or to gain more meaning in life. Married women understand these benefits because they currently have children. The lesson would seem to be that marriage and children are a great source of satisfaction for women. Wouldn't it be advisable for single women to marry and for childless married women to have children?

The Negatives of Having Children

What are the disadvantages?

Next, let's consider the factors that prevent people from having children. What makes a child a burden rather than a blessing? Table 5-5 shows the reasons why couples have fewer than their desired number of children, classified by wife's age. Note that the survey is of couples whose planned number of children is lower than their

Table 5-5 Reasons why couples do not have their desired number of children by age of wife

Couples whose planned number of children is below their desired number *(%)*

Age of wife	(n)	Too expensive to raise and educate children	Don't want to give birth late in life	Can't bear more mental/physical burden from childrearing than already have	Interferes with work (job or family business)	Health reasons	Want to have children, but cannot	Home is too small	Cannot get husband to cooperate in housework and childcare	Social context is not conducive to children growing up carefree	Want last child to be an adult by the time husband reaches retirement age	Husband does not want more children	Want to focus on our life as a couple or as individuals	Other
Under 25	(20)	80.0	—	20.0	20.0	—	—	15.0	25.0	5.0	5.0	10.0	10.0	10.0
25–29	(115)	83.5	6.1	20.0	27.8	4.3	7.8	20.0	20.0	16.5	5.2	13.0	13.0	13.0
30–34	(329)	78.7	18.2	24.6	21.9	12.5	10.6	19.8	19.1	18.2	7.0	12.5	11.9	11.2
35–39	(464)	75.0	40.1	26.5	17.9	16.4	16.8	17.9	17.0	16.2	8.0	9.7	8.6	8.2
40–44	(485)	56.3	52.8	20.8	14.6	21.9	20.4	12.6	10.5	9.7	12.0	7.2	7.2	5.2
45–49	(412)	51.2	44.9	15.0	13.8	19.7	18.4	9.5	7.5	11.4	7.5	3.4	3.9	9.2
Total	(1,825)	65.9	38.0	21.6	17.5	16.9	16.3	15.0	13.8	13.6	8.5	8.3	8.1	8.5

Note: Subjects are first-marriage couples whose planned number of children is below their desired number of children. Respondents were permitted to give multiple answers so the percentages total more than 100.

Source: Based on National Institute of Population and Social Security Research (2007, vol. I, 38, table 4-7).

desired number, and not of couples who have no children. It might be best to consider this table, then, as a presentation of the reasons why couples with one child hesitate to have a second.

The most frequently cited reason is that it is "too expensive to raise and educate children." This reason was cited by 65.9 percent of the couples surveyed, a rate higher by far than that for any other reason. The high cost of education and other expenses in raising children in Japan today constitute the most serious factor for couples in deciding whether to have a child. "Home is too small," another factor that can be considered a financial issue, stood at 15.0 percent.

The second highest response, "don't want to give birth late in life," was cited by 38.0 percent of all couples, and "can't bear more mental/physical burden from childrearing than already have" was also quite high at 21.6 percent. As might be expected, the percentage of couples citing "don't want to give birth late in life" rose dramatically among couples where the wife was age thirty-five or higher. "Can't bear more mental/physical burden from childrearing than already have" is similar to the fifth-ranked "health reasons." We can say that the mental and physical strain of childbirth and childrearing weighs heavily on wives in all age groups.

We see that "interferes with work (job or family business)" was cited by 17.5 percent of couples, making this factor a real block to having children. More particularly, it was frequently cited by couples where the wife was in the 25–29 or 30–34 age group, a time when women are struggling to balance work with childrearing responsibilities. Such results are natural for these two age groups.

In addition, we should not overlook the fact that 16.3 percent of couples cited "want to have children, but cannot." These couples want to have children, but either cannot conceive or cannot sustain a pregnancy to term. There is increased awareness of such issues in Japan today, with much debate over the ethical issues involved in artificial insemination and surrogate birth, as well as general recognition that infertility treatments are very expensive for ordinary citizens. In light of the low birthrate, concrete policies are certainly called for in this area.

Next, let's turn to table 5-6, based on Fujita (2001), which presents the disadvantages that women in their thirties—both married and single—see in having children. The findings are quite similar to those in the previous table on the reasons for not having children. The most serious factor is the economic burden of having children, as shown in the concern over childrearing expenses, school fees, and housing expenses.

Quite a high percentage of women also cite the psychological and physical strain of childrearing, but single women demonstrate a greater apprehension about this than married women do. It is somewhat odd that single women who have not yet given birth or

Table 5-6 Disadvantages of having children as reported by women in their thirties

(%)

		Raising and educating children is a great financial strain.	I will not be able to do what I want anymore.	The home will feel crowded.	Raising children is a great psychological strain.	Raising children is a great physical strain.	Having children makes it hard to divorce.	Children do not grow up the way you hope.	Pregnancy and childbirth are a great physical strain.	I cannot have the career I want.	I cannot get my spouse to cooperate.
Overall	n=182	53.3	44.5	33.0	28.6	24.7	24.2	22.5	17.0	15.4	8.8
Never-married	n= 20	60.0	55.0	55.0	50.0	35.0	10.0	35.0	5.0	0.0	15.0
Married	n=154	42.9	53.9	26.0	31.2	26.0	17.5	7.8	20.1	22.7	16.9
Married: age 30–34	n= 65	36.9	63.1	23.1	27.7	21.5	23.1	6.2	23.1	32.3	16.9
Married: age 35–39	n= 89	47.2	47.2	28.1	33.7	29.2	13.5	9.0	18.0	15.7	16.9

Source: Based on Fujita (2001, 43, table 2-5).

raised a child have such great misgivings—maybe they have heard other women talk about their experiences or read something in a book or magazine. A positive finding in this chart is that married women do not feel childbirth and childrearing to be so much of a burden, so I would like those who are not yet married not to be so apprehensive either.

A somewhat higher percentage of married women than single women cite the physical strain of pregnancy and childbirth as a negative of having children, a finding opposite to the two groups' assessment of the psychological and physical strain of raising children. In either case, childbirth and childrearing are a great strain on women, and the support of their husbands and others around them is crucial.

We should take special note that "I will not be able to do what I want anymore" stands at 44.5 percent, second only to the economic burden of having children. This likely reflects women's dissatisfaction with the fact that they will have to sacrifice their jobs or will not be able to enjoy their own lives or leisure time because their time and money will be taken up with childrearing, including children's education. In this table, "I cannot have the career I want" is counted separately. If we add the 15.4 percent of women who cite this item with the 44.5 percent who cite the previous one, the total is 59.9 percent, making it the highest on the table. In table 5-5, the percentage of women who cited "interferes with work" was not very high, but this difference can be explained by the fact that table 5-6 is of women in their thirties, the age group that struggles the most to balance work and childrearing.

Another interesting finding is that the statement "having children makes it hard to divorce" is cited as a negative of having children by 24.2 percent of respondents, quite a high figure. Although having children and creating a new family was cited earlier as one of the aims of getting married, here survey respondents are saying that having children will make it hard to divorce. This gives the sense that a new era is dawning. We have already seen that the divorce rate has risen in Japan; people are less reluctant to divorce and they perhaps enter marriage with the possibility somewhere in their minds that the marriage might end in divorce. The idea that having children has the disadvantage of lowering a couple's ability to divorce is completely opposite to the traditional view that "a child cements a marriage." I would like to emphasize that this in itself heralds a new age.

Health concerns

Women are the ones who must bear babies so we cannot ignore health issues related to pregnancy and childbirth. If women were to encounter major health problems during pregnancy or childbirth, it would be natural for them to decide to forgo the experience. How much is this contributing to the decline in the birthrate?

First, let's look at maternal mortality. According to the statistics, there were 176 reported maternal deaths for every 100,000 births in 1950, and this has dropped to around 5 deaths for every 100,000 births today. Since there are about 1.1 million births per year in Japan, the number of maternal deaths nationwide can be calculated to be around 55. Thanks to the dramatic advances in the field of medicine, maternal mortality has been virtually eliminated. We can conclude, therefore, that women are not avoiding pregnancy and childbirth because they are afraid they will die.

What about fetal deaths, cases of babies being stillborn or dying at birth? In 1950 there were 216,974 fetal deaths, versus 34,365 in 2004. The fetal death rate—fetal deaths per 1,000 live births + fetal deaths of twelve completed weeks of gestation and over—was 84.9 in 1950 but stood at 30.0 in 2004. The fetal death rate thus has gone down, but not as much as has the maternal mortality rate. However, at the risk of sounding callous, I would venture to say that a fetal death is a less serious matter than a maternal death, and that a certain number of such deaths are inevitable even with the advances in medicine.

A more serious problem is women having some kind of health issue during pregnancy or childbirth. There are various menstrual disorders that women can have from a comparatively young age, and gynecological problems increase as women get older. According to *Wagakuni fūfu no kekkon katei to shusshōryoku* (Marriage process and fertility of Japanese married couples), a report released by the National Institute of Population and Social Security Research, one out of every four married women suffers from some kind of health issue, quite a high figure. Moreover, the report reveals that one in every four women had a health problem during pregnancy.

Of particular concern is the fact that the longer the work hours of married women, the higher the percentage who have a health issue related to pregnancy and childbirth, as can clearly be seen in table 5-7. We observe a steady progression, culminating in women with health issues skyrocketing to 26.2 percent in the category of fifty or more work hours a week.

The problem of overwork—sometimes even leading to death (*karōshi*)—among young and middle-aged men is well established in the popular consciousness, but little attention has been paid to overwork and related gynecological problems. This must change. It is a sad state of affairs indeed when women, the bearers of the future generation, hesitate to become pregnant and have children because of overwork.

Table 5-7 Health as related to pregnancy and childbirth by wife's work hours

(Multiple answers permitted; %)

Wife's work hours per week (women aged 30–39)	Total (%)	(n)	Have some kind of health problem	Problem with menstrual cycle	Have gynecological disorder	Have menopausal symptoms	Have problems with sex life	Prone to miscarriage	Other
Nonworking	100.0	(1,160)	20.2	7.6	7.7	0.3	3.4	3.3	2.7
0 to <20 hours	100.0	(231)	19.9	7.4	6.5	1.3	3.9	0.9	3.5
20 to <30 hours	100.0	(293)	20.8	9.6	7.9	0.3	4.8	2.7	1.0
30 to <40 hours	100.0	(240)	21.7	8.3	6.7	0.4	5.4	2.9	2.5
40 to <50 hours	100.0	(407)	22.6	8.1	10.1	0.5	4.2	3.2	1.5
50 or more hours	100.0	(107)	26.2	8.4	10.3	0.0	6.5	1.9	2.8

Note: Subjects are first-marriage couples. The data of wives for whom the number of work hours is not known (139 cases) are not shown, but are included in the total. "Gynecological disorder" includes ovulation disorders, ovarian cysts, fibroids, endometriosis, and infectious diseases.

Source: Based on National Institute of Population and Social Security Research (2007, vol. I, 54, table 6-2).

Childbirth and work

Next, I would like to present some data that bring into focus the distinctive features of the disparities among women in Japan in relation to pregnancy and childbirth. Figure 5-2 compares women's type of employment before pregnancy and then one year after giving birth. The main aim is to show how health issues during pregnancy affect a woman's employment one year later, but the figure also provides valuable information on the impact of employment type on postpartum employment.

First, let's look at the impact of health issues during pregnancy on women's employment after childbirth. We see a major difference in postpartum employment according to whether or not the woman had a healthy pregnancy only in the case of women who were self-employed before their pregnancy. Self-employed women who

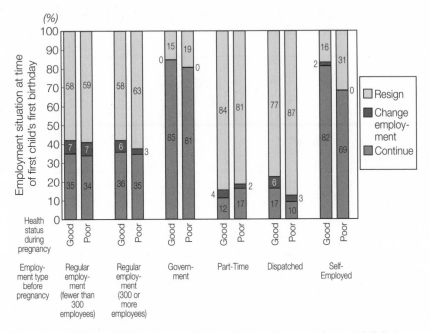

Fig. 5-2 Women's employment situation one year after childbirth by employment type before pregnancy and by health status during pregnancy

Note: Subjects are wives in first-marriage couples who have given birth to one or more children and who were employed before pregnancy. "Continue" refers to those wives who had the same type of employment at the time they learned of the pregnancy and at the time the child turned one year old. "Change employment" refers to those wives who had a different type of employment at the time they learned of the pregnancy and at the time the child turned one year old. "Resign" refers to wives who were nonworking or were students at the time the child turned one year old.

Source: Based on National Institute of Population and Social Security Research (2007, vol. I, 56, fig. 6-4).

had health trouble during pregnancy quit their work at a rate a full 15 percentage points higher than those who had a healthy pregnancy.

Second, we see in this figure that the type of employment has a major influence on whether a woman is still working one year later or not. In particular we observe that over 80 percent of women working in government are still working at the same job when their baby turns one year old, in other words, continuing to work after pregnancy and childbirth. This is made possible by the maternity leaves and childcare leaves guaranteed to government employees. The private sector is also required by law to offer maternity and childcare leaves, but the percentage of private companies that actually have such systems in place is quite low, as we will see later.

I do not see such provisions as preferential treatment in some sort of civil servant paradise. On the contrary, maternity and childcare leave should be available to all women; such laws should also be enforced in the private sector. The real problem is that the private sector falls so far short of the public sector in this respect.

There is another reason why large numbers of female public servants continue their employment after childbirth: they want to hold on to their jobs since the government offers various work conditions that are "woman-friendly," such as no transfers, equal wages, reasonable work hours, and good benefits. In principle, women working at private companies should also have these things. It is also true, though, that private companies face tough competition and their employees do not have as many benefits as public servants do.

We see that a high percentage of women in the self-employed category also continue working after childbirth at the same job they had before pregnancy, although the rate is somewhat below that for public servants. Since self-employment covers a wide range of circumstances, this cannot be explained by any one reason. However, if we think of farm families or mom-and-pop stores, for example, we can imagine that the women cannot quit their jobs despite maternity and childcare leave systems being practically nonexistent for them. Indeed, their continuing to work at close to the same rates as public servants without the support system enjoyed by the latter would strongly suggest a lack of choice in the matter.

We noted that, compared with the other categories, there is a larger gap in employment continuation rates between those with healthy pregnancies and those with health problems during pregnancy among the self-employed, as mentioned earlier. Perhaps their work is hard and so sometimes it is impossible for them to continue. However, such women may return to work again after they have regained their health.

Next, roughly 35 percent of women in regular employment at private companies are in the same employment before pregnancy and one year after childbirth, making this category the highest after public servants and the self-employed in this regard. This figure is much lower than the public servant figure of over 80 percent, but it does mean that about one in three women remain in their positions as regular employees after giving birth. More significantly, though, around 60 percent of these women resign, no doubt because of the inadequate maternity and childcare leave provisions at companies.

Since large corporations are more likely than small and medium-sized ones to have such provisions, one might expect a higher percentage of women working at large corporations (300 or more employees) than at smaller ones to continue their jobs. In fact, however, figure 5-2 shows no difference in the continuation rate between the two sizes of companies. Why is this? Perhaps we can get a hint in the fact that both register a high resignation rate, as noted. In other words, women who work in the private sector have relatively little to lose if they quit their job so they do so in high numbers regardless of the size of the company. Another factor is the common choice to resign at the time of pregnancy and childbirth and then to work again after the children are older. It is not easy for public servants to return to their jobs once they have quit, and so a high percentage of women working in the public sector continue their employment in order to retain their status as public servants.

The most shocking piece of data in this bar chart, however, is that no more than 17 percent of women working as part-time or dispatched workers continue their same employment after pregnancy and childbirth. Some 2 to 6 percent change jobs so the remaining 80 percent or so of women resign. This means that these women retire from the labor market. The fact that about 80 percent of married women employed as nonregular workers quit their jobs vividly reveals one face of Japanese society.

The great disparity in wage and other work conditions between regular and nonregular workers is well known, and a later chapter will examine this topic in detail in relation to women. What we can say here, though, is that there is a vast discrepancy between regular and nonregular working women in relation to whether they continue their employment after pregnancy and childbirth or not. Generally speaking, a high percentage of public servants and regular employees working at private companies continue their employment, although there is a great difference between the figures for these two groups. In contrast, the majority of nonregular workers, such as part-time and dispatched workers, leave the labor market entirely.

Since nonregular workers lose almost nothing even if they resign, around 80 percent of them quit at pregnancy or childbirth. From the beginning, their working conditions are inferior to those of regular workers and so rather than push themselves to continue their jobs, it seems these women decide to devote themselves to raising children for the time being. They can put off thinking about whether to return to work or not until after they have finished raising their children.

This is an important part of our examination of the inequalities among women in Japan today. We see that the type of employment a married woman has when she gets pregnant plays a crucial role in whether she will continue her employment after pregnancy and childbirth—this is a crossroads where those who continue working and those who do not part ways. Thus, one key disparity among women is between regular and nonregular female employees and the impact of children on their work life.

Having Children: The Major Turning Point in a Woman's Life

A generation ago, a woman's life changed when she married. As captured in the common saying *eikyū shūshoku*, or that "marriage is a lifetime job," it was a woman's dream to resign and become a full-time homemaker when she married. Of course, not all women wanted to be full-time homemakers. A good number of women continued working, and many returned to part-time work after marrying and focusing on childrearing for a time.

Marriage was, without doubt, though, the major life turning point for a woman. Although women did find jobs after finishing with school, this work, sometimes referred to as a *koshikake tsutome* or "stepping-stone job," was abandoned once the woman found a marriage partner, at which time she resigned in what was called a *kotobuki taisha*, or "auspicious resignation," and married. Women who finished school but did not find jobs busied themselves with *hanayome shugyō* or "training for married life," staying home until marriage and learning domestic skills like cooking. The term *kaji tetsudai*, or "household help," was also used to describe these women. While there was a distinction between women who worked after graduating from school and those who did not, marriage was the major turning point for all women in the sense that their highest priority was on finding a marriage partner and becoming a full-time homemaker once they married.

Today, however, the major turning point in a woman's life is not marriage, but pregnancy and childrearing. The abovementioned phrases—"marriage is a lifetime job," "stepping-stone job," "auspicious resignation," and "training for married life"—still exist, but are used much less frequently than before.

One proof of this change can be found in a glance at figure 5-2 on female employment: namely, the survey compared women's employment situation at the time they discover they are pregnant with that at the time their child turns one—not before and after marriage. The focus was on how pregnancy and childbirth affect a woman's employment, not on how marriage does. Those carrying out the survey perceptively sensed a societal change; they realized that people were more interested in the impact of pregnancy and childbirth on employment than in the impact of marriage and designed the survey accordingly. In other words, the societal focus has shifted to the problem of having children and deciding whether to quit working or to stay in the labor force.

Let's turn now to the impact of pregnancy and childbirth on a woman's life overall. Single women were surveyed about what kind of life they wanted and were given the following five options to choose from:

1. Full-time homemaking: Get married and have children; resign from work at the time of marriage or childbirth; do not work outside the home after resigning.

2. Return to work: Get married and have children; resign from work at the time of marriage or childbirth; return to work after raising the children.
3. Both work and family: Get married and have children without resigning from work; work for one's entire working life.
4. DINKS: Get married, but do not have children; work for one's entire working life.
5. Single and working: Do not get married; work for one's entire working life.

The first three of the five choices all include getting married and having children, but having children is a greater determinant of a woman's later life than getting married is. The discussion here will proceed as though the phrase "get married" were excluded from those three definitions.

The fourth option clearly states the intention not to have children. The fifth option states "do not get married" and thus can also be seen as a clear decision not to have children. Of course, a woman may simply live with someone and not marry, and women can have children without marrying. At least in present-day Japan, however, option 5 can be seen as not planning to have children. Although 15 percent of single women did indicate "single and working" as their expected life course, those choosing the last two options still constitute only a small minority of the respondents, so leaving these two groups out of our study should not have a major impact on our findings. We can therefore discuss how having children affects the rest of a woman's life by focusing on the first three options.

Figure 5-3 shows the trends over the past two decades. The percentage of women who see their ideal life as having children and becoming full-time homemakers has dropped considerably, falling from almost 34 to 19 percent over the past two decades. Moreover, we see that the expectation of being able to do so has also declined over the years. Over all of the survey periods, the percentage of women who expect that they will be able to become full-time homemakers is roughly 10 percentage points lower than the percentage who indicated this as their ideal life. This implies that women are not able to have their dream life and that a considerable number of women still would prefer to be stay-at-home wives. Although some 20 percent of women today say that their ideal is to become a full-time home-maker, they realize that they may have to be a working wife.

It is the next option—"return to work"—that garnered the highest percentages as both the ideal life and the expected life. Roughly 40 percent of single women expect to resign from work at pregnancy or childbirth, focus for a time on childrearing, and then return to work after the children are older. It is clear that this is what most Japanese women expect their life to be like.

On the other hand, the percentage of women who see having "both work and family"—where women do not quit their jobs at childbirth—as the ideal life course has increased from 19 to 30 percent. The figures for women expecting to do this, however, have

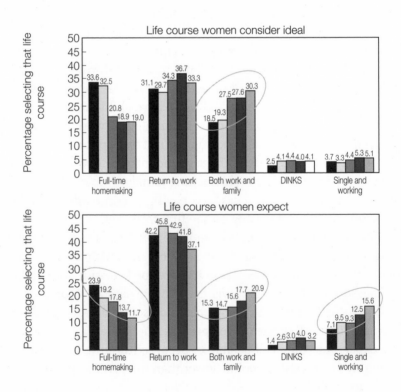

risen much less. In every era, we see a gap of some 4 to 10 percentage points between ideal and expected for this option. In other words, many women would like to balance work and children if they could, but realize the obstacles to doing so and settle for the path of "return to work" as a more realistic life option.

Let's take a moment to review what we have seen so far. About 10 percent of women expect that they will be able to become full-time homemakers, somewhat less than half expect to return to work, and about 20 percent expect to balance work and children. "Return to work" gathers the highest percentage as the expected life course, but both the "full-time homemaking" and the "both work and family" options are selected by a substantial percentage of the survey pool. This suggests that women with children take a variety

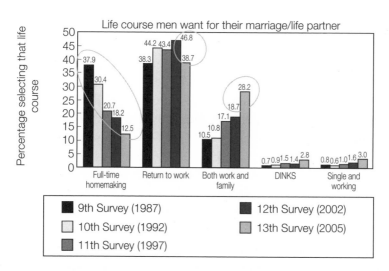

Fig. 5-3 Never-married women's views on their ideal and expected life course and men's views on the life course they want for their marriage/life partner, by survey

Notes: 1. Female subjects are never-married women aged 18–34.
2. The survey questions were as follows: For women's ideal life: "What would be your ideal life course?" For women's expected life: "Setting aside your ideal, what kind of life course do you expect you will actually have?" For men (9th through 12th surveys): "What kind of life course do you want for women?" For men (13th survey): "What kind of life course do you want for the woman who will be your partner (or wife)?"

Source: National Institute of Population and Social Security Research (2007, vol. II, 59, fig. 7-1).

of future life paths. In addition, we should note that in the most recent survey as many as 15 percent of single women respondents expect to remain single and keep working.

What I find particularly interesting is that the survey also looks at the question of what path men—women's marriage and life partners—would like their wives' lives to take. In other words, the creators of the survey regarded this as a matter of interest.

Somewhat under half of men indicated that they expect their wives to resign at childbirth and then return to work after raising the children. Since this is about the same figure as we saw for women, it seems that couples plan for wives to follow this course. We can thus assess this life path to be a desirable one that increases the couple's level of happiness.

One other finding that deserves special comment is that the percentage of men who desire for their wives to be full-time homemakers has decreased drastically from just under 40 percent to around 13 percent or so, while those who would like their wives to balance both work and children has risen dramatically from 10 percent to 28 percent. Earlier we saw large changes concerning these two life courses in the responses of women as well, revealing, more than the variety of paths that women's lives take after childbirth, the magnitude of the changes in the times over the past twenty years. We should also note that the kind of life men consider desirable for their wives has changed more drastically than the life path women themselves expect to have after childbirth—women are changing, but men are changing even more in their expectations.

We see, then, that somewhat under half of both men and women expect that wives will combine work and children by resigning from their jobs at childbirth, focusing on childrearing for a time, and then returning to work after the children are older. The expectation of being a full-time homemaker has declined substantially for both genders, while the percentage hoping women can balance both work and children simultaneously has shown a considerable increase. In addition, the changing times have brought a greater shift in the thinking of men than of women.

Proposals for Raising the Birthrate

The low birthrate is a major issue in Japan today. Broadly speaking, there are two ways to view the matter. One is that whether to have children or not is up to the couple or the woman herself, period. If the declining birthrate has a negative impact on Japan's standard of living or the national economy, so be it. The other line of thinking, on the contrary, regards the low birthrate as a serious problem that society has no choice but to address.

Discouraging abortions

Rather than present my personal views on the low birthrate, I would like to propose two possible remedies. My first proposal starts with the fact that there are women who, after getting pregnant, decide for a variety of reasons not to go through with the birth and to have an abortion. It stands to reason that the number of births would increase considerably if such people were to have their babies rather than terminate their pregnancies. Let's look at this in some detail.

First, we need to know how many elective abortions are performed in Japan. Table 5-8 shows trends in the number of abortions since World War II. We see that in the early years after the war there were more than 1 million abortions a year, but the number has subsequently declined to about 300,000 a year today. We must remember, though, that these figures only include abortions that are reported and that unreported abortions do take place. The abortion statistics shown in the table are minimum figures, then, and the actual figures are no doubt considerably higher.

Obviously, pregnancies are terminated because they are unwanted. The circumstances will differ for each woman or couple, but we can imagine several likely scenarios—the couple is not married; their birth control failed; they are too young to raise a child; they don't have the money to raise a child; they already have all the children they want.

Rather than asking which reasons are most common, though, here I want to focus on whether it would be possible to devise policies to persuade pregnant women—as well as their male partners,

Table 5-8 Reported induced abortions and sterilizations

Year	Induced abortions			No. of sterilizations
	No.	Rate per 1,000 women aged 15–49 (‰)	Abortion-birth ratio (%)	
1954	1,143,059	50.2	64.6	38,056
1964	878,748	42.1	51.2	29,468
1974	679,837	22.4	33.5	10,705
1984	568,916	18.5	38.2	8,194
1994	364,350	11.8	29.4	4,466
2004	301,673	10.6	27.2	2,875

Notes: 1. Statistics are from Statistics and Information Department, Ministry of Health, Labor, and Welfare, *Eisei nenpō* (Annual report on public health), *Botai hogo tōkei hōkoku* (Maternal protection statistics), and *Eisei gyōsei hōkokurei* (Report on public health administration and services).
2. Data prior to 1972 do not include Okinawa Prefecture.
3. The "abortion-birth ratio" is the number of induced abortions to 100 births.

Source: Based on National Institute of Population and Social Security Research, *Jinkō tōkei shiryōshū 2006* (Population statistics of Japan, 2006), 68, table 4-21.

if possible—to have the baby rather than an abortion. If successful, this may well increase the number of births considerably.

But how can we convince people not to choose abortion? Having doctors and others talk with them is unlikely to be effective. What is needed is the disbursement of childbirth, childcare, and other allowances. If the birth mother is not in a position to raise a child, adoption or foster, residential, or some other form of state care should be available. The costs would have to be covered by tax revenues, except in the case of adoption. After all, it is Japanese citizens who are concerned about the low birthrate and want to see the population increase.

Europe has introduced "baby hatches" where unwanted babies can be left anonymously, and this system has been set up at some hospitals in Japan as well. The idea behind baby hatches is to give parents who cannot raise their child a way to have society raise the child either temporarily or semipermanently. So that women will carry their pregnancies to term rather than seek abortions, what I would like to suggest here is to pledge to the parents before the baby is born that society will take responsibility for the child they bear. This is the equivalent of taking the baby hatch concept and applying it at a slightly earlier stage, namely, during the pregnancy.

I am fully aware that implementing this policy would be attended by various challenges. How should the custody of the child be handled? How can taxpayers be convinced to cover the high costs of such a system? People can understand baby hatches because they deal with children who have already been born and it is clearly inhumane to abandon a baby. If the baby hatch concept is implemented in the pregnancy stage, however, the baby is not yet born and abortion is still possible. People will say my proposal is entirely different from baby hatches.

The question of whether children should be viewed as private property or as public assets also comes into play here. In economics, the term "private property" refers to property that a person purchases using his or her own funds for his or her own use. Groceries and automobiles are examples of private property. In contrast, "public assets" are purchased using tax money contributed by many individuals for use by society as a whole. Bridges and roads are examples of public assets. Children are usually considered to be private property and so parents invest their own funds in rearing them to adulthood. As I have already pointed out, however, the next generation performs functions that are of a similar nature to those of public assets because they will become part of the work force and contribute social insurance premiums in the future. It can be assumed, then, that people will be able to accept viewing children as public assets in some respects.

As proof, we have the fact that compulsory education is financed entirely by tax revenues and that a considerable amount of taxes is allocated to higher education as well. The state also disburses child allowances and other tax-financed benefits to support childrearing. Such expenditures offer support for viewing children as being of a similar nature to public assets. Although it would not be easy to determine what percentage of a child is private property and what percentage is public assets, it is clear that children are not 100 percent private property. If children are viewed in this way, then there should be no grounds to fight against the allocation of tax revenues to the raising of children whom women agree not to abort.

The Catholic prohibition against abortion is another perspective that supports this proposal. People who oppose abortion on religious grounds may support the idea of having babies who were carried to term raised in some way by society. From the standpoint of biology, there is no hard-and-fast way to say when life begins: at fertilization of the egg by the sperm, at the time that the fetus takes on a recognizable human form, or at birth. In the earlier discussion of baby hatches, I noted that it is unethical for babies to be abandoned. If life is considered to begin when the fetus has a recognizable human form, however, many abortions would also be considered unethical. This also could serve as a persuasive argument against abortion and for societal responsibility for those children who would otherwise have been aborted.

We can also cite historical validation of policies to have society raise children in the experience of other parts of the world. Not so long ago, Israel had the kibbutz system of raising its precious children communally. A similar system also existed in Taiwan. We must keep in mind that such frameworks were created in times of emergency with the additional aim of ensuring that there would be soldiers to fight for the survival of the country. Nonetheless, these places did take a communal approach to childrearing at one point, reflecting the concept of children as public assets.

I realize that this proposal to persuade couples from having elective abortions and to use tax revenues for the children born raises serious issues; it certainly cannot be introduced immediately. From the fact that baby hatches have been set up in Japan, however, the proposal outlined here may be something that can be considered in the future. My aim has been simply to point out that such an option to raise the birthrate does exist and is not beyond the realm of possibility.

Encouraging out-of-wedlock births

Fortunately or unfortunately, marital births make up the absolute majority of births in Japan. "Legitimate" is the legal word used to refer to children born to a couple who are lawfully married to each other. Such children are recognized under the law and their rights are guaranteed in terms of taxation and social insurance as well as inheritance.

In contrast, children born to a couple who are not lawfully married to each other are referred to as "illegitimate," a term that gives the impression that the children were born out of something illicit. *Shiseiji*, a word with a negative connotation, was once widely used in Japan to refer to such children, and these children were seen as undesirable.

As mentioned earlier, out-of-wedlock births constitute only 2 percent or so of all births in Japan. This is a very small figure. We can assume that the abortion figures cited above include many people seeking abortions out of fear of the stigma of having an illegitimate child. The increase in the number of marriages where the bride is pregnant (*dekichattakon; sazukarikon*) can also be interpreted as the desire to make an out-of-wedlock child a wedlock child. This is a new trend.

In contrast, recently it was reported that more than half of the births in France are to couples who are not legally married to each other—children born to couples living together or in a love relationship are now the majority. Europe has always had a high number of out-of-wedlock births, and now things have reached this point in France.

Why has such a situation arisen in Europe and particularly France? We can give several reasons. First, more and more men and women do not see any particular merit in the legal institution of marriage. Behind this lie freedom in relationships, sexual freedom, and people's desire not to be tied down. Another major factor is that quite a number of couples live together and get legally married after they have a child.

Second is the emergence of people who want children, and not marriage, although there are still not all that many people who fall into this category. These people simply want their own child and are not particular about the man or woman with whom they have it. This is seen more in women than in men; an extreme example is a woman who has a baby using sperm from an unknown donor.

We must also note that there is almost no difference now in European countries in the rights and benefits granted to children born in wedlock and those born out of wedlock. Since there is no longer any legal difference between the benefits received from the education or social security system or in the inheritance of property, couples now have children without getting legally married.

We can foresee that this trend will have a major impact on other countries as well; it is even possible that out-of-wedlock children will become the mainstream in industrialized countries. Many times things that happen in the West happen in Japan a few decades later, so it is likely that marriage customs will change here as well, both as a natural development and as a result of influence by the example of trends abroad.

Such a change in attitudes would be welcome in terms of the birthrate problem as well. The first step would be to eliminate the legal differences between the rights of children born in wedlock and those of children born out of wedlock, and that is already under way, in fact.

It is important to create a cultural climate in Japan where there is no prejudice or discrimination whatsoever against children born to parents who are not lawfully married. To the extent that traditional views of the family are still strong in Japan, this will not be easy to achieve. Japan can change little by little, however. The fact that there is less stigma attached now to being a single mother or to being a pregnant bride is proof of movement in that direction.

Chapter Six

Full-Time Homemakers and Working Women

I t would seem at first glance that full-time homemakers have an advantage over working women. People tend to think that full-time homemakers enjoy carefree lives because they do not have to work to make a living. This idea is captured in an older Japanese phrase once used to describe such women: sanshoku hirunetsuki, literally, "three meals and naps included." In other words, a homemaker is guaranteed three meals a day without working because she can live off her husband's money, and she also has the luxury of taking naps because she has lots of free time.

Full-time homemakers actually do work, though. A very small number of wealthy families may have housekeepers, but most full-time homemakers handle the housework and childcare. Their work hours may not be as long as those of working women, but they are not short either. The key difference is that working women earn wages because they work outside the home, while full-time homemakers are not paid for their labor.

What about working women? Such women do earn wages for their labor outside the home, but working wives are still responsible for housework and, often, childcare—unpaid labor in the home. A woman trying to do both will have very long work hours indeed unless her husband helps her at home. It is very hard both mentally and physically on a woman to have work responsibilities both at home and at the office. To avoid overextending themselves, wives sometimes shorten the number of hours they work outside the home by taking part-time positions, or they may pay an outside party to help with the housework and childcare.

It is not easy to determine whether full-time homemakers or working women are more fortunate. Comparing the two groups, we find that each has different responsibilities, and the decision of who is luckier also depends on how monetary remuneration and unpaid labor are viewed. I would like to explore this question in more depth below, considering these two groups from various perspectives in order to reach a more informed judgment.

To Become a Full-Time Homemaker:
A Woman's Dream of Yesteryear

An historical perspective

If we say that it used to be a Japanese woman's dream to be a full-time homemaker, how will people today react? Highly educated career women might think that being stuck at home taking care of a husband and children would be boring. They might find it intolerable to end their days having done only that—to them that would be not a dream but a nightmare.

Other women might think that it would indeed be a dream to live the carefree life of a full-time homemaker—as captured in the phrase *sanshoku hirunetsuki*—rather than feeling run down physically and mentally by working outside the home. A surprisingly large number of overworked men might also agree.

Some might assert that it is noble to dedicate oneself to caring for a husband and children. To raise children who will be capable members of society in the future is a necessary human act, and being able to fulfill such a role as a mother is a very special opportunity. Raising children well can be a way for a woman to realize her own dreams.

And it might be anyone's dream life to marry a very wealthy man, live in a huge mansion, have servants to take care of the housework and children, wear beautiful clothes, go on trips, and enjoy life in general. Since early times, Japan has had the expression *tama no koshi* ("she married into money" [literally, "bejeweled palanquin"]), which aptly describes this last scenario.

I have attempted here to portray some of the dreams and nightmares people might associate with being a full-time homemaker, but let's turn our attention to the time when this was a woman's dream life. Women dreamed of being full-time homemakers before World War II and then again after the war until Japan's period of high economic growth.

In pre–World War II Japan, there was a wide gap between the rich and the poor. Japan had clear social stratifications, with people categorized as peerage, former samurai, or commoners. Women raised in wealthy, upper-class families did not go on to university or other higher education, but they did attend *jogakkō* (girls' schools that provided post-elementary education) and *kōtō jogakkō* (girls' secondary schools that were the counterpart of boys' middle schools). On the other hand, women raised in poor, lower-class families ended their education at graduation from *shōgakkō* (a six-year compulsory elementary school) or *kōtō shōgakkō* (a two-year supplemental elementary school).

Women raised in poor, lower-class homes had to work, generally in hard labor, to help support their family. Usually they engaged in farming, but they also might work at a factory or store or as a maid in a wealthy household. The work conditions at factories were harsh; in fact, a book entitled *Jokō aishi* (The sorrowful history of female factory workers) was published in 1925 depicting the extremely poor conditions for female workers at textile mills. The term *jokō aishi* was used thereafter to refer to women's harsh labor conditions. And we should note that these women continued to work even after they married, as their marriage partners also were not very affluent; such couples needed the wife's wages as well to make ends meet. Farming, retail trade, and home-based businesses were the main industries in those days, and they required the wife's labor whether the couple lived at the workplace or in homes near the workplace.

The birth of children added the extra work of childcare. In those days, the ideal woman in Japan was the *ryōsai kenbo* ("good wife and wise mother") so there was not much pressure for husbands to help with the housework and the children. Rather, husbands were seen as working hard outside the home. Since lower-class women carried the triple burden of working, doing the housework, and raising the children, it is clear that wives had hard lives. There was one source of support, however. Thanks to the extended family system in those days, grandparents lived in the same house or neighborhood as the family and so grandfathers and particularly grandmothers helped with housework and childcare. Even with such support, however, there is no question that women led lives of unceasing labor, often caring for elderly parents as well.

On the other hand, women raised in wealthy, upper-class families—and some well-off, middle-class families—generally stayed at home and prepared for marriage after graduating from *jogakkō* or *kōtō jogakkō*, although there were some women who found employment after graduation. A woman prepared for married life at home by learning household skills and waited for an arranged marriage with a university-educated man, the son of a good family that would be appropriate for her family line. Once married, she followed the path of the *ryōsai kenbo* and dedicated herself to domesticity, doing housework and raising the children. In the case of a small number of very wealthy families, servants performed the housework and childcare.

Although the dichotomy between working married women and full-time homemakers has been described here in absolute terms, there were some exceptions to the rule. For example, a tiny number of highly educated women pursued professional careers. Some women born in poor, lower-class families fell in love with and married men in the upper class and thus instantly became members of the upper class themselves. In most cases, however, the division between the two categories was very distinct, and the vast majority of women had to continue working after marrying. And since Japan was still a poor country, many women labored long hours under very harsh conditions.

Under such circumstances, it would have been only natural for overworked women to dream of becoming full-time homemakers. If her husband had the financial means, a woman would not have to work but could stay at home and devote herself to taking care of her husband and raising her children like the ideal woman, the *ryōsai kenbo*. Or she could daydream of picking the "easy" path of having a carefree life without having to do mentally and physically taxing labor.

Before World War II and then again after the war until the period of Japan's rapid economic growth, women who were able to realize this dream were in the minority. Japan was not affluent and so was not the kind of society where many could be full-time homemakers. This dream was truly nothing more than a dream for most women.

Changes with Japan's economic miracle

Many things related to women's lives changed, however, in the period of high economic growth from 1955 to 1973. During this time, Japan's growth rate was nearly 10 percent a year on average, bringing major changes throughout Japanese society. Let me briefly summarize those changes that affected women.

First, high economic growth resulted in a corresponding rise in wages. As salaries rose, it became possible for families to get by on the husband's income alone, meaning it was no longer necessary for the wife to work.

A second effect of such rapid economic growth was a new geographical mobility of workers. In response to the rising demand for factory and office staff in the cities, workers, particularly young people, moved from the countryside to urban areas in droves. Before that time, it had been common for young people raised in families engaged in farming, retail trade, or home-based businesses to inherit their parents' occupation. As work opportunities in cities increased and people realized that the wages for such work were higher, they naturally chose to move to urban areas. As a result, there was a great migration of workers from the countryside to the city.

The nature of employment also changed. An industrial structure centered on farming, retail trade, and home-based businesses requires that all members of the family work to support the family business. In the case of manufacturing and service industries in the city, however, help from family members is not required. As Japan converted to an industrial and employment structure centered on workers in urban areas, employment based on the individual came to be mainstream. This did not eliminate two-income couples where both the husband and the wife worked as employees, but, as I have already said, the husband's income rose so it became possible for families to choose whether the wife would work.

Another new development in this period was that, when young people working in the cities married and created new families, they lived in company or public housing. In particular, they lived in *danchi*, a housing development composed of a group of apartment buildings of a particular style and design. Although each residential unit was small, *danchi* did make it possible for couples to have their own home. Some who were a little better off were even able to have their own house rather than an apartment. This marked the dawn of the urban couple composed of a "salaryman" (white-collar corporate employee) and his stay-at-home wife.

This is how there came to be many full-time homemakers, particularly in the cities, during Japan's economic miracle. Let's look at some numbers in table 6-1, which traces the percentage of working married women from 1965 to 1992. In 1965 and 1971, during Japan's rapid economic growth, roughly 39 percent and 42 percent, respectively, of married women were engaged in work, but after this period ended the figure rose to over 50 percent. We see that there were many stay-at-home wives—nonworking women—during the time of high economic growth.

Table 6-2, which shows women engaged in full-time housekeeping as a percentage of all women aged fifteen years and over who are not in the labor force, also indicates that the percentage of stay-at-homes rose during the period of high growth, increasing from 29.8 percent in 1960 to 36.9 percent in 1975. The percentage of full-time homemakers peaked that year and has been on an overall decline since then.

Table 6-1 Percentage of married women engaged in work

(%)

Year	Those engaged in work	Of which, those mainly engaged in work	Of which, those engaged in work on the side
1965	38.7	64.7	35.3
1971	42.0	52.9	47.1
1982	50.2	50.1	49.9
1992	53.3	50.6	49.4

Source: Based on Statistics Bureau, Ministry of Internal Affairs and Communications, *Employment Status Survey*.

Table 6-2 Women engaged in full-time housekeeping as a percentage of women aged 15 years and over who are not in the labor force

	(%)
Year	
1960	29.8
1965	31.6
1970	33.8
1975	36.9
1980	34.0
1985	31.4
1990	29.2
1995	30.3
2000	31.1
2005	29.6

Source: Based on Statistics Bureau, Ministry of Internal Affairs and Communications, *Labor Force Survey*.

Of course, not all women became full-time homemakers. As these two tables show, there were two-income couples during this period and many women went back to work after a time of full-time homemaking during their childrearing years. Nonetheless, it is clear that Japan's economic miracle enabled a considerable number of women to realize their "dream life."

The larger meaning of full-time homemaking has been analyzed from various standpoints. In her Marxist-feminist analysis, Ueno (1990) sees the "salaryman" and full-time homemaker as products of patriarchy and capitalism. Patriarchy creates a male-centric society where wives are subordinate to their husbands and families are centered on the father and the sons, particularly the eldest son; and capitalism creates relationships where workers/husbands slave away at companies and are exploited by capitalists. The home, then, is where the wife backs up the husband who is exhausted body and soul from working himself to the bone for the company. Ōsawa Mari (1993) offers a similar analysis.

Ochiai (1994) also sees full-time homemakers as providing behind-the-scenes support for Japan's economic growth, although she does not take a Marxist perspective. Workaholic male employees were able to give their absolute all at the workplace, and corporations were able to enjoy high productivity, because full-time homemakers were at home taking care of all housework and childrearing duties. Japan was able to achieve high productivity because the division of labor in households (Becker 1981) operated exceptionally well.

Beyond Full-Time Homemaking

As we have seen, the period of high economic growth enabled many women to fulfill their dream of becoming a full-time homemaker. Later, however, the percentage of women, particularly married women, engaged in work increased once again and the number of stay-at-home wives correspondingly declined. Does this mean that women had ful-filled their dream of becoming full-time homemakers and no longer held such a goal?

Looking at the numbers, we see in table 6-1 that the percentage of married women engaged in work rose in the 1980s, with the 1990s figure standing roughly 15 percentage points higher than that of the 1960s. This represents a rather dramatic increase in the percentage of working wives.

Why the increase? We can cite several reasons a woman might decide to give up on her "dream life" of comfort as a full-time homemaker and enter, or reenter, the labor force.

1. Income: Although incomes had been rising during the period of high growth, the oil crises of the 1970s brought a time of lower growth and ended large rises in family income. Households did not have a sufficient income with the husband's salary alone so more wives worked to supplement the family finances.

2. Desire for a better standard of living: The Japanese had enjoyed rather affluent lifestyles during the period of high economic growth and began to desire even better lifestyles. They wanted to live in as large a house as possible. They

wanted as high a standard of living as possible. They wanted to give their children as good an education as possible. Couples started to realize that, to fulfill such desires, the wife needed to work and add to the household income.

3. Education level: As we have already seen, more women were going on to higher levels of education. It is natural for highly educated women to want to work, and women who had strong work qualifications could find meaningful positions with high wages. And it is an economic principle applicable to men and women alike that a worker's desire to work goes up as wages increase. The second part of what is known as the Douglas-Arisawa theory in Japan (in which a hypothesis advanced by the American economist P. H. Douglas in the 1930s was later applied to Japan by the Japanese economist Arisawa Hiromi) relates this to the case of Japanese women; the work of Ōsawa Machiko (1993) also supports this principle.

Since I have mentioned the second part of the Douglas-Arisawa theory, let me also present the first part of the theory: the lower the husband's income, the more likely it is that the wife will work. If the husband's income is high, then there is little need for the wife to work. This long held true in Japan, but it has not proved to reflect the situation since the 1990s, as shown by Kohara (2001) and Ōtake (2005), among others. In other words, the question of whether a woman works is unrelated to her husband's income. We should note that some, like Abe and Ōishi (2006), claim that the first part of the theory is not entirely invalid, but the trend seems to be toward discarding it as no longer relevant.

Tachibanaki and Urakawa (2006) and Abe (2006) have shown that today (1) the higher the husband's income, the more likely it is that the wife will work and (2) the more education a wife has, the more likely it is that she will work. If both husband and wife are highly educated, they will earn high wages, resulting in a very healthy family income. On the other hand, lesser-educated couples will have a low household income. In the chapter on education, we noted that the correlation between the educational attainment of the husband and the wife is gradually decreasing. Nonetheless, couples where the husband and wife have roughly the same level of education still make up the majority, leading to a growing inequality in household income among two-income couples depending on their level of education.

Talking about education and women in the labor force, we should further note that the situation in Japan differs from that in other industrialized nations. As shown in figure 6-1, over 80 percent of females who completed four-year universities or graduate schools are in the labor force in other countries, but only 70.5 percent of women with the equivalent education in Japan work. Thus, a lower percentage of highly educated women work in Japan than in other industrialized nations. In all nations surveyed, however, the rate of participation in the labor force increases with the amount of education.

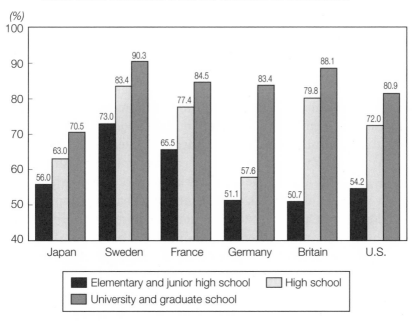

Fig. 6-1 International comparison of women's labor force participation by educational attainment (age 25–64)

Source: Ministry of Health, Labor, and Welfare, *Heisei 16 nen ban josei rōdō hakusho* (2004 white paper on women in the labor force), 35, fig. 2-4.

If only 70 percent or so of highly educated Japanese women work, this means that the remaining 30 percent are full-time homemakers, with important implications for our study of disparities among women. Highly educated women are marrying highly educated men, but sometimes both the husband and wife work and sometimes the woman stays home. This has a subtle impact on household income, producing a disparity between women in the two different circumstances. This phenomenon will be considered in more detail later.

• Lifestyle dissatisfaction: Women started to be dissatisfied with spending their entire lives shut up in the home caring for their husbands and children. As the feminist movement started to take root in Japan with its tenet that women are the equals of men, women decided to be less dependent on their husbands and to earn their own income.

Women's Employment: An Overview

The "M-curve"

Having compared the situation of full-time homemakers and working married women, let's now turn our attention to the various factors that determine female employment in contemporary Japan.

Today most women work in the paid sector after finishing their schooling. This is a change from a generation or so ago, when quite a few women did not work outside the home, but were *kaji tetsudai*, or "domestic help." They stayed at home and prepared for marriage by observing their mothers and doing household chores. Today, however, the majority of women work after finishing their studies. In figure 6-2 we see the participation of women in the labor force by age bracket from 1960 to 2006, while figure 6-3 compares singles[*] and married women. These two figures will help us to discover the changes that have taken place in the area of women and work.

---

[*] Note that "singles" (*mikonsha*) refers to "singles who have never married," as in the other surveys cited in this book.

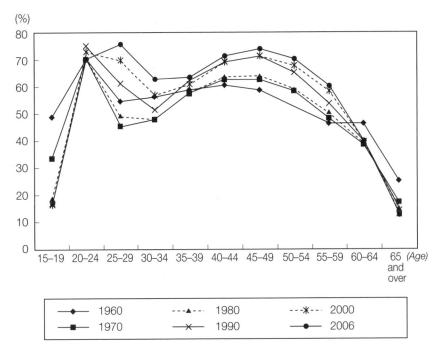

Fig. 6-2 Women's labor force participation rate by age bracket

Source: Based on Statistics Bureau, Ministry of Internal Affairs and Communications, *Labor Force Survey*.

Let's look first at employment after leaving school. According to figure 6-3, about 90 percent of single women aged 25–34 worked in the paid sector in 1996 and 2006—only 78.6 and 72.9 percent of single women aged 20–24 worked in those two years, but these lower numbers are due to many women in this age bracket still being in school. The percentage of single working women remains high over the age of thirty-five as well since these women must make their own living.

More interesting is the change over the years in the percentage of working women in the 25–29 and the 30–34 age brackets. Figure 6-2 shows us that less than half of women in these two age categories worked in 1970 but that this percentage rose over time until in 2006 it stood at 75.7 percent for the 25–29 age bracket and 62.8 percent

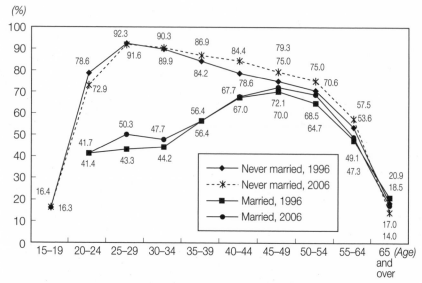

Fig. 6-3 Women's labor force participation rate by marital status and by age bracket

Source: Based on Statistics Bureau, Ministry of Internal Affairs and Communications, *Labor Force Survey* (1996 and 2006).

for the 30–34 age bracket. We can assume that many in the 25–29 age group have yet to marry, as women are marrying later these days, and that this has resulted in the particularly high rate—almost 76 percent—in this age group.

We see that women in the labor force increase again in the 35–49 age group. In other words, the rate is high when women are in their twenties, declines from the late twenties through early thirties, and then rises again in the late thirties and forties as women reenter the labor force. Women's labor force participation thus traces what is referred to as an "M-curve." The middle dip in the M curve—when women are in their late twenties and early thirties—corresponds to the period when women quit work for a time to focus on marriage and, more particularly, children. Quite a number of women shift from being working women to being full-time homemakers during these years and then later return to the ranks of working women. For more information regarding women's reentry into the labor force, see the work of Tomita and Wakisaka (1999), Higuchi (2000), and Suruga and Nishimoto (2001).

In figure 6-2 we see that the dip in the M has gradually lessened and become flatter since 1960. This signifies a decrease in the percentage of women who resign from work at the time of marriage or childbirth. In some Western countries, the dip in the curve has disappeared so that the curve has the shape of a bell—women are no longer temporarily withdrawing from the labor market but are continuing to be employed through their marriage and childbearing years. The curve for Japanese women still features a dip, but chances are that it will take on the shape of a bell in the not-too-distant future. With the declining birthrate and projected labor shortage, there will be increased societal pressure on women to work; women may well want to work, and increased childcare assistance is expected to be offered to make it easier for them to work.

Let's take a closer look at the flattened dip in the M-curve. What has changed for women aged 25–34? Figure 6-4 shows the percentage of women in this age bracket engaged in work, the percentage wishing to work, and the percentage of those wishing to work who are able to find jobs. The percentage engaged in work has risen more or less steadily since 1962, with more than 60 percent working in 2002. This proves that the middle dip in the M-curve is gradually lessening.

The key factor behind this is the rapid rise over this period in the number of full-time homemakers in the 25–34 age bracket who want to work. In 1962, a mere 30-plus percent wanted to work versus roughly 62 percent in 2002, a dramatic rise. Such an increase in the desire to work among women aged 25–34 is impressive indeed.

What percentage of women in this age group who wish to work are able to find employment? As figure 6-4 shows, more than 60 percent of women who wished to work were able to find employment in the 1960s and early 1970s. After that time, however, the percentage able to find work decreased. The percentage started to rebound markedly in the 1990s, and slightly over 70 percent of women in this age group who wished to work were successful in finding it in 2002. (It is interesting that the curve that traces the

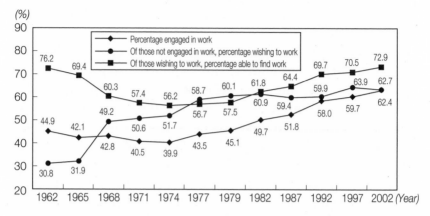

Fig. 6-4 Percentage of women aged 25–34 engaged in work

Source: Based on Statistics Bureau, Ministry of Internal Affairs and Communications,
Employment Status Survey.

percentage of women who are able to fulfill their wish to work also takes the form of an M like the curve for the female labor force participation rate.) The key nugget of information revealed in figure 6-4, however, is that almost 30 percent of women in the 25–34 age bracket who wished to work could not find jobs in 2002.

If these women were to succeed in finding work, it would substantially alleviate the labor shortage anticipated with the decline in the birthrate. One likely reason these women were not able to find employment is the lingering recession in Japan. Another reason, however, is that workplaces have not met the needs of women who must balance children and career. Employment support measures targeting women would be an effective step here.

It is important to look further into why almost 30 percent of women in the 25–34 age bracket who wish to work cannot find employment. In one sense, we could say that there is no need to concern ourselves with women who do not want to work; after all, such women have chosen that path themselves. However, the women may have decided not to work because there seemed to be no job possibilities open to them. In this case, we need to determine why they anticipated they would have no opportunities. The reasons why about 30 percent of women in this age group cannot work even though they want to and the reasons why other women in the same age group anticipate from the start that there are no opportunities and so do not wish to work may be surprisingly similar. Let's examine this question more closely.

Childcare leave systems

Childcare leave allows mothers or fathers to be absent from work for up to eighteen months for childrearing and then to return to their jobs. In Japan, a law for childcare leave was first enacted in 1991, and it is overwhelmingly women who take advantage of this system: a mere 0.50 percent of men avail themselves of it.

Figure 6-5 gives two key pieces of information related to this issue. First, we see an increase of about 25 percentage points in companies offering childcare leave schemes from 1996 to 2005, from 36.4 percent to 61.6 percent for small companies and from 60.8 percent to 86.1 percent for larger firms. This is indeed a positive development. The problem, though, is that the figure has yet to reach 100 percent.

Second, the percentage of companies with childcare leave provisions differs greatly depending on the company's size. Almost all large companies—those with 500 or more employees—have such a scheme; however, a rather low 57 percent or so of small firms—those with only 5–29 employees—have one. This means that slightly over 40 percent of workers have no childcare leave program.

Why is there such a discrepancy by size? Under childcare leave programs, employees who take leave are paid wages (40 percent of full wages) through unemployment insurance. Companies and employees must meet various conditions, however, to enroll in unemployment insurance: firms that have five or fewer employees and workers with employment contracts with a term of less than one year are not eligible to enroll in unemployment insurance. As a result, some small companies do not offer leave and some workers are not eligible for it.

More importantly, small companies in particular find it difficult to temporarily replace employees on childcare leave. For such companies, it is more convenient if the worker quits the company altogether, and so there is often tangible and intangible pressure prompting her to

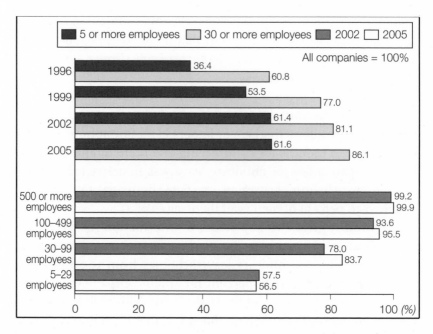

Fig. 6-5 Percentage of companies with a childcare leave system

Source: Based on Ministry of Health, Labor, and Welfare, *Josei koyō kanri kihon chōsa* (Basic survey of employment management of women).

resign before the birth. It is less trouble to hire a new worker to replace one who resigns than to find a temporary replacement for a woman going on childcare leave or to figure out what to do with someone who returns after her childcare leave ends.

What percentage of workers actually takes childcare leave? A decade or so ago, approximately 50 percent of female workers took advantage of the system, and this figure rose to 72 percent as of 2005. This means that nearly one in three women do not use the childcare leave system. Shigeno and Ōkusa (1998) and Morita (2003) examine in more detail the impact of the Childcare Leave Act.

To summarize, quite a high percentage of married women in the 25–34 age bracket quit their jobs because they cannot, for various reasons, take childcare leave. Once a woman resigns, however, she cannot easily find a good job again even if she searches for one.

As a result, quite a few women continue as full-time homemakers after childbirth even if that is not their first choice.

Disparities among women: education

The M-curve for women in the labor force that we looked at earlier has two intriguing aspects. First, the shape of the M changes depending on women's education level, and, second, the M also changes with the geographical area in which women live.

Such differences in the M-curve by education level can be seen in figure 6-6. A much higher percentage of university-educated women—those who have earned a degree from a four-year university or graduate school—are working in their twenties compared with high school or junior college graduates. In fact, the university graduate figure is higher than that of high school graduates by about 17 percentage points in the 25–29 age bracket. The bottom of the dip in the M for university-educated women comes in the 35–39 age bracket, and from there the graph remains relatively flat. In fact, the M-curve for high school graduates shows a steeper rise. We see that in the 45–49 age group, the percentages of high school and junior college graduates engaged in work are about 5 percentage points higher than that of women who completed university and graduate school.

Why does the percentage of women engaged in work change by age group depending on the woman's level of education? First, let's look at the gap in the rate for women in their twenties. Many university-educated women work because they have a greater desire to work and they receive higher wages than those with less education, but the situation is reversed for high school graduates—they cannot expect high wages and are not so enthusiastic about working. A considerable percentage of high school graduates in the 25–29 and the 30–34 age brackets become full-time homemakers when they marry or have children. (One factor behind this trend is that the percentage of high school graduates who are engaged in work in their twenties is low to begin with.)

The same is true for university-educated women. In fact, the percentage of these women who are engaged in work after marriage and particularly childbirth drops more precipitously than that of high

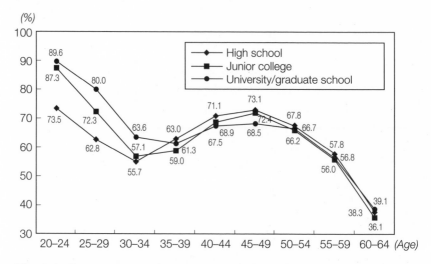

Fig. 6-6 Percentage of women engaged in work by age bracket and by educational background (2002)

Source: Based on Statistics Bureau, Ministry of Internal Affairs and Communications, *Employment Status Survey* (2002).

school graduates. We can see from figure 6-6 that junior college graduates, who are between high school and university graduates in terms of education, also fall between them in terms of percentage engaged in work. In other words, the middle dip of the M for this group at marriage and childbirth lies between that for university graduates, which is rather sharp, and that for high school graduates, which is slightly flatter.

The differences in the upturn in the M-curve from the 30–34 and 35–39 age groups when women start to return to work are interesting. The percentage of high school graduates engaged in work rises quite sharply from the low of 55.7 percent in the 30–34 age group to a peak of 73.1 percent in the 45–49 age group. In contrast, the rate for university-educated women rises a mere 7 percentage points from its low of 61.3 percent in the 35–39 age group to peak of 68.5 percent in the 45–49 age group. That is to say, quite a number of high school graduates return to work, but few university-educated women reenter the labor force.

This represents a unique and striking feature of disparities among women in Japan. A higher percentage of highly educated women—those who have finished university or graduate school and thus have high qualifications—work in their younger years than women whose studies ended with a high school diploma. Both highly educated and lesser-educated women resign from their jobs when they marry or, more particularly, when they have children. If we focus on the trend after the M-curve reaches its low point—in other words, when women start to rejoin the work force—we find that a lower percentage of university-educated women than high-school–educated women return to work. Highly educated women are more likely to remain full-time homemakers in their middle-aged years than lesser-educated women.

This can rightly be considered a disparity among women that is unique to Japan. Compared with other industrialized nations, a lower proportion of highly educated Japanese women are working. Highly educated Japanese women in their forties are not working outside the home as much as could be expected.

Why is this? First, the husbands of highly educated women are making quite a good salary by that age so there is no pressing need for the wives to help out financially. As has already been discussed, highly educated women have a greater probability of marrying a highly educated man.

Second, highly educated women who have left work to raise children end up losing valuable work skills during their time away from the workplace. Even if they try to return to the work force, they are unlikely to find a desirable job. They thus abandon the idea of looking for a job because they are not in economic hardship and they know that they will not find satisfying, high-paying work. Wakisaka and Okui (2005) discuss this issue.

A third factor in the relatively low figures for highly educated women is that lesser-educated women have a greater financial need to work. Quite a high percentage of lesser-educated women return to the labor force once their childrearing responsibilities have decreased because their household income is low and they are forced to return to work for economic reasons. Many lesser-educated women thus work to supplement the household budget, and the decisive factor is the difference in income between the husbands of lesser-educated women and of highly educated women. Coming into play here is the fact that a high percentage of lesser-educated women are married to lesser-educated men.

Disparities among women: geographical area
The second interesting aspect of the M-curve is the differences in the shape of the M by region, i.e., the disparity among women by region. Japan's *Heisei 16 nen ban josei rōdō hakusho* (2004 white paper on women in the labor force) contains a good analysis of this issue that we will find useful.

In figure 6-7 we can see the relationship between the percentage of women in the 25–54 age bracket engaged in work and the depth of the dip in the M by prefecture. According to this figure, the percentage of women working is high and the dip in the M is shallow in the regional areas of Hokuriku, Tōhoku, San'in, and Kyūshū, which include Fukui, Ishikawa, Yamagata, Akita, Shimane, Tottori, and Kumamoto prefectures. This means that a higher percentage of women in regional areas work than in urban areas and that more of them continue to work after they marry and even after they have children.

Conversely, in urban areas, such as Kanagawa, Osaka, Chiba, Saitama, and Hyōgo prefectures, the percentage of women engaged in paid work is somewhat low and the depression in the M-curve is deeper. This means that a low percentage of city women are engaged in work, and that many stop working at the time of marriage and particularly at childbirth and childrearing.

Putting these facts together, we see that in regional areas women's labor force participation rate is high and many women continue their employment through marriage, childbirth, and childrearing, whereas in city areas women's presence in the labor force is low and many women quit their jobs at the time of marriage, childbirth, or childrearing. What might be behind such differences between country and city women?

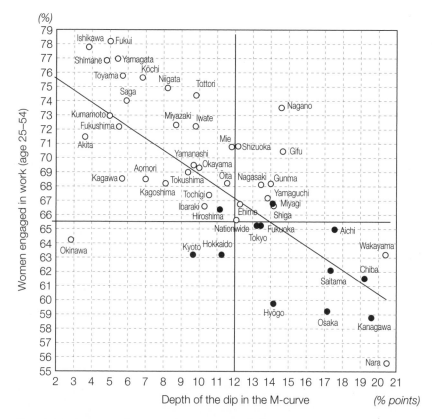

Fig. 6-7 Percentage of women aged 25–54 engaged in work and the M-curve, by prefecture (2002)

Notes: 1. "Depth of the dip in the M-curve" is the difference between the highest percentage of women engaged in work (first peak in the M-curve) and the figure at the lowest point in the dip in the curve.

2. Solid dots represent Tokyo (special wards) or prefectures that are home to an ordinance-designated city. (See the notes of the next figure for explanations of "Tokyo [special wards]" and "ordinance-designated city.")

Source: Based on Statistics Bureau, Ministry of Internal Affairs and Communications, *Employment Status Survey* (2002).

Let's look at differences between urban and regional areas that might explain this disparity in women and work by geographical location. First, there is a difference in industrial structure. Compared with urban areas, regional areas have a higher percentage of agriculture, retail trade, and home-based businesses. Not only are many women engaged in these industries, but a high percentage of women continue to work even after marriage and childbirth due to the nature of such industries. In contrast, manufacturing and services are the main industries in urban areas, so it is not surprising that many women quit when they get married or have children.

Another factor enabling women living in the countryside to continue working after marriage and childbirth is that, in many cases, they live in the same home as their parents or in-laws, or else parents, in-laws, or other relatives live nearby. The extended family means these women have their own private system of childcare support. In contrast, most women in the city lack this support system as family and relatives live far away. Daycare centers and other assistance have the potential to remedy the situation but are not yet fully in place. It is thus easy to see why many women living in the city quit their jobs when they have children.

Also in regard to married women, we find that there are comparatively more women with high-income husbands in cities than in regional areas, and, as a result, there is not a very strong need for wives in urban areas to find work to help out financially. In contrast, the income of husbands in country areas is relatively low, and there is a strong expectation that wives will work and thus boost the household income.

Earlier we looked at the percentage of women wishing to work who were successful in finding work, and we can see regional differences in this respect as well. Figure 6-8, which shows this percentage in urban areas, indirectly reveals the difference in this regard between urban and regional areas. According to this figure, the percentage of women aged 25–54 living in one of Japan's major cities (known as ordinance-designated cities) who wish to work and are successful in finding it is lower than the national average of 77.0 percent in nearly every case; Tokyo is the one exception. Since in cities other than Tokyo, the percentage of women who would like to work but cannot find employment is higher than the national average, it follows that the percentages of women who wish to work and

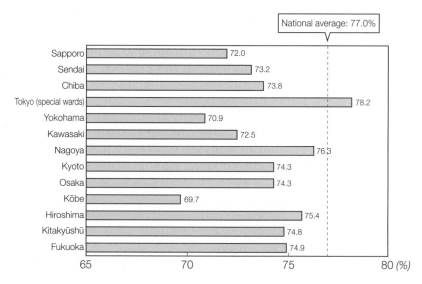

Fig. 6-8 Percentage of women aged 25–54 wishing to work able to find work in ordinance-designated cities and Tokyo (special wards)

Notes: 1. An "ordinance-designated city" is a city that has a population greater than 500,000 and that has been designated as such by an order of the Cabinet of Japan under Article 252, Section 19 of the Local Autonomy Law.

2. "Tokyo (special wards)" refers to the 23 municipalities that together make up central Tokyo.

Source: Based on Statistics Bureau, Ministry of Internal Affairs and Communications, *Employment Status Survey* (2002).

are successful in finding it are higher in many regional areas than the national average.

While urban women have difficulty finding employment even if they want to work, it is comparatively easy for women living in regional areas to find a job. This gap likely arises from the difference in industrial structure between regional and urban areas, as has already been mentioned. Moreover, the wages that women expect are likely somewhat lower in country areas than in the city, so that women are more likely to be hired by regional companies than by urban companies—supply and demand are more evenly matched in regional labor markets.

One additional comment must be made about Tokyo, the one urban area that is higher than the national average in terms of the percentage of women wishing to work who are able to find jobs. Women find work comparatively easily in Tokyo because the national capital has many job opportunities. Although Nagoya is a close second, Tokyo is the nation's center economically, far ahead of the rest of the country by almost every measure. Tokyo also has solid childrearing-support measures, such as daycare centers, but the high demand for labor can be viewed as the more important factor in the high percentage of women successfully finding employment.

Chapter Seven

Women and Japanese Companies I:
Career Tracking and Promotion

W omen face various choices regarding their work lives. First they have to decide whether or not to work. If they decide to work, they then have two major choices: (1) whether to work in a management-track position or a clerical-track position and (2) whether to work as a regular, full-time employee or as a nonregular employee (part-time worker, dispatched worker, contract employee, etc.). There are also the questions of whether to be hired by a company or to be self-employed, what occupation to take up, and what industry to enter. The first two choices of employee status—management track versus clerical track; regular employee versus nonregular employee—are of particular interest in our study of disparities among women. In this chapter, we will, therefore, look more closely at the role of career tracking in Japanese companies, as well as at how Japanese companies choose who to promote and how this affects women. The question of regular and nonregular employment will be taken up in the next chapter.

The Management Track and the Clerical Track

Tracked personnel systems establish distinct categories of employee status and assign work duties and work conditions accordingly. The most common such system in Japan has two tracks—management (*sōgōshoku*) and clerical (*ippanshoku*)—where employees are assigned to one or the other track at the time of their hiring. Some corporations, however, have a variety of hybrid tracks that lie between these two, such as the region-based management track (*chiki gentei sōgōshoku*) and the quasi-management track (*Junsōgōshoku*). Depending on the corporation, the exact definition of the management track and the clerical track and their administration may differ; they might be called by other names. For this reason, our discussion will focus only on the core differences between the two tracks and will not look at fine details.

There are two key differences between the management track and the clerical track: work duties and work transfers. Those in management-track positions are involved in comparatively high-level work, much of which relies on the judgment of the employee. In contrast, clerical-track workers engage in comparatively simple and routine support work and generally defer to the judgment of superiors or management-track employees. Internal promotions are open to those in the management track, whereas such opportunities are limited for clerical-track personnel.

Let's turn now to the second difference: job transfers. Corporations that operate nationwide sometimes request employees to transfer to another location, and management-track employees must accept such requests, barring some good reason. Those in clerical positions usually are not asked to transfer, however. Those in the region-based management track or the quasi-management track perform work duties that are equivalent to those of management-track employees, but they are guaranteed not to be asked to transfer across country. Based on this condition alone, these two hybrid tracks can be seen as lying between the management and clerical tracks.

How many companies in Japan have adopted a dual-track employ-ment system? Figure 7-1 shows the percentage of companies with such a system, by company size. What do we learn from this figure? First, the most recent statistics reveal that a very small percentage—a mere 11.1 percent—of all companies have such a system.

Second, looking at the data by company size, we find that 55.0 percent of very large corporations (5,000 or more employees) have adopted such a system whereas a mere 6.3 percent of small com-panies (30–99 employees) use tracking. Slightly less than half, or more precisely 43.6 percent, of all large corporations—i.e., those with 1,000 to 4,999 employees—have a dual-track system. Therefore, the larger the company size, the higher the percentage of companies that

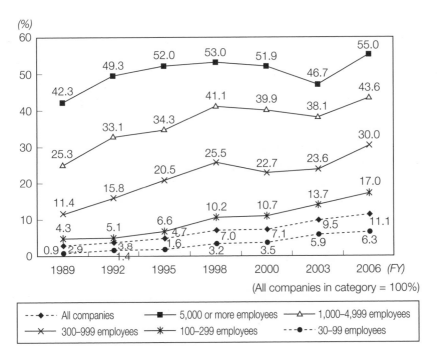

Fig. 7-1 Percentage of companies with a dual-track employment system by company size

Source: Ministry of Health, Labor, and Welfare, *Heisei 18 nendo josei koyō kanri kihon chōsa* (Basic survey of employment management of women, FY2006), 11, fig. 5.

engage in career tracking. From this, we can conclude that the tracking system is characteristic of large companies, but that, since only
slightly over half of very large companies (5,000 or more employees)
have adopted it, not all large corporations use such a system. In other
words, companies have differing views on career tracking.

We can also see in this figure the long-term trend over the past
twenty years or so and note that the percentage of companies adopting a dual-track system increased gradually from 1989 to 2006.
The career-tracking system, therefore, is definitely not falling out
of favor; rather, it is gradually taking stronger and stronger hold.
I mention this because some claim that the system has served its
purpose and is falling out of use because of the various problems
associated with it. Let's just note that the system of career tracking
is problematic for many.

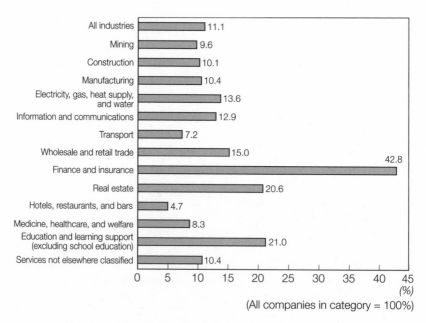

**Fig. 7-2 Percentage of companies with a dual-track employment
system by industry (FY2006)**

Source: Based on Ministry of Health, Labor, and Welfare, *Heisei 18 nendo josei koyō kanri kihon chōsa* (Basic survey of employment management of women, FY2006), 12, fig. 6.

We have seen that career tracking is primarily found in large corporations, but to gain insight into its particular characteristics, let's look more closely at the industries and job areas where such a system is used. Figure 7-2 shows the percentage of companies that have adopted a dual-track personnel system by industry. According to this figure, over 40 percent of companies in finance and insurance have this system, a much higher percentage than in other industries. Next highest are education and learning support (excluding school education), real estate, and wholesale and retail trade. The figures for these latter service industries roughly fall between 15 and 21 percent. Thus we can conclude that career tracking is frequently adopted by companies in the financial and services industries.

Next, let's look at what job areas are subject to career tracking. Table 7-1 lists the job areas or work duties of female management-track and clerical-track employees. Although the data is slightly old, we can see that women in the management track work in a variety of job areas, with a slightly higher percentage in marketing, planning and research, and research and development. That is, they are not concentrated in a specific job area but rather are in many different areas. One reason for this is that companies make a point of rotating management-track employees among different departments quite frequently so they will gain experience in the full range of company operations and be prepared for future promotions.

In contrast, a very high percentage—85.2 percent—of women on the clerical track are in general affairs and accounting. This job area includes secretarial positions, though, so typical clerical-track work should be seen as routine, support duties performed in various departments.

The History of Career Tracking

An overview of tracking

Wakisaka (1997) offers a detailed discussion of why companies introduced the dual-track employment system. According to Waki

Table 7-1 University-educated women and female management-track and clerical-track employees, by job area

(%)

Job Area	Ministry of Health, Labor, and Welfare Survey (FY1990)	Japan Institute of Workers' Evolution Survey (1993)	Tokyo Labor Research Institute Survey (1993)	
	University-educated women*	Management-track women**	Clerical-track women***	Management-track women***
Personnel, education, and training	13.6	11.3	85.2	34.2
General affairs and accounting(1)	28.0	6.9		
Planning and research	8.4	13.5		
Corporate communications	3.1	4.0		
Research and development(2)	6.9	10.2	1.4	9.0
Data processing	5.4	4.4	3.5	20.0
Marketing	9.4	21.9	5.3	19.2
Sales and services(3)	5.0	1.9	2.2	3.6
Production(4)	1.2	2.2		
Other(5)	19.0	20.2	2.4	14.0
No response		3.6		
Total	100.0	100.0	100.0	100.0
n	521	744	771	731

Notes: 1. Single asterisk (*): University-educated regular employees. Double asterisk (**): Educational background unknown. Triple asterisk (***): Job area of first employment position. (1) Called the "clerical" category in the Tokyo Labor Research Institute survey. (2) "Technology" category in the Tokyo Labor Research Institute survey. (3) "Sales" category in the Tokyo Labor Research Institute survey. (4) "Production technology" category in the Japan Institute of Workers' Evolution survey. (5) Includes "legal" (2.8%) and "corporate accounting (finance)" (1.5%) categories in the Japan Institute of Workers' Evolution survey and "specialized track other than technology" and "other, including technical track" categories in the Tokyo Labor Research Institute survey.

2. Based on Ministry of Health, Labor, and Welfare, *Heisei 2 nendo joshi koyō kanri kihon chōsa* (Basic survey of employment management of women, FY1990); Japan Institute of Workers' Evolution, *Sōgōshoku josei no shūgyō jittai chōsa* (Survey of the work situation of management-track women); and Tokyo Labor Research Institute, *Daisotsu josei no shokugyō sentaku kōdō to shokugyō seikatsu chōsa* (Survey of occupational choice and occupational lifestyle of university-educated women).

Source: Wakisaka (1997, 259, table 7).

saka, companies started to introduce career tracking around 1985, but what triggered its introduction at that particular time?

It was in 1985 that the Equal Employment Opportunity Law, or EEOL, was first enacted in Japan. This law banned, albeit in adequately, discrimination against women in hiring, promotion, and wages. Companies responded by dividing women into two groups: (1) women who were career-oriented and wanted to do the same work as men and (2) women satisfied with routine, support work. Prior to the EEOL, men generally had the management-track jobs and women had the clerical-track ones. By codifying the system and opening the management track to women, companies hoped to reduce the discriminatory air of the system in which women were overwhelmingly relegated to subordinate positions. In this way, companies demonstrated their willingness to comply with the EEOL.

An alternative interpretation of the advent of the dual-track system involves women's education. As we saw in chapter 3, by 1985 more women were graduating from university; more women had high-level skills and a strong desire to work. Companies attempted to satisfy these women's ambitions by offering them management-track positions. At the same time, many women were content with clerical work—they did not desire a career but only wanted to work until marriage and children. To effectively respond to this dichotomy in women's life plans and choices, companies adopted the policy of placing the first group in the management track and the second group in the clerical track.

Which of the two reasons carried the most weight in the emergence of the tracked personnel system? Wakisaka suggests that the two were about equal in importance; it is impossible to say whether one of the two was decisive or not.

As for what percentage of female workers are actually in management-track and clerical-track positions, I will cite the findings of the various surveys in Wakisaka (1997 and 2001). Although the exact figures differ depending on the survey, the percentages in the two tracks are roughly fifty-fifty. At companies with career tracking, half of female workers are in management-track positions and half are in clerical-track jobs on average. In some industries, including construction as well as finance and insurance, however, the percentage of women in clerical-track positions is very high. Earlier, we noted that a particularly high percentage of companies in finance and insurance have a dual-track management system. This then means that these two industries have many female clerical-track workers.

Education and tracking

Next, I would like to talk about educational background and the dual-track employment system in Japanese companies. In short, women with high school or junior college diplomas are almost all in clerical-track positions, as are most women graduating from average universities. Women with degrees from top universities generally have management-track jobs.

Wakisaka (2001) broadly divides female university graduates into two groups—he says that graduates of Japan's national and public universities are in the management track while graduates of private universities are in the clerical track. I find these classifications a little too simplistic, however. Top female graduates of average private universities are found in management-track positions while quite a few women who have graduated from prestigious private universities know from the start that they want to take the clerical path. The matter is not so clear-cut. Let me add, though, that the *Kōgakureki josei to shigoto ni kansuru ankēto chōsa* (Questionnaire survey on highly educated women and work) conducted by Wakisaka found that no women graduates of the University of Tokyo were in clerical-track positions.

Let's now consider the matter from the perspective of disparities among women. We have noted that large corporations adopted a dual-track employment system to respond both to the EEOL and the diversification of women's career plans with the rise in their education level. We have also found that schooling has a major impact on whether a woman will be in the management track or the clerical track.

The first split is between high school and junior college graduates, on the one hand, and women who went to university and graduate school, on the other. Management-track positions at large corporations are virtually closed to female high school and junior college graduates; a woman who has not graduated from university has no chance of entering the management track. High school or junior college graduates who work hard and want to pursue a career are more likely to find satisfying work at small and medium-sized companies.

The second split is based on the university from which the woman received her undergraduate or graduate degree. Many women in management-track positions are graduates of national and public universities or famous private universities that have difficult entrance exams. In chapter 3, we saw the increasing competition among women to earn a good education—Japan is a society that puts great stock in educational attainment. One result of this is the divide between women who enter the management track at large companies and those who must be content with clerical work.

Women who know from the start that they do not want the management track may not necessarily need to attend a high-level university. On the other hand, if a career-minded woman has not been able to attend a famous university, she might be better off working at a small or medium-sized company that does not have career tracking. She may feel dissatisfied at a large company where she would be on the clerical track with its discriminatory terms compared with the management track.

My personal opinion is that an employee's work performance depends on the person's ability and effort, which are not related to academic achievement. As mentioned in chapter 3, however, Japanese corporations focus on educational background at the time of hiring. If the management track is closed off to an employee at the hiring stage, though, that employee should be prepared to work the system to find the best conditions available to her.

To summarize, from the perspective of disparities among women, the university a woman graduates from is critical, as it determines whether she will be on the management track or the clerical track. We should remember, though, that some university-educated women—even graduates of prestigious universities—deliberately choose to enter the clerical track. Since this decision is directly related to how they view family and work, it is not up to me to judge whether such a choice is right or wrong. Each person is free to decide how she will live.

Why, though, do these highly educated women choose sub-ordinate, clerical-track positions? One reason is that wages and other work conditions are good at a large company even for such positions. Moreover, there are many opportunities at such companies to meet men who would make excellent marriage partners. Men working at the huge, well-known companies listed on the stock exchange are ideal candidates for marriage: they are highly educated, capable, and have a good earning potential.

The conventional wisdom is that women want to work at corporations located in the geographical triangle formed by Kasumigaseki, Nihonbashi, and Ōtemachi in Tokyo, where many prestigious corporations are located, and the "three-meter rule" became a popular term at top trading companies at one point because of the large number of marriages between young management-track men and clerical-track women whose desks were within three meters (roughly ten feet) of each other. With these kinds of real-life stories, we cannot criticize university-educated women for wanting clerical positions at prestigious companies. We cannot fault women for trying to find a marriage partner when, as we have seen in chapter 4, traditional arranged marriages have virtually disappeared in Japan. Even if a woman cannot meet a man at her workplace, the fact that she is working at a prestigious company will be to her advantage in her search for a husband.

From the standpoint of the company, however, there may be some question about whether it makes good business sense to have university-educated women in clerical positions. Every workplace has routine, support work that needs to be done. Rather than hire university-educated women, though, companies could have high school and junior college graduates perform such tasks. This is the very reason why many female high school and junior college graduates are hired for clerical work, as we have already seen. There is also a good chance that the work could be done more efficiently and at lower cost by part-time or dispatched workers. To reduce costs during the recent recession—known as the "lost decade" or the "lost decade and a half"—corporations took on part-time and dispatched workers for these clerical positions that had formerly been given to university graduates, resulting in a decrease in the numbers of clerical-track female employees. We will be looking in more depth at part-time, dispatched, and other nonregular workers in the next chapter.

Shifting to a different track

An interesting question here is whether women continue in the track they were first hired for or switch to the other track after working for a while. At the time of first hiring, the company decides whether a woman will be in the management or the clerical track. No doubt some women who are hired in the clerical track actually want to be in the management track. If such women want later to shift to the management track, how do corporations handle the situation? Our interest here is in the different life paths women take after being assigned to one of the two tracks. Of course, we will also look at women who resign at marriage or childbirth.

The Tokyo Labor Research Institute (1994) and Wakisaka (1997) have produced some very interesting findings on this issue. Figure 7-3 shows the results of a Tokyo Labor Research Institute survey conducted of women who graduated from university in 1987 and joined a corporation in the management track or in the clerical track or joined a company with no track distinctions. The survey looks at the women's views on work before graduation from university and then seven years later. "Long term" here means the woman hopes to work for as many years as possible or until retirement whereas "short term" means the woman plans to resign as soon as possible or just to work until marriage or childbirth.

For the survey, the Tokyo Labor Research Institute created six categories, gave each a catchy name, and then asked women to select the one that best described them. This is quite unusual in the sense that a conservative government institute tried to make its report appealing to the outsider by developing categories with clever names.

A "Career Woman" is a woman who both in university and seven years later intends to continue working through the life stages of marriage and childbirth, while a "Chameleon" thinks during her university days that she would like to have a career but then changes her mind while in the work force. A "Broken Dream" is someone who in university definitely wants a career, but then resigns when

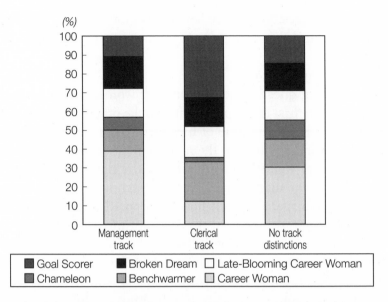

**Fig. 7-3 Changes in views on work continuation (1987 female
university graduates)**

Notes: 1. Six categories of women based on changes in their views on work continuation at the
time of their job search during university and seven years later

	Work views during university	Work views/status seven years later
Career Woman	Long term	Long term
Chameleon	Long term	Short term
Broken Dream	Long term	Not working
Late-Blooming Career Woman	Short term	Long term
Benchwarmer	Short term	Short term
Goal Scorer	Short term	Not working

2. "Long term" includes those who responded "hope to work as many years as
possible" or "hope to work until retirement." "Short term" includes those who
responded "hope to resign as soon as possible," "hope to work until marriage," or
"hope to work until childbirth."

Source: Wakisaka (1997, 263, fig. 2), based on a special tabulation of Tokyo Labor Research
Institute (1994).

she gets married or has children. As the name indicates, a "Late-
Blooming Career Woman" plans to work until she marries or has
children, but then becomes career-oriented while in the work force.
On the other hand, a "Benchwarmer" is a woman who both in university and seven years later has the intent of resigning from work

soon. Finally, the "Goal Scorer" intends from the start to work until marriage or childbirth and then does just that.

In figure 7-3 we see that, of women holding management-track jobs, about 40 percent have chosen to call themselves Career Women. This is the highest percentage for this category, reflecting the strong work commitment of this group of women. Career Woman was also the choice for quite a high percentage—about 30 percent—of women at companies with no dual-track system. Perhaps companies that have not adopted a career-tracking system can be seen as treating all employees as management track. To that degree, women at these companies are highly career-oriented.

On the other hand, slightly over 30 percent of women in clerical-track jobs are Goal Scorers. This is the largest group in the clerical track, followed by the 20 percent or so of Benchwarmers. We can say that these figures realistically portray clerical-track women, who enter the work force planning to work only until marriage or childbirth. Since those who succeed in achieving this goal make up the highest percentage, many seem to have the lives they intended. These findings also agree with the image of a clerical-track employee as a woman who entertains ideas of resigning even while she is employed.

What is intriguing here, and Wakisaka emphasizes this as well, is that there are quite a few Chameleons, Benchwarmers, and Goal Scorers in management-track positions; an amazing 25 percent— one out of four—hope to or actually do work short term. This means that there are quite a few management-track women who hope to resign midway through their career.

In contrast, quite a few clerical-track women hope to work long term, as shown by the percentages of Career Women and Late-Blooming Career Women in this category. Many of these women may have sought management-track positions when they joined the company, but were denied and so now hope to shift to that track midcareer. Or, perhaps they did seek a clerical-track position from the start. The important thing is that it is inaccurate to assume that all clerical-track women hope to work short term. We should recognize that many women want to work long term even if they are in clerical-track positions performing routine tasks. It is very valuable to have clerical-track workers who have a strong desire to work because companies will always have routine, support duties that need to be performed.

Career Tracking and Inequality

How does the Japanese dual-track employment system affect disparities among women? As we have seen, the management track involves comparatively sophisticated work that often requires judgment calls, whereas clerical-track work is largely routine and repetitive. From the perspective of disparities, it is clear that those in management-track jobs are in a superior position to those in the clerical track.

Equal opportunity?

What about wages? If two employees are the same age, have worked for the same number of years at the same company, and have the same educational background, the management-track employee will receive higher wages than the clerical-track one. In light of the difficulty of the work and the amount of responsibility, it is not illogical for there to be a gap in wages. In addition, internal promotions are available to those in the management track. As these employees get older and their number of years of service to the company increases, some of them will be promoted to managerial positions, such as subsection manager, section manager, or division manager, widening the wage differential with clerical workers even further. Here too the wage gap is not unfounded given that those in managerial positions are entrusted with greater responsibility and must possess leadership skills.

The question is whether equal opportunity is guaranteed at the time of hiring, i.e., when the worker enters one of the two tracks. Companies, and particularly large corporations, hire women in accordance with the career plans of the applicant. In other words, they select the best candidates for the management track from the pool who apply for that track. The same is true for the clerical track. We can conclude, then, that equal opportunity is guaranteed at least at the time of hiring, because it is the applicants who are making the decision regarding the track for which they want to apply. Whether they are actually hired or not depends on their skills and capabilities, although there is some luck involved as well.

However, under the terms of this system, employees must stay on the track—either management or clerical—decided when they entered the company. This is the employee's permanent status as long as she works at that company. As we saw in figure 7-3, quite a number of female university graduates in both the management and clerical tracks change their minds about whether they want to work long term or short term. This implies that there may be women who would like to transfer from the clerical track to the management track and vice versa. It is easy to imagine that quite a few women would like to shift to the management track for more challenging and responsible work with the chance to exercise managerial skills. On the other hand, it may seem a little odd for a woman in the management track to give up her privileged position within the company and move down to the clerical track. If we see it, though, as a desire for shorter hours and somewhat less responsibility, it becomes more understandable.

Given such circumstances, it would certainly be desirable for companies to give employees the opportunity midcareer to shift between the two tracks. Even if it would be impossible to do so frequently, considering the administrative burden and cost of arranging tests and employee interviews as well as the difficulty of changing staff rota, such a chance could be offered, say, once every five or ten years. Reportedly, some companies are already allowing their employees to change tracks.

Of particular relevance for our discussion is the point that factors unique to women's lives may render problems in the dual-track employment system. We have already noted several times in this book the complicated impact that marriage and particularly childbirth and childrearing have on a woman's work career. This is also true in regard to the dual-track personnel system, as we saw in figure 7-3. From a corporation's perspective, it is clearly inconvenient if management-track women resign at marriage or childbirth; the loss of employees being groomed for management is a negative for a company. Of course, the resignation of clerical-track employees is also a negative, but the impact is not as great—companies sometimes hire clerical employees with the assumption from the start that they will resign midway through their career. And if we add in the potential for some employees wanting to switch to the other track midcareer, we can see why some feel that the dual-track personnel system is not optimal.

However, the pros and cons of the dual-track employment system can no longer be discussed by talking about the case of women alone. It is a problem that female employees in both tracks—even the management track—are resigning, but in this era of labor mobility men are also quitting their jobs. The trend away from lifelong employment at one firm means that all personnel systems, including the dual-track system, will need to be reevaluated and refigured to fit the new age.

Envisioning a woman-friendly employment system

How can the dual-track employment system be reconceived? Let's summarize the issue and then consider this question more closely.

First, the two key factors that led to the creation of this management system were the EEOL and the impact on companies of the diversification of women's lifetime work patterns resulting from their increasing levels of education. If these two reasons still exist today, there is no need to consider abolishing the system. The EEOL has been amended over the years since its introduction in 1985 but is still far from adequate. The situation is similar in regard to the diversification of women's work paths: no major changes have been seen in the past twenty-plus years other than (1) a slight lessening of the dip in the M-curve tracing the two stages of women's work lives divided by their marriage and childrearing years and (2) the introduction of some childcare support measures. We can conclude, therefore, that the historical reasons for a dual-track personnel system are still present.

A second point involves the social ramifications of the system—some say that the career-tracking system should be abolished because its stratification of employees into two ranks promotes inequality.

I believe, however, that it is not necessary to completely abolish the system. My reasons are as follows. First of all, this system gives employees in both tracks a fair degree of employment security because they are regular employees. I see the gap between regular and nonregular staff (discussed in the next chapter) as a much more serious issue. Second, the complex nature of corporate operations means that companies will always have both work duties that require high-level skills and judgment and other duties that are routine and do not require much thought. For this reason, there is some validity to distinguishing the two types of workers and awarding them compensation packages accordingly, provided that, as discussed above, there is equal opportunity in initial choice of track and later chances to change one's track.

We could also rightly question why in practice the management track and clerical track seem to apply only to women while men are all in the management track. Having a dual-track management system only for women can be seen as discriminatory. The response might be that the tracking system is intended to accommodate the differing decisions of women on whether or not to continue working after marriage or childbirth. Women in the management track are expected to pursue a lifelong career, whereas clerical-track women are expected as a matter of course to leave the labor force. Those in clerical positions who do continue to work are not asked to work long hours or to transfer to other locations. In these ways, the career-tracking system addresses the diversity found among women and offers the advantage of giving women positions based on their wishes.

However, women in management-track positions might disagree with the above line of reasoning, wanting to know why married women with families cannot have a career too. Naturally enough they also want to be exempt from work transfers and to be able to raise their children while continuing to work. The transfer problem is already being addressed, although in a limited way, as some corporations have created the region-based management track or the quasi-management track. Awareness is also increasing in Japanese society of the need for policies to help women balance work with childcare responsibilities, so we can expect improvements in this area in due course. If the Japanese people truly want a gender-equal society, there should be little opposition to such measures. We do see, however, some ambivalence and resistance to creating such a society so this remains something of a gray area.

Another development of relevance to the future of the dual-track management system is that the amount of routine and support tasks to be performed by clerical-track workers has dropped at many workplaces. With the spread of automation and computerization, a single management-track employee can efficiently perform routine work at the same time as core duties. Moreover, as already suggested, it may be more efficient to have part-time and dispatched workers perform such tasks. Since work terms for part-time and dispatched workers often are inferior to those for regular workers, however, any such shift from clerical-track workers to part-time or dispatched workers should retain the labor and wage conditions of regular workers. We will look at this issue later. It would certainly be undesirable if companies were to replace clerical-track employees with part-time and dispatched workers just to cut costs, thus acting against the interests of workers.

Rather, the best way forward is to shift clerical-track employees to the management track as much as possible. If they are committed to their work and are given the necessary training, these workers should be able to perform management-track tasks adequately. At the same time, management-track employees can continue in their regular work while taking care of routine tasks at the same time thanks to the computer.

It is only natural that gaps will appear among management-track employees between the capable and the less capable and between those who work hard and those who do not. The capable, hardworking ones can be paid higher wages and be promoted at a faster pace while the other type can be given wages appropriate for their work and be promoted at a slower pace. With more employees on the management track, there will inevitably be those who perform well and those who do not, and it is natural for them to be treated differently.

In fact, this kind of personnel policy can be observed in companies that do not track their employees, the category cited as "no track distinctions" in figure 7-3. Almost all employees at such companies are management track, and they perform routine, support tasks themselves as they do their core duties. That said, a workplace will not function optimally if all employees do management-track work, so it is appropriate for there to be a small number of clerical-track employees. To conclude, the ideal personnel policy is to reduce the number of clerical-track employees as much as possible and to have most employees on the management track.

Advancing up the Ranks

At companies with a dual-track employment system, opportunities for advancement to managerial positions are open to almost all employees on the management track but to very few on the clerical track. At companies that do not use a career-tracking system, on the other hand, promotion is open to most employees. As is widely known, few women advance to managerial positions in Japan, and in this section we will look at the reasons why. As part of our study of the disparities among women in contemporary Japan, we will also consider the wage and other disparities that arise between women who receive promotions and those who do not.

Two key questions in looking at the career advancement of women are (1) the impact of factors unique to women and (2) the type of person promoted, whether of either gender. What qualities do those promoted possess? How is their work performance? Before looking at the question of gender, we first need to know more about what type of person does well and is regularly promoted through the ranks at a Japanese company.

Who gets promoted?
Let's first look into this question, referring to key portions of Tachibanaki (1997b).

The company section manager (*kachō*) is the epitome of middle management, and white-collar employees generally want to rise at least to this rank. For some, this will be the highest position they ever attain, and they will retire as section managers. For certain capable and ambitious employees, however, section manager is no more than a stepping-stone to a higher position. In terms of corporate structure, section manager is a midway point, as the worker is neither an executive nor a rank-and-file employee. The section manager leads and manages the members of his or her section while at the same time being led and managed by the division manager and board members who are above him or her. It is a delicate position. The joys and sorrows of the section manager are often the focus of Japanese popular novels about white-collar office workers.

What are the factors that determine promotion to section manager or above? (Position titles other than section manager are often used today, such as *manējā* [manager]. Here, though, I am using the title of section manager to represent all middle management.) In table 7-2 we see the key factors behind promotions, as ranked in a questionnaire survey of white-collar employees at large corporations.

We see that for promotion up to the level of section manager, "employee evaluations," at 40.9 percent, stands out among the choices for the number-one factor in determining promotions. Next most frequently cited as number one are "age/length of service" at 20.0 percent and "educational background" at 18.0 percent. "Age/length of service," at 27.8 percent, is top-ranked as the number-two factor in promotions. Next in this category are "influence of superiors" and "employee evaluations." As the number-three factor, we find "influence of superiors" ranking first at 22.9 percent, although "character" is close behind at 21.5 percent.

Putting it all together, we find that "employee evaluations" are of key importance, clearly standing out above the other factors. Next in importance is "age/length of service," and third is the "influence of superiors," followed by "character." We should not overlook "educational background," either, which is quite high as the number-one factor at 18.0 percent. The factors determining promotions up to the level of section manager then can be listed roughly in the following descending order: employee evaluations, age and length of service, influence of superiors, character, educational background, and exam results.

Turning to the choice of the number-one factor in determining promotions above the position of section manager, we see that "employee evaluations" and "influence of superiors" are at about the same level. However, the statistic for "evaluations" is lower here than in the case of promotions up to the rank of section manager. In the category of the number-two factor, we find, similarly, that "influence of superiors" and "evaluations" are about the same in weight and "character" is also quite high. As the number-three factor, "character" heads the list at 27.2 percent, far above the others. Overall, "age/length of service" is quite low as a factor in higher-level promotions while "educational background" should not be overlooked as a contributing factor. To summarize, the factors determining promotions to positions above section manager are, in descending order, as follows: employee evaluations and influence

Table 7-2 Key factors in determining promotion

(%)

	Employee evaluations	Age/length of service	Influence of superiors	Exam results	Educational background	Character	No response	n
Up to Rank of Section Manager								
No. 1 factor	40.9	20.0	12.1	2.4	18.0	3.5	3.1	1,816
No. 2 factor	20.5	27.8	22.4	7.4	9.2	8.6	4.1	1,816
No. 3 factor	16.7	14.9	22.9	8.3	10.5	21.5	5.2	1,816
Above Rank of Section Manager								
No. 1 factor	34.1	6.3	33.1	0.3	16.1	6.4	3.5	1,816
No. 2 factor	22.4	14.0	26.3	3.4	11.8	17.6	4.6	1,816
No. 3 factor	17.5	17.6	17.8	3.5	10.2	27.2	6.2	1,816

Note: Underlined figures are the highest in their row.

Source: Tachibanaki (1997b, 70, table 4-2), based on *Howaito karā chōsa* (Survey of white-collar workers).

of superiors, character, educational background, age and length of service, and exam results.

Using the above survey information on what it takes to get ahead, we can create the following scenario of a successful career. Since employee evaluations are especially important in becoming a section manager, employees need to show their superiors and colleagues that they are competent and are working hard to improve. Age and length of service are also quite important, however, so employees must wait their turn no matter how competent they may be or how outstanding their work record is. On the other hand, low-performing employees will also automatically move up thanks to the seniority system.

We should also note in this regard that the employee's level of competency and job performance remain on the record in employee evaluations and will play a key role in determining future promotions. And of course, people become section manager at differing ages—the speed of promotion differs even under the seniority system.

After becoming section manager, the results of an employee's evaluations before and after becoming section manager are compiled and are key to future promotions. Moreover, after the rank of section manager, the opinion of superiors becomes crucial. The section manager's actual job performance is important, but having a powerful superior lobby on one's behalf is often decisive in promotions to higher ranks. This could be considered the good fortune of having an influential mentor. The next most important factor in further promotions after reaching the rank of section manager is character. The higher a person rises in the organization, the better his or her character is expected to be.

Criteria used to evaluate employees

Considering the importance placed on employee evaluations, let's examine what factors are given the most weight in the performance review itself, or, more specifically, what factors the employees being evaluated felt were being measured in the assessment.

Figure 7-4 offers this data. Let's look at the top three factors and the bottom five. Towering above the other factors in importance is "leadership skills," at 60.8 percent. This shows that performance

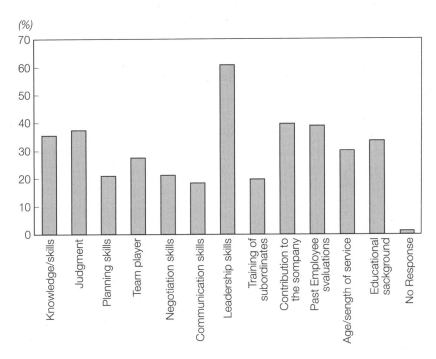

Fig. 7-4 Key items evaluated in performance reviews

Note: Respondents were permitted to give up to four responses.
Source: Tachibanaki (1997b, 75, fig. 4-1), based on *Howaito karā chōsa* (Survey of white-collar workers).

reviews place the highest priority on how well employees can form and lead groups. Ranked second is "contribution to the company." At 39.6 percent, however, this is more than 20 points lower in importance than the first-ranked factor. Third is "past employee evaluations." This means employees sense that a favorable assessment in the past continues to have a positive impact long into the future and vice versa—that an unfavorable past assessment will continue to haunt an employee and that it may be impossible for the employee to redeem him or herself. "Judgment," obviously an important factor, is ranked fourth.

Turning to the factors that are given the least weight in performance reviews, we find that "communication skills" ranks the lowest. A polished presentation alone is not enough. Although it is often said that communication skills are important in life, it seems that they do not carry much weight in personnel assessments at corporations. Second from the bottom is the "training of subordinates." Third and fourth from the bottom are "planning skills" and "negotiation skills," which are at roughly the same level. Fifth from the bottom is "team player." All of these qualities may be considered very important interpersonal or social skills, but we are looking at them here from the perspective of a company performance review.

Next, let's consider from a different angle the reasons why workers are promoted at different speeds. If these reasons are not convincing, dissatisfaction among employees may increase, the atmosphere at the workplace may deteriorate, and this may lead, in turn, to a decline in productivity. We have already looked at the factors emphasized in promotion to the managerial ranks, but exactly what work-style characteristics and objective facts are promotions based on? What yardstick or criteria are used in these all-important assessments? What is the basis for differences in evaluations between employees performing the same work?

Table 7-3 shows the main items in evaluations that result in disparities in wages and promotions. The factor that greatly outweighed the others in impact is "has achieved excellent results." A total of 68.4 percent of respondents said that it was "very important." Adding those who said it was "somewhat important," the total figure rises to 92.9 percent. Here "results" should be seen as concrete, tangible results—in other words, increase in sales volume for workers in the sales department, development of efficient production technologies or reduction of costs for workers in the production technology department, development of new products for workers in the development department, hiring of many talented professionals for workers in the human resources department, or creation of a hit advertisement for workers in the publicity department. Others should be able to see the results for themselves; creating visible results has a positive impact on assessments by superiors and clears the path to career advancement.

The second most important factor is "has trained subordinates and junior employees." There is a big price to pay for focusing exclusively on improving one's own results and ignoring subordinates and junior employees. Also, employees dislike superiors who claim subordinates' work as their own. In other words, good superiors must earn the trust of those working under them. Developing outstanding subordinates and creating junior employees who can be promoted is a good accomplishment for the superior as well.

The next most important factors are "has gained skills and knowledge" and "has done more work than others." These two are ranked much lower in importance than the first two factors, however, as is also indicated by their relatively high totals for "not very important" and "not important at all," 20.9 and 24.6 percent, respectively. One could say that enhancing one's knowledge and skills only improves one's own qualifications, or that it is meaningless if a person performs more work than others but does not produce results.

Table 7-3 Factors leading to disparities in wages and promotions among employees performing the same job

(%)

	Very important	Somewhat important	Not very important	Not important at all	No response	n
Has taken a serious attitude toward work	23.3	45.5	25.0	4.6	1.7	1,816
Has done more work than others	26.8	47.0	21.0	3.6	1.7	1,816
Has gained skills and knowledge	24.4	52.9	18.8	2.1	1.7	1,816
Has achieved excellent results	68.4	24.5	4.8	0.6	1.7	1,816
Has trained subordinates and junior employees	35.7	50.6	10.0	2.0	1.7	1,816

Source: Tachibanaki (1997b, 77, table 4-3), based on *Howaito karā chōsa* (Survey of white-collar workers).

Another interesting finding presented in this table is that "has taken a serious attitude toward work" is not very highly valued. No matter how hard a person works, even taking on more work than others, it does not have much impact on promotions and wages. This teaches the lesson that a worker who is somewhat casual about work and even slacks off a bit will rise up in the ranks provided he or she produces results.

Women and promotion: why so few managers?

Using this information on the promotion process, let's now look at the advancement of women at Japanese companies today. As has already been mentioned, corporations use a variety of titles for positions these days. Not so long ago, the standard managerial titles of *kakarichō* (subsection manager), *kachō* (section manager), *buchō* (division manager), *yakuin* (officer), and *jūyaku* (executive) were the only ones used for the various ranks. Today, however, position titles taken directly from English, such as *chīfu* (chief), *manējā* (manager), *heddo* (head), and *direkutā* (director), have come into use, as well as new Japanese titles, including *shunin* (senior staff member), *shuseki* (key member of staff), and *riji* (director). As a result, the amount of responsibility for a given managerial position and the number of subordinates overseen are not uniform either. Government statistics resolve this problem by using the three titles of subsection manager, section manager, and division manager as general managerial categories typified by these positions.

Figure 7-5 shows that the percentages of women in these three managerial classes have been rising. Of the three categories, the division manager class has the lowest percentage, with women making up between 1 and 2 percent at most. It is no exaggeration to say, then, that virtually no women are promoted to the position of division manager. Moreover, the percentage of women in this class has risen only very slightly over the past two decades or so.

The percentage of women in the section manager class has seen a slight rise, climbing from 2.1 percent in 1989 to 3.6 percent in 2006. Basically, though, the figures for this managerial class are not very different from those for division manager: women make up

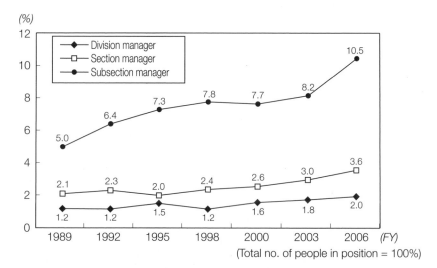

Fig. 7-5 Trends in the percentage of women managers by position

Source: Based on Ministry of Health, Labor, and Welfare, *Heisei 18 nen do josei koyō kanri kihon chōsa* (Basic survey of employment management of women, FY2006), 16, fig. 12.

only a tiny percentage of such managers. This situation is somewhat offset by the fact that the percentage of women in the subsection manager class has doubled over the past two decades, increasing from 5.0 percent to 10.5 percent. Subsection manager is the lowest managerial position and the first managerial promotion. Even here, though, the figure for women is only one in ten. We must conclude that the glass ceiling is very difficult to break through.

Next, let's look at figure 7-6 to see if female promotion differs by company size. The statistics are as you might expect: the smaller the company, the more female managers. Similarly the higher the position and the larger the company, the fewer female managers there are. For example, in the most recent figures, women make up less than 1 percent of division managers and 2.4 percent of section managers at very large corporations that have 5,000 or more employees—miniscule percentages indeed. In contrast, women make up about 15 percent of subsection managers at companies with 30–99 employees although even this figure is by no means high.

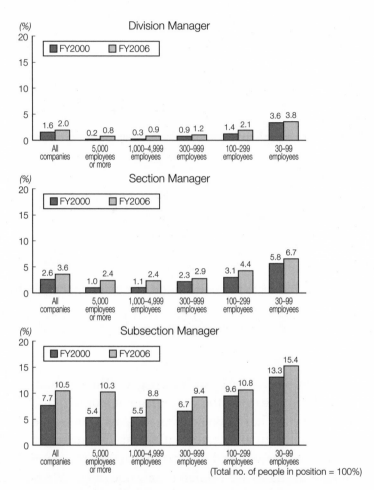

Fig. 7-6 Trends in the percentage of women managers by position and by company size

Source: Based on Ministry of Health, Labor, and Welfare, *Heisei 18 nendo josei koyō kanri kihon chōsa* (Basic survey of employment management of women, FY2006), 17, fig. 13.

Why are so few women in the managerial class at Japanese companies? Figure 7-7 offers the corporate response to this question, as given in answers to a Ministry of Health, Labor, and Welfare survey. (Note that companies were permitted to give more than one response so the totals exceed 100 percent.) The main

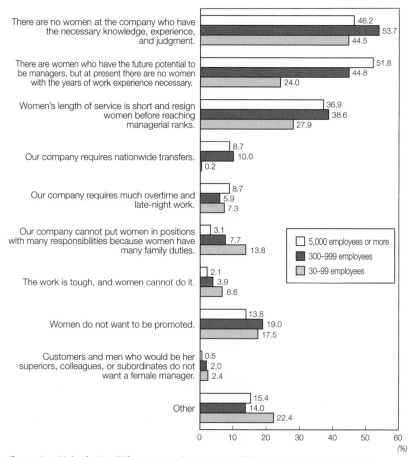

(Companies with few [under 10%] or no women in one or more of the managerial categories = 100%)

Fig. 7-7 Companies with few or no women managers by reason and by company size

Note: Respondents were permitted to give multiple responses.

Source: Based on Ministry of Health, Labor, and Welfare, *Heisei 18 nendo josei koyō kanri kihon chōsa* (Basic survey of employment management of women, FY2006), 18, fig. 14.

reason, according to this survey, why companies have very few or no women in management positions is that there are no women with the appropriate qualifications: there are no female employees who possess the necessary knowledge, experience, and judgment. That is a harsh assessment, but not utterly baseless since, as we saw in our discussion above on how the promotion process works, employee evaluations and job performance are key.

And yet it must be admitted that schools, companies, and society have not shown much commitment to fostering such women. Schools have not encouraged women to pursue majors that would help them in corporate careers, although women themselves bear some responsibility for not pursuing such studies. Companies also have failed to groom their female employees for management, although once again we cannot hold the corporate world solely responsible for the situation since it is true that many women have resigned early in their work lives, giving companies little incentive to train them. And the lukewarm stance of society as a whole can no doubt be laid to the persistence of traditional views that the male is the breadwinner and the place of woman is in the home, raising the children.

The second most frequently cited reason by companies for the low percentage of women in management positions is that although there are qualified women, they do not yet have the years of work experience necessary to be promoted to manager. This is the case particularly at very large corporations, reflecting the fact that the age of promotion tends to be later at larger companies. And, as we have seen, women in Japan tend to work for a short number of years. This response also confirms our finding above that length of service is a major factor in promotions.

Overlapping with the lack of sufficient experience is the third reason: many women resign before they are promoted. As has been mentioned many times, many women in Japan resign when they marry and particularly when they have children. Even if they return to work after they have raised their children, they will almost certainly lack the qualifications for a managerial position because of the deterioration of their work skills during the five to ten years that they are absent from the work force.

Other barriers cited to the promotion of women to managerial positions—they cannot accept transfers or perform overtime work; they cannot be placed in a busy managerial role because of family duties; they themselves do not want managerial positions—show that women are struggling to find a proper work-life balance and may not themselves desire to become managers. According to this survey, quite a high percentage of women—close to 20 percent—do not desire promotion. It is not surprising that there are women who do not see the point in subjecting themselves to the long hours and other burdens of managerial life in Japan; not a few men share that perspective. There is nothing wrong with thinking that there is more to life than work and getting ahead at the company.

Career advancement and disparities among women

We have looked at what kind of person is promoted to managerial positions at Japanese corporations and the criteria upon which they are promoted. We found that promotions are generally based on employee evaluations and on length of service. We found that important items in performance reviews included leadership skills, job performance, and training of subordinates. Turning to the promotion of women to managerial roles, we found that length of service is a major barrier. Not only are there few women in management-track positions—positions where promotion is possible—but many women resign when they marry and particularly when they have children. This means that there are few women who could be deemed candidates for promotion. In other words, there is a very limited number of women in the pool for possible promotion to managerial positions.

Very few women are in managerial positions at Japanese companies today. Let's look at this reality from the perspective of disparities among women. If the majority of women are rank-and-file employees and very few are in the managerial class—and since average wages for women overall are quite low—it means that the distribution of wages will be greatly weighted to the low-end bracket.

Figure 7-8 compares the wage distribution of men overall with that of women overall. Most women fall into the low-wage range; women's average wages are low, and very few receive high wages. Although men also cluster in the low-wage range, the clustering is not as extreme as in the case of women. Moreover, the average wages of men are higher than those of women, and quite a few

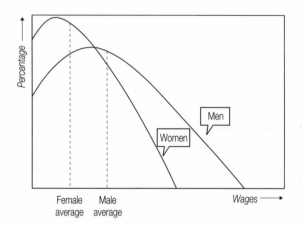

Fig. 7-8 Wage distribution by gender

men are in the high-wage bracket. One of the main reasons for this gender gap is that so few women are in managerial roles. Wages increase considerably with promotion to subsection manager, section manager, and division manager as financial compensation is quite hefty for managerial work. See Tachibanaki (1995) for more information on this point. In terms of disparities among women in Japan, then, the low rate of female promotion leads to a situation where the vast majority of women are low-wage earners and very few are high-wage earners.

Chapter Eight

Women and Japanese Companies II:
Regular and Nonregular Employees

More and more women are working outside the home these days, but what form does that employment take? Considering their family responsibilities and varied motives for working, we can expect no one uniform pattern of employment for all women. This chapter will look into these differences in more detail, paying particular attention to the divide between regular, permanent employees and the large number of employees in nonregular work situations—contract workers, dispatched workers, part-time workers. As the life goals, work styles, and labor conditions of these various types of nonregular workers differ quite a bit, it is inappropriate to lump them all together as exploited employees working under less-than-desirable terms. Nonetheless, nonregular employment has a major impact on inequalities among women, so we will look at this issue in some depth.

In terms of supply and demand in the labor market, the number of nonregular workers, particularly nonregular female workers, has increased due to factors related to both workers and employers. What exactly are these factors? Are the supply-side or the demand-side factors stronger? Of course, we cannot ignore the role of the recession that has plagued Japan for the past ten to fifteen years and must also consider the future impact of broader economic and societal trends, such as the decreasing birthrate and the aging of society. After examining these issues, I will offer a brief outlook for the future.

Types of Employment

Nonregular workers

Before turning to the situation of female nonregular workers, let's first look at women's employment status overall. We can broadly divide employment into three categories: (1) self-employed workers, (2) unpaid family workers, and (3) paid employees. Self-employed workers own and operate unincorporated businesses, such as a farm or store. Family workers engage in piecework at home for businesses that are operated by a member of their family.

Figure 8-1 shows trends in women's employment over the past twenty years or so. In 1986, self-employed workers and family workers together totaled 31.7 percent of all female workers. In 2006, however, their combined total had fallen to 13.6 percent—little more than one in ten working women. In contrast, women employed at com-

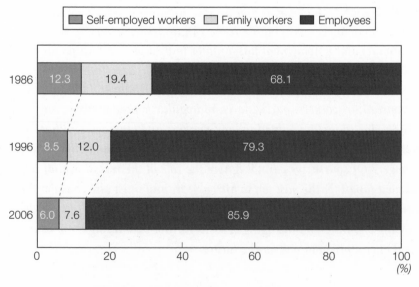

Fig. 8-1 Working women by employment status

Source: Based on Statistics Bureau, Ministry of Internal Affairs and Communications, *Labor Force Survey*.

panies accounted for 85.9 percent of working women that year—the vast majority of women who work are employees of outside firms. Self-employed workers and family workers can set their work hours comparatively freely, but employees do not have much freedom in this regard since they must follow the company rules. However, this does not exclude the possibility of employment with shorter work hours, such as part-time work, as well as employment that offers more flexibility in regard to employment period and contract conditions. Such types of employment are very important in the case of women, as we will see.

Let me say a word about terminology before going into the main discussion. I have chosen generally to use the terms "regular employment" (*seiki rōdō*) and "nonregular employment" (*hiseiki rōdō*) in this book. Some researchers and government statistics, however, use the terms "regular employees" (*seishain*) and "nonregular employees" (*hiseishain*) or "standard work" (*tenkei rōdō*) and "nonstandard work" (*hitenkei rōdō*). There are no major differences among these three sets of terms so I have chosen to retain the term used in the original source I am quoting from.

In the case of regular employment, the employee works the full-time work hours prescribed by the company, and the employment term is indefinite. Although this is not spelled out in Japanese employment contracts, there is a tacit understanding between the worker and management that the employment term is unlimited. This is often referred to as "lifetime employment" (i.e., employment until retirement). In economics, such agreements are known as "implicit contracts."

The use of implicit contracts explains various phenomena unique to the Japanese labor market. For example, companies dismiss regular workers as rarely as possible, and workers do not casually quit their jobs. Candidates for promotion are selected from the pool of regular workers, and these workers benefit from the seniority system. These things have somewhat lost their centrality today, but implicit contracts are a classic symbol of labor-management relations in Japan. This stands in contrast with the formal written contracts used in the West.

What kinds of nonregular employment are there? Table 8-1 defines the different types and gives the percentage for women as well as the combined percentage for both genders for each type. The categories of nonregular employment are determined based on the work contract, employment period, and work hours. Unlike regular workers, who have implicit contracts, dispatched workers, contract

Table 8-1 Categories of standard and nonstandard employment and percentages of employees

(%)

	Women (total)	Description	Men and Women (total)
Standard employment (regular employees)	44.4	Employees whose term of employment is not fixed; regular workers	65.4
Nonstandard employment (nonregular employees)	55.6	Employees other than regular employees	34.6
Part-time workers (*pātotaimu*)	42.5	Workers with fewer prescribed working hours per day or fewer prescribed working days per week than regular employees; those with an employment term that is more than one month or is not fixed	23.0
Dispatched workers from temporary labor agencies (*haken*)	3.4	Workers dispatched by temporary labor agencies based on the Worker Dispatching Act	2.0
Contract employees (*keiyaku*)	2.9	Employees contracted for a fixed period to perform a specialized task in a specified job area	2.3
Short-term contract employees (*shokutaku*)	0.9	Workers reemployed typically after retirement for a fixed period of time	1.4
Daily employees (*rinjiteki*)	0.8	Workers employed on a daily basis or with an employment term of less than one month; *Arbeit* (*arubaito*; temporary workers)	0.8
Seconded employees (*shukkō*)	0.6	Employees seconded from other companies based on a secondment contract, regardless of whether they retain their post at their original company	1.5
Other	4.6	Workers other than the above	3.4

Source: Based on Ōsawa and Harada (2006, 156, table 11-1), compiled from Ministry of Health, Labor, and Welfare, *Heisei 15 nen shūgyō keitai no tayōka ni kansuru sōgō jittai chōsa* (General survey of the diversification of types of employment, 2003).

employees, short-term contract employees (*shokutaku*), daily employees, and seconded employees usually enter into a contract that clearly states the employment period at time of hiring. The contract is not necessarily written; the two parties might enter into an oral agreement if the contract period or work hours are very short. Needless to say, nonregular workers work fewer hours than full-time workers.

Here it should be noted that the situation of part-time workers is much the same as that of workers with limited-term contracts, such as dispatched workers and contract employees, in that there are no guarantees regardless of whether or not the period of part-time employment has been explicitly set in advance. If the company suffers a business slump, part-time workers are the first to be let go. This means that these workers lack job security.

Looking at the column for women in table 8-1, we detect a great difference in the percentage of regular workers between men and women. A total of 44.4 percent of working women are regular workers and 55.6 percent are nonregular workers, so that more than half of working women have nonregular work. In contrast, roughly 80 percent of men are regular workers and 20 percent nonregular workers.

Part-time workers make up 42.5 percent of all female workers, or slightly over three-fourths of all female workers. In other words, most female nonregular workers are part-timers. Next are dispatched workers at 3.4 percent and contract employees at 2.9 percent, for a total of 6.3 percent of female workers. The remaining types of employment—short-term contract employees (*shokutaku*), daily employees, and seconded employees—each make up a very low percentage, less than 1 percent.

In Japan the category of part-time worker includes at least three different types: (1) persons who have fewer working hours/days per month than regular employees, (2) those who work fewer than thirty-five hours per week, and (3) those who are referred to at their workplace as "part-time workers." Types 1 and 2 require no explanation, but type 3 workers are called part-time in contradistinction to full-time, regular employees even though their working hours/days per month or working hours per week in actuality differ little, if any, from those of full-time workers. These are "nominal part-timers" (*koshō pāto*), as it is customary in Japan for any employee who has low wages, a short employment contract, a changeable number of working hours, and a comparatively low level of responsibility to be called part-time. According to Nagase (2003), 26 percent of part-time workers were nominal part-time workers in 2000.

Some researchers refer to nominal part-time workers as "pseudo" or "core" part-timers because they are not working part-time according to the traditional definition. The term "pseudo part-timer" (*giji pāto*) carries the connotation that the practice is undesirable, as employees who should be considered full-time workers are being given somewhat inferior terms of employment. The term "core part-timer" (*kikan pāto*), however, interprets the practice positively, highlighting that these part-time workers are given important responsibilities at the workplace and are considered for promotion alongside full-time workers. Nakamura (1990) uses this latter term.

Dispatched workers have a work contract, not with the client company where they actually work, but with the temporary labor agency that dispatches them. The relationships among the three parties are depicted in figure 8-2. When first enacted in 1985, the Worker Dispatching Act limited worker dispatching to highly specialized jobs. Since then, however, restrictions on the type of work have been eased and the dispatch period extended to up to three years—changes representative of the deregulation of Japan's labor market.

With contract employment, workers with specialized skills in specific areas are hired for a fixed period. Companies use contract employment for work that they need only occasionally for set periods, and they frequently pay comparatively high wages to such employees. Not all contract employees perform particularly highly skilled work; sometimes they are hired to cover busy periods, as in the case of seasonal factory workers.

Since companies hire dispatched and contract employees to meet their need for talented, trained professionals with specialized skill sets, it is not correct to view these two categories as simply being low-wage workers. Of course, sometimes the wages are low, as dispatched work now is permitted in more job areas and contract workers are being hired for a diverse array of jobs. The real problem

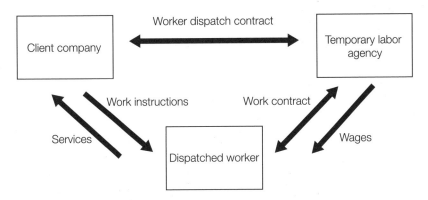

Fig. 8-2 Worker dispatching

Source: Ōsawa and Harada (2006, 141, fig. 10-1).

with dispatched and contract labor, however, is the lack of access to social insurance and the lack of job security—there is no guarantee of long-term employment.

Social insurance: another cause of inequalities among women
What percentage of nonregular workers have social insurance and other benefits? Figure 8-3 shows corporate provision of the three main social insurance programs—unemployment insurance, health insurance, and employee pension insurance—as well as of company pension schemes, retirement allowances, and bonuses. Virtually all regular employees are enrolled in the three social insurance programs, so their data in those areas were not collected.

Figure 8-3 tells us that the percentage of companies enrolling their contract employees in the three social insurance programs falls in the 73 to 80 percent range; the remaining 20 to 27 percent of companies do not. Many fewer companies offer these programs to their part-time workers, with 53.2 percent providing unemployment insurance; 36.0 percent, health insurance; and 33.1 percent, employee pension insurance. The figure for unemployment insurance is just over 50 percent, but those for health insurance and employee pension insurance are under 40 percent, meaning that more than 60 percent of companies do not enroll their part-time workers in these

(% of companies)

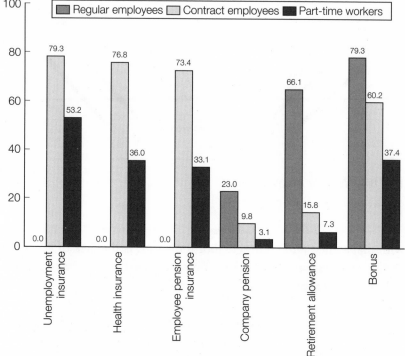

Fig. 8-3 Corporate provision of social insurance and employee benefits (2003)

Notes: 1. For definitions of the types of employment, see chapter 1 of Japan Institute for Labor Policy and Training (2006).
2. The survey asked companies if they currently had the various programs. For details regarding the survey questions, see the FY2003 questionnaire in the attachments to Japan Institute for Labor Policy and Training (2006).
3. The survey did not inquire about unemployment insurance, health insurance, and employee pension insurance for regular employees.

Source: Based on Japan Institute for Labor Policy and Training (2006, 71, fig. 2-4-1).

programs. In a word, the level of social insurance coverage for part-time workers is deplorable.

It is very rare for firms to offer their contract employees and part-time workers a company pension plan or retirement allowance. This means that these workers do not have a secure post-retirement income through these programs. Few corporations offer their regular employees a company pension scheme so it is no surprise that the percentage is low for nonregular employees. What about retirement allowances? There is quite a gap between the percentage of companies that provide this to their regular employees and the percentage that do so for their nonregular workers. I am not going to insist that companies pay the same retirement allowance to nonregular employees as they do to regular employees, but it is important to note that most nonregular employees receive no retirement allowance.

Thus we see that few companies provide their part-time workers with social insurance. And because women make up the vast majority of part-time workers, this means that a sizable gap arises between full-time and part-time working women in terms of safety net. This is one face of inequalities among women in Japan.

However, a married woman who works part-time is covered by her husband's health insurance as his dependent if she keeps her work hours below a certain number and, of course, if her husband is enrolled in health insurance in the first place. So not all married part-timers are uninsured. A woman also will have a pension if she herself is enrolled in the national pension plan (*kokumin nenkin*, a separate system from the employee pension, which is *kōsei nenkin*). Some married women, though, are not entered in the employee pension insurance at their place of employment or in their husband's health insurance as his dependent, meaning that not all married part-time working women are fully guaranteed these safety nets. Such disparities among women will not be eliminated unless the social insurance system is converted into one where married part-time working women enroll in the programs independently.

Let me also say a word about full-time homemakers in relation to social insurance. Full-time homemakers are not working for pay so they cannot join a company-related social insurance program and have the company cover part of the insurance premiums. They must join their husband's health insurance plan as his dependent and also must rely on pension payments made to their husband. The basic pension is the minimum that wives themselves are guaranteed. As with married women who are working part-time, the safety net is insufficient for full-time homemakers. And if a full-time homemaker divorces, her safety net is rendered almost nonexistent. What should be done about social insurance for full-time homemakers? This question goes to the very roots of Japan's social insurance system and is too large to tackle here. As a general principle, though, it would be desirable to shift coverage in social insurance, such as healthcare and pension, from a system based on the family unit to a system based on the individual. This would be a complicated matter involving adjustments among the various programs and the resolution of various technical issues.

Education and employment type

Let's turn our attention now to the educational background of female nonregular workers. Table 8-2 gives the distribution by educational background for each type of employment. The chart divides dispatched workers into the two categories of hired and registered so let me offer a brief explanation. Hired dispatched workers are employed by a job agency under an indefinite-term work contract and are subcontracted to other companies, while registered dispatched workers are enrolled on a job agency's available staff list but not on the agency's payroll. The latter enter into a work contract with the temporary labor agency only when they are dispatched to a client company. Employment is less stable for registered dispatched workers than for hired ones.

We see in the table that 13.4 percent of all working women have completed university or graduate school and 21.5 percent are graduates of a junior college or college of technology. These figures are rather low because they include women of all age groups, including many women who finished their schooling a number of years ago when not very many women went on to higher education. A total of 51.5 percent—or more than half of all working women—are high school graduates. A very low 3.6 percent ended their education at graduation from junior high school. These percentages will likely change in the future: since more and more women are going on to higher education, the percentage of high school graduates should fall while that of university graduates increases. In addition, 10 percent of working women are graduates of specialized training colleges.

Table 8-2 Women's educational attainment by employment type
(FY2003)

(%)

		Junior high school	High school	Special-ized training college	Junior college or college of tech-nology	University or gradu-ate school	Total
Working women	Total	3.6	51.5	10.0	21.5	13.4	100.0
	Regular employees	1.1	44.7	10.1	27.0	17.1	100.0
	Contract employees	6.7	40.4	14.4	19.5	19.0	100.0
	Seconded employees	4.8	46.8	11.1	23.5	13.7	100.0
	Hired dispatched workers	2.9	44.0	10.8	25.4	16.9	100.0
	Registered dispatched workers	1.0	33.2	11.3	30.3	24.2	100.0
	Daily employees	18.8	41.1	5.8	7.2	27.2	100.0
	Part-time workers	6.3	62.7	9.3	14.5	7.3	100.0
	Other	8.4	55.4	10.0	16.2	9.9	100.0

Notes: 1. For definitions of the types of employment, see chapter 1 of Japan Institute for Labor Policy and Training (2006).
2. Completed questionnaires in which the respondent did not indicate gender, employment type, or age were excluded.

Source: Based on Japan Institute for Labor Policy and Training (2006, 24, table 1-3-3).

Now let's examine the percentages in each type of employment. Many university graduates work as regular employees, contract employees, seconded employees, hired dispatched workers, registered dispatched workers, and daily employees. Few work in the other types of employment. It is particularly striking that many university-educated women work as registered dispatched and daily employees. Also, university-educated women make up 13.4 percent of working women overall, but only 7.3 percent of part-time workers, so we can say that university graduates are underrepresented in this category.

A markedly high percentage of junior college graduates work as hired or registered dispatched workers. The percentage working as regular employees is also rather high, and a higher percentage of junior college graduates than university graduates is in part-time work. Overall, though, female junior college graduates are mainly engaged in dispatched work.

Turning now to female high school graduates, we find that they are spread quite evenly over all the various types of employment, as indicated by the fact that all the figures are slightly below the percentage of high school graduates in the female work force overall. Particularly noteworthy is that over 60 percent of part-time workers are high school graduates. The figure for junior high school graduates is also somewhat high compared with the percentage of these graduates in the female work force overall.

To sum up what we have found here, regular employees are distributed almost evenly across the various education levels. We know this because the figures for regular employees are close to those at the top of the table showing the distribution of total female workers by level of education. There is a comparatively large number of university graduates working as daily employees and dispatched workers, while high school graduates make up a high percentage of part-time workers. The higher a woman's education level, the more likely she is to be engaged in dispatched work. Conversely, the lower her educational background, the more likely she is to be in part-time work. This gap arises from the difference in skill level of university and high school graduates. Since a higher percentage of university graduates have specialized skills, they can do dispatched work that requires such job skills, while high school graduates tend to be concentrated in part-time work that does not demand high-level specialization.

Table 8-3 illustrates this. It shows the percentage of regular employees, contract employees, registered dispatched workers, and part-time workers across eight job areas. Looking at female regular employees, we see that a high 69.6 percent are in clerical work. The next most frequent job areas are markedly lower—professional/technical work at 9.9 percent and sales at 7.4 percent—and lower still are services and skilled manual work/manufacturing at less than 5 percent each. We can see then that the majority of female regular workers are engaged in general clerical work and that professional/technical work and sales are somewhat low, each under 10 percent.

The breakdown for contract employees is completely different. A high 57.8 percent of contract employees are engaged in professional/technical work. This is markedly higher than the next most frequent

Table 8-3 Women's job areas by employment type (FY2003)

(%)

	Professional/technical	Managerial	Clerical	Sales	Services	Police/Security	Transport/ communication	Skilled manual work/ manufacturing
Regular employees	9.9	3.7	69.6	7.4	4.4	0.0	0.4	4.6
Contract employees	57.8	0.5	20.5	3.6	7.4	0.1	0.6	9.5
Registered dispatched workers	7.5	0.4	80.5	1.8	3.9	0.0	2.1	3.7
Part-time workers	7.6	0.4	27.7	14.6	29.1	0.1	3.1	17.4

Notes: 1. For definitions of the types of employment, see chapter 1 of Japan Institute for Labor Policy and Training (2006).
2. For details regarding the job areas, see Japan Institute for Labor Policy and Training (2006) as well as the FY2003 questionnaire in the attachments.
3. Completed questionnaires in which the respondent did not indicate employment type or job area or selected "other job area" were excluded.
4. The job area or percentages for each employment type total 100.

Source: Based on Japan Institute for Labor Policy and Training (2006, 29, table 1-4-3).

job area—clerical work, at 20.5 percent. Female contract employees are engaged in highly skilled work, and their remuneration is commensurately high. In addition, services and skilled manual work/ manufacturing are 7.4 percent and 9.5 percent, respectively, and so should not be ignored.

The vast majority of registered dispatched workers—80.5 percent—are engaged in general clerical work. Indeed, it would be no exaggeration to consider registered dispatched workers as synonymous with clerical staff. The next most frequent is professional/ technical work at 7.5 percent. This, however, should be regarded as very low and as further evidence that registered dispatched workers are doing clerical work.

Part-time workers are not concentrated in any particular job area, unlike contract employees (professional/technical work) and registered dispatched workers (clerical work). Rather, part-time workers are spread over a broad range of job areas, although services at 29.1 percent and clerical work at 27.7 percent are comparatively high. An example of a part-time employee in services is the supermarket worker. Next in line are skilled manual work/manufacturing and sales, both of which are between 14 and 18 percent. These job areas involve comparatively simple tasks that do not require very high-level skills. We can conclude, then, that part-time workers are involved in a variety of job areas, but the vast majority are performing comparatively simple tasks.

The Wage Gap

The differing positions of regular workers and nonregular workers in Japan can be measured by a variety of criteria: length of employment, work hours, coverage in social insurance systems, wages and bonuses. We have already considered the first three, so in this section we will look into wages and bonuses.

Bonuses

Let's focus first on bonuses, which are disbursed in Japan to workers two or three times a year in addition to wages. It is generally thought that bonuses are only given to regular workers, but is that really so?

Figure 8-3, which we looked at earlier in our discussion of social insurance, shows the percentage of companies offering bonuses. We saw that company pensions and retirement allowances are beyond the reach of most nonregular workers, but the situation is different for bonuses. Some 60 percent of companies award bonuses to contract employees and 37 percent even give them to part-time workers. The latter might not seem like a large percentage, but we must remember that part-time workers far exceed contract and dispatched workers in number. By the same token, however, over 60 percent of companies do not have a bonus system for their part-time workers, meaning that most part-time workers—who are many in number and almost all women—do not receive a bonus. Part-timers work fewer hours than full-time workers, so a system where part-time workers are given a bonus of three months' salary (as might be typical for regular employees), for example, would not be sustainable. If bonuses were awarded, the amount would be quite low, perhaps one month's salary. As a result, we may say that the great majority of part-time workers effectively receive no bonus at all.

Hourly wages

How do women's hourly wages compare? Table 8-4 gives women's hourly wages adjusted for hours worked, by employment type. The hourly wages in this table have not been adjusted, however, for factors differentiating workers such as age, years of service, educational background, and job area, so we must keep in mind that these figures are the average wages of all workers in a given employment type.

We see that seconded employees receive the highest hourly wage at 1,515 yen, while part-time workers receive the lowest, 881 yen. Seconded employment is often short term, but these workers who are sent from one corporation to work at another are paid high wages. While there are relatively few seconded employees, regular employees, who are many in number, have the second highest wage, 1,258 yen. Contract employees and hired and registered dispatched workers are next with hourly wages that range from 1,000 to 1,200 yen, somewhat lower than those of regular employees on average. In some job areas, however, these three employment types sometimes have better pay than regular employees.

Most women are in part-time positions, and the wages of part-time workers are the lowest of any employment type. To put this in perspective, we need to compare the wages of part-timers with those of other workers, especially regular employees. When we do so, we find that full-time workers make 1,258 yen an hour while part-time workers make 881 yen, or roughly 70 percent of what full-time workers earn.

Opinions differ on whether this is too high or too low. First, let's look at what part-timers themselves think about this wage differential. According to the Japanese Cabinet Office's Research Committee on Family and Lifestyle (convened in 2001), 72 percent of part-time workers judged their wages to be low compared with

Table 8-4 Women's hourly wages adjusted for hours worked, by employment type

(Yen)

	Average	
	1999	2003
Regular employees	1,418	1,258
Contract employees	1,370	1,134
Seconded employees	1,440	1,515
Hired dispatched workers	1,192	1,045
Registered dispatched workers	1,346	1,168
Daily employees	922	888
Part-time workers	956	881
Other	1,029	940
Total	1,221	1,096

Notes: 1. For definitions of the types of employment, see chapter 1 of Japan Institute for Labor Policy and Training (2006) as well as the FY2003 questionnaire in the attachments.
2. Completed questionnaires in which the respondent did not indicate gender, employment type, or wages were excluded.
3. Figures have been adjusted for inflation using the consumer price index (2000 = 100, excluding imputed rent).

Source: Based on Japan Institute for Labor Policy and Training (2006, 104, table 3-4-10).

those of full-time workers performing the same work. The phrase "same work" is key: part-timers are aware that their wages are lower even though they are doing the same work. Interestingly, though, 43 percent of those same part-time workers said that they could understand why there was a wage difference while 39 percent said they could not. Thus slightly more were accepting, but the percentages are not so far apart. As for the reasons for accepting the difference, 33 percent mentioned differences in responsibility and 24 percent cited differences in work content. Full-time employees are expected to take more responsibility and, while the work may be the same, full-time workers perform the more difficult aspects. Full-time workers also must work overtime during busy periods while part-time workers can decline such work. This difference in loyalty to the corporation is one reason why part-time workers can accept the wage difference.

Those not seeing the pay differential as a major problem often point out that nonregular workers choose part-time work of their own volition. Since they intentionally choose not to take on work with heavy responsibilities, that means they do not desire a high wage. As we will see later, the percentage who voluntarily choose to be part-time workers is quite a bit higher than the percentage who actually want to work full-time but have ended up taking part-time work. We cannot say, then, that this view is completely wrong.

According to Nitta (1993) and others, part-time workers do not aspire to make high wages. Moreover, Satō (1998) and the Japan Institute for Labor Policy and Training (2006) claim that female part-time workers are not particularly unhappy with their job or work life and may even have a higher level of satisfaction than regular workers in some respects. Quite a few people hold the opinion that there is no need for others to be concerned that part-time work is paid less than full-time work if part-time workers themselves are not particularly dissatisfied and do not desire better compensation. Even very recently, Satō and Koizumi (2007) again found that most non-regular workers are satisfied with their work life and took the position that classifying all nonregular work as insecure employment or as exploitation of workers is too simplistic and fails to take into view the whole picture. I will share my personal views on this later.

Earlier it was mentioned that age, length of service, educational background, job area, and other factors contribute to the wage differential between full-time and part-time workers. Would that wage gap still exist if differences in these factors were eliminated? In other words, if a full-time and part-time worker had the same characteristics in terms of age, education, etc., would there still be a difference in their wages? Nagase (1997 and 2003) and the Japan Institute for Labor Policy and Training (2006) have conducted some helpful econometric analyses in this regard. I will not present that research in detail here, but only cite their findings: even when such factors are controlled for, the wage differential between full-time and part-time workers decreases only slightly. The basic pay gap still exists. Such factors as age, educational attainment, and job area prove to have only a small impact on the wage disparity between full-time and part-time workers.

Trends in the wage gap

Next, let's look at how the wage differential between female full-time and part-time workers has changed since 1980. Figure 8-4 depicts these trends. Age, education, job area, and other factors have not been controlled for here, so the comparison is of average wages for full-time and part-time workers, with the former referred to in the figure as "ordinary workers" (*ippan rōdōsha*). As noted earlier, the impact of such personal attributes is small so the wage gap shown in the figure is close to the actual gap.

According to the figure, part-timer wages were 76.2 percent of full-timer wages in 1980, but the gap gradually widened so that in 2002 part-timer wages were down to 64.9 percent of those of full-time workers. In the years leading up to 2002, the Japanese economy was plagued by a recession that hit companies very hard. Rather than any increase in pay, many part-timers experienced a pay cut. Of course, full-time workers were also affected by the recession, but the drop in their pay was smaller, so the gap between the two widened.

Why does the wage gap between full-time and part-time workers expand during a recession? Let me offer several reasons. First, companies feel the need to tighten the purse strings at such times, and it is easier to lower the wages of part-timers because they perform noncore support work. Moreover, it is thought that lowering their pay will not have a major impact on productivity. Companies are more afraid that they will face a decline in productivity if they lower the wages of full-timers.

Second, during a recession, it is hard for workers to change jobs and hard for those newly entering the employment market to find a job. This means that companies can secure the number of workers they need even if they offer low wages. Since this particularly applies to part-time workers, their wages become comparatively lower.

Another factor affecting the wage gap is that many full-time workers, and particularly full-timers at large corporations, are members of a labor union. Corporations cannot make major changes to the work conditions for these employees because they are bound by a collective labor agreement and the union would certainly protest. Most part-time workers, however, are not part of a labor union so

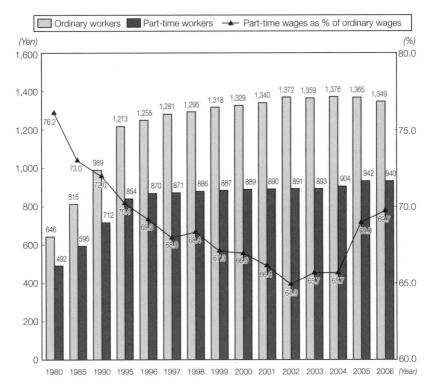

Fig. 8-4 Wage gap between female ordinary and part-time workers

Note: Hourly scheduled cash earnings for ordinary workers were calculated as follows:
hourly scheduled cash earnings = scheduled cash earnings / actual number of scheduled
hours worked.

Source: Ministry of Health, Labor, and Welfare, *Chingin kōzō kihon tōkei chōsa* (Basic survey on
wage structure).

corporations can change their wages and other work terms comparatively easily.

Looking at figure 8-4, we see that the wage gap between full-
time and part-time workers peaked in 2002 and contracted after
that point, as Japanese entered a period of economic expansion that
would turn out to be even longer than the Izanagi boom (November
1965 to July 1970). The reasons just mentioned for the widening of
the wage gap between full-time and part-time workers during reces-
sions operate in reverse during expansionary periods. Corporate
solvency improves, and companies must increase wages to attract

part-time workers because it is now easy for them to change jobs. In this way, the wage gap between full-time and part-time workers starts to contract.

Although the economy is expanding, not all companies have seen improved solvency. It is large corporations in city areas and some manufacturing firms that are enjoying economic recovery. As a result, the wage gap between full-time and part-time workers has not narrowed to earlier levels.

How the wage differential will develop in the future will depend on the economic recovery. The lesson here is that the gap in wages between full-time and part-time workers moves in tandem with economic trends: generally, the wage gap expands during economic downturns and contracts during upturns. However, it seems that the wage gap will never be zero even if an economic recovery lasts for a very long time and is strong enough to create inflation because, as we saw, a wage gap exists between full-time and part-time workers even if we adjust for factors such as age and experience. As a result, even economic expansion cannot eliminate the wage gap between full-time and part-time workers entirely.

Why Are There So Many Nonregular Workers?

So far we have discovered that more than half of female workers are nonregular workers and that the employment terms—especially wages—of such workers are quite a bit inferior to those of regular workers. What has given rise to this state of affairs? Once we know this, we will be in a better position to consider possible policies to ameliorate the situation.

We can say that labor issues involve supply-side factors—i.e., workers—and demand-side factors—i.e., companies. Through a process of negotiations and adjustments between workers and management, wages and job numbers are set at the point where supply and demand meet. For this reason, we first need to examine demand-side and supply-side factors in why there are so many nonregular workers in Japan.

What companies say

Why do companies—the demand side—say they want to hire non-regular employees? Table 8-5 lists the reasons given by companies for hiring contract employees, dispatched workers, and part-time workers. Interesting here is that the reasons differ greatly for the three worker types.

Let's look at contract employees first. There are essentially four reasons that corporations hire contract employees: "for specialized work," "to hire capable, trained human resources," "to reduce personnel costs," and "to reemploy older workers." Each of those was chosen by over 30 percent of companies, in contrast to the 10 percent or so for the other reasons. In other words, contract employees offer the key advantage of trained, highly skilled personnel who can be put on the job immediately whenever necessary. Contract work is also a good way for firms to reemploy older workers who have reached retirement age. Since contract employees receive high wages, "reduction of personnel costs" may appear contradictory at first glance. However, the term of employment is limited for these workers, as their employment is terminated when the work runs out; companies can lower their personnel costs because they do not employ unnecessary workers.

In the case of dispatched workers, the most important factor is "to reduce personnel costs," with 41.7 percent of firms citing this reason. Next is "to hire capable, trained human resources" at 38.0 percent. Hiring dispatched workers results in a reduction in personnel costs because such workers are not taken on unless needed. Moreover, hiring dispatched workers is a good way to acquire workers that can immediately perform up to par. We see that around 25 percent of companies chose "to adjust the size of the work force to economic fluctuations" and "for specialized work." "Specialized work" was also cited for contract employees, but "economic fluctuations" was not a major factor there. Dispatched labor is convenient for companies because they can hire these workers during upswings and release them in the event of a downturn.

The key advantage for businesses in hiring contract employees and dispatched workers, therefore, is that they can immediately

Table 8-5 Reasons companies hire nonregular employees (FY2003)

(%)

	Contract employees	Dispatched workers	Part-time workers
1. Because we cannot find regular employees	10.4	16.2	11.8
2. To have our regular employees concentrate on core duties.	11.4	16.6	12.2
3. For specialized work	39.5	24.9	9.7
4. To hire capable, trained human resources	38.1	38.0	11.8
5. To adjust the size of the work force to economic fluctuations	14.3	25.4	22.4
6. To handle long operating hours	6.5	2.7	19.6
7. To adjust to fluctuations in work volume over the course of a day or week	2.6	7.7	33.5
8. To handle temporary or seasonal changes in work volume	6.4	13.8	14.8
9. To reduce personnel costs (see reasons 12 and 13 and note 3)	33.6	41.7	61.2
10. To reemploy older workers	33.1	1.7	6.1
11. To replace regular employees on childcare or family care leave	1.2	8.4	2.0
12. To save on wages	27.2	25.2	52.6
13. To save on labor costs other than wages	9.0	25.6	22.9

Notes: 1. For definitions of the types of employment, see chapter 1 of Japan Institute for Labor Policy and Training (2006).
2. For details regarding the reasons for employment, see chapter 1 of Japan Institute for Labor Policy and Training (2006) as well as the FY2003 questionnaire in the attachments.
3. The figures for "9. To reduce personnel costs" are the total percentages of companies that selected either reason 12 or 13 or both.
4. Respondents were permitted to give multiple responses.
Source: Based on Japan Institute for Labor Policy and Training (2006, 60, table 2-2-1).

employ competent, trained employees when they need them. In addition, hiring such employees results in a lowering of labor costs.

Turning to part-time workers, we find that the reasons companies employ them are quite different from those for hiring contract and dispatched workers. The most frequently cited reason by far was "to reduce personnel costs," selected by 61.2 percent of companies in the survey. It is safe to say that companies hire low-paid part-time workers primarily to save on labor costs. The next most frequent reasons were "to adjust to fluctuations in work volume," at 33.5 percent, and "to adjust the size of the work force to economic fluctuations," at 22.4 percent. Firms have busy periods and slow periods that cycle in step with business trends; they have busy and slow times of day. Employing part-time workers is a good way to handle these fluctuations—and their comparatively low wages make them even more ideal.

We have learned why companies like to hire part-time workers. Now let's look at what kinds of industries and corporations hire them. Figure 8-5 shows that part-time workers make up 62.8 percent of the work force in hotels, restaurants, and bars; 37.3 percent in wholesale and retail trade; and 22.0 percent in services. This highlights the nature of these industries to have busy and slack seasons and times of day. Part-time workers also make up 15.5 percent of the work force in real estate and 12.7 percent in manufacturing, a significant presence.

Next, let's turn to figure 8-6 and see if nonregular workers as a percentage of a company's work force differs by company size. This figure gives percentages for part-time workers only, but since contract employees and dispatched workers make up a mere 2 to 3 percent of corporate workers, and since this makeup percentage varies very little by corporate size, the statistics can be considered as representative of the percentages of all nonregular workers by company size.

The key finding shown in this figure is that firms of every size hire nonregular workers. Part-time workers make up the highest percentage—25.3 percent—of the work force at small companies with 5–29 employees, and have the smallest presence—18.1 percent—at medium-sized corporations with 500–999 employees. The difference between the high and low figures, however, is a mere 7 percentage points: part-time employees are distributed fairly evenly throughout the work force regardless of company scale.

This implies that businesses of all sizes have busy and slack seasons and times of day and have set the reduction of personnel costs

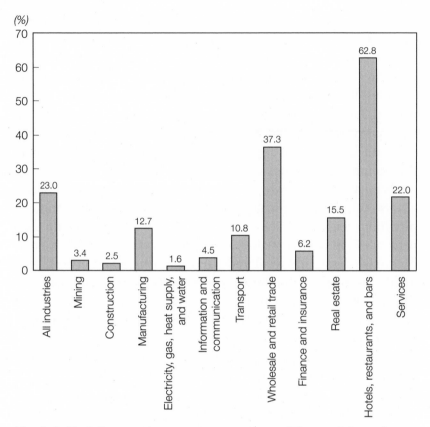

Fig. 8-5 Part-time workers as a percentage of the work force by industry (FY2003)

Notes: 1. For definitions of the industrial classifications, see chapter 1 of Japan Institute for Labor Policy and Training (2006).
2. For the definition of part-time workers, see chapter 1 of Japan Institute for Labor Policy and Training (2006).

Source: Based on Japan Institute for Labor Policy and Training (2006, 48, fig. 2-1-5).

as an important goal. Further, large corporations are not exempt from being concerned about reducing personnel costs or regarding this as an important policy objective. At the same time, we see that cutting personnel costs is not the number-one priority of all small companies. Overall, employing part-time workers is a key management technique for firms of all sizes to reduce labor costs.

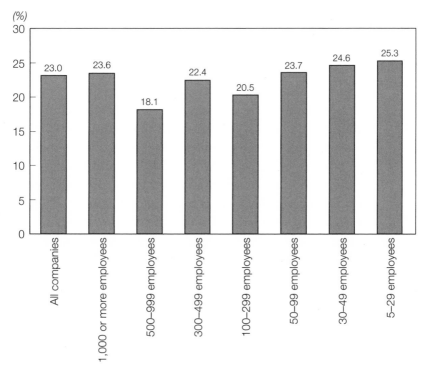

Fig. 8-6 Part-time workers as a percentage of a company's work force by company size (FY2003)

Note: For the definition of part-time workers, see chapter 1 of Japan Institute for Labor Policy and Training (2006).

Source: Based on Japan Institute for Labor Policy and Training (2006, 50, fig. 2-1-9).

What companies don't say

Drawing on a government report, we have just looked at several reasons why companies employ part-time workers. Now let's think about the reasons that are not stated explicitly. Some of these are in line with the reasons given by the companies themselves while others are of another dimension altogether.

- Impact of economic fluctuations: It has already been noted that the wage gap between full-time and part-time employees fluctuates in tandem with the economy; however, a weak economy and a strong economy both act to simultaneously decrease and increase the number of part-time workers. Let's take the example of an economic downturn. When the economy is poor, corporate sales and production fall and companies are likely to have more workers than they need. In such cases, companies first reduce the number of part-time and other nonregular workers. At the same time, however, companies want to lower costs by having part-time and other nonregular workers perform work that regular employees have handled up to that point, which will serve to push up the number of part-time workers. Whether a net decrease or increase in the number of part-time workers will result depends on which of the two opposing forces is stronger. The same mechanism operates in reverse in periods of economic upturn. Whether there is a net decrease or increase in part-time workers is influenced by the following two factors: (1) the level of the economic downturn or upturn—if the economy is very bad, the need to cut labor costs will be strong and part-time workers will be let go; and (2) the ease with which companies can replace regular workers with part-time workers—this varies from business to business so we cannot say categorically which direction that will go.

- Wages: Although more and more corporations are adopting ability- and merit-based personnel systems for regular employees, the seniority system remains intact in Japan. The wages of regular employees increase with seniority, but seniority has very little impact on the wages of part-time workers. Since the pay of part-time workers stays the same even if they work at the same company for many years, there will be a wage gap between regular and part-time employees. Similarly, regular workers are promoted, whereas most part-time workers are not—also a major factor behind the wage differential.

- Social insurance: Such considerations of seniority and promotions combine with a third component—social insurance—to become a significant reason for companies to hire part-time workers. As already discussed, nonregular workers are often either not eligible or are not signed up for certain social insurance programs. If workers at the company are not in such programs, then, the company can save the portion of the premiums payable by it. This is appealing to firms as it reduces their labor costs considerably.

Part-time workers are eligible to enroll in these social insurance programs if they fulfill certain conditions. For unemployment insurance, the workers' prescribed work hours must be at least twenty hours per week, and they must expect to be employed for not less than one year. For employee pension insurance, the workers' weekly work hours must be 75 percent or more of those of full-time workers. Part-time workers who do not meet the above qualifications are outside the system so companies do not have to pay their share of the premiums. In the case of health insurance, if the employee is a dependent of another family member (such as a husband), the employee does not need to pay separate health insurance premiums and the company will also be exempt from its portion. Employing part-time and other nonregular workers thus means that a company can lessen its social insurance premiums, an incentive to hire many such workers.

Companies are not alone in thinking carefully about social insurance premiums in making employment decisions. Workers also think about this. For reasons related to social insurance premiums, many married part-time working women adjust their working hours to ensure their annual income does not exceed 1.03 or 1.3 million yen. (This will be discussed later as a supply-side factor.)

- Benefits: Nonregular workers are usually excluded from various employee benefits, such as company housing, company pensions, and retirement allowances. This has already been discussed to some degree, and readers are invited to refer to Tachibanaki (2005) for further details. Hiring nonregular workers is thus attractive to firms because they are not required to disburse employee benefits and this helps them save on labor costs.

- Legal restrictions on the dismissal of regular employees: Japan has regulations to prevent companies from abusing their rights and casually firing regular employees. Under the Labor Standards Act, companies are allowed to release regular employees if certain rather stringent conditions are fulfilled, but many firms find these conditions too strict and so they try to pare down their number of regular employees and instead hire many part-time and other nonregular workers, whom they can legally dismiss or have quit comparatively easily.

  Japan needs to consider whether its employee dismissal regulations should be adjusted. Labor law specialists, with the exception of a certain group, generally feel that Japan's employee dismissal legislation is not too strict. Many non-Marxist labor economists, though, are calling for the restrictions to be eased, saying this will promote economic revitalization by freeing up the movement of labor. On the other hand, most Marxist and a few non-Marxist economists say the rules related to dismissals should not be touched. Japan is moving toward an American style of economic and corporate management, though, so we can expect that such regulations will gradually be relaxed.

- Recruitment: Companies can observe and assess a worker's skill level and attitude during the period of part-time, dispatched, or contract employment. Workers found to be competent can be taken on as regular employees. The period of nonregular employment thus serves as a trial period.

  In the case of dispatched workers, the company receiving the services is obligated under the Worker Dispatching Act to make efforts to offer regular employment to any worker whose period of dispatching has exceeded a certain period. This provision can serve to encourage firms to promote employees from dispatched to regular status after using the dispatch period as a trial. Some corporations do not want to upgrade the worker's status, however, and dismiss the employee right before the term of dispatching is to end and then rehire the employee as a dispatched worker after some time has passed.

Companies are not obligated by law to change the status of part-time workers to regular status, but the period of employment as a part-time worker can in effect function as a trial period during which the company can monitor the part-timer's performance.

- Structural changes: As is widely recognized, Japan is moving away from manufacturing and becoming a service economy. In figure 8-5 we saw that part-time workers make up a large percentage of the work force in hotels, restaurants, and bars; wholesale and retail trade; and services. All of these are service industries in the broad sense, and part-time workers are particularly suited to this sector. As Japan's service economy has grown, the number of people working in the service industry has increased as well, and, as a result, the number of part-time and other nonregular workers has risen overall.

Why women choose part-time work

Let's now examine factors on the supply side, i.e., workers. We have looked in detail at why the demand side—companies—wants to hire nonregular workers. On the whole, companies are not singling women out for nonregular employment but simply want to reduce their labor costs and hire people for short-term, short-hour work and jobs in services, clerical areas, and unskilled manual work. Since women fulfill such conditions, there are many female nonregular workers. The question, rather, is why women choose to take nonregular positions.

Women's participation in the labor force has already been taken up in past chapters so the discussion here will focus on why women seek part-time work. (Contract and dispatched work is also open to women seeking nonregular work, but part-time work is by far the most popular type of nonregular work among women so it will be simpler if we limit our discussion to part-time work.)

Why do women want part-time work? This type of employment is particularly common among married women as well as single women who plan to resign at the time of marriage or childbirth. We can understand this more easily if we think about the motivations of these women.

- Traditional attitudes: Not all Japanese women think that women should work outside the home and build a career, although attitudes are changing. Figure 8-7 shows the changes over the past thirty years or so in women's support of the traditional view on the family and the gender-based division of labor. In 1979, roughly 70 percent of women supported the traditional view that the husband should be the bread-winner and that woman's place is in the home. That figure had dropped to slightly over 40 percent in 2004—over half of women support the idea of women working outside the home. Clearly the attitudes of Japanese women have changed dramatically. The younger the woman, the less likely she is to support the traditional view of the family, so we can expect the number of working women to increase in the future. Data for men are not presented here, but the statistics indicate that a somewhat higher percentage of men than women adhere to the traditional view of the family, although that figure has also declined over the past thirty years. While the percentage of women who are interested in working is increasing, two constraints remain: First, who will raise the children? Second, how seriously do women commit to a career?

- Family responsibilities: In Japan the woman has the greater share of the housework and childrearing in many families. This is true even in couples who believe that, in principle, both partners should commit equally to these tasks. Traditional views on the gender-based division of labor linger, and the long hours men spend at work limit the time they have for housework and childrearing. Perhaps because they bear the children, women seem to feel a stronger dedication and sense of responsibility toward nurturing and raising them. Many women thus believe that work is a woman's second rather than first priority, and they prefer to take part-time positions if they work.

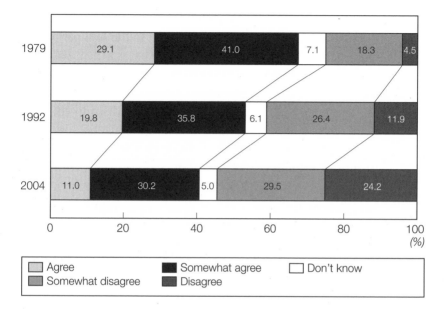

Fig. 8-7 Japanese women's views on the statement "The husband should be the breadwinner and the wife should take care of the home"

Source: Based on Cabinet Office, *Danjo kyōdō sankaku shakai ni kansuru yoron chōsa* (Public opinion poll on a gender-equal society).

- **Limited opportunity**: Unfortunately, women still tend to have less education than men and most are in clerical-track positions, as has already been discussed. This means there are few women in high-level jobs and many in work that involves simple routine tasks. Women's wages are not very high, and discrimination against women still exists as well. It is no surprise, then, that many women find the idea of seeking a career underwhelming and decide to keep their paid work to a moderate level. One outward sign of this is their turning to part-time work.

- **Lack of incentive**: If the husband is making an income that is adequate for the family to live on, the wife will not feel a very strong incentive to work and earn money. If the husband's income is low, however, the wife will naturally be moved to work full-time to increase the household income. This has been true in Japan for a long time and is captured in the first part of the Douglas-Arisawa theory, which states that married women's employment is influenced by their husband's income level. Although this part of the theory is gradually losing its validity, as mentioned earlier, it has not been entirely discounted: quite a few wives seek work to supplement the household income, and part-time work is well suited to such a goal.

- Bridge to regular work: As mentioned above, companies sometimes view the period of nonregular employment as a trial period and then promote workers to regular employment if they find them to be capable, and this same motivation operates on the worker side as well—workers sometimes first try out the work on a nonregular basis and later seek regular employment. In such cases, the worker intentionally seeks a nonregular position as a first step. These workers do not necessarily seek regular employment at the same company; they are open to being hired as a regular employee at a different company. Their goal in taking a part-time position is essentially to acquire skills.

  In Europe it is common for people to take nonregular work with the hope that it will lead to a regular position. See Ōsawa and Houseman (2003) for more details about countries where nonregular work plays a significant role in this regard. Tachibanaki (2004a) and the Japan Institute for Labor Policy and Training (2006) offer some information about whether nonregular positions lead to regular work in Japan. When questioned, around 30 percent of young people working as freeters and other nonregular workers reported that they ended up taking nonregular work because no regular position was available; 70 to 80 percent of these young people said they would prefer regular employment if it were available. This indirectly implies that nonregular work is a bridge to regular work in Japan.

- Structural reasons: Japan's tax and social insurance systems also encourage married women to take part-time work. If a married woman's annual income is between 0.9 and 1.03 million yen, her income is tax free. In addition, if she is her husband's dependent and her annual income is under 1.3 million yen, she does not have to pay social insurance premiums. Consequently, married women try to limit their income to the levels just mentioned. According to Nagase (2003), 29 percent of married women deliberately keep their income below the income tax threshold and 10 percent try to avoid social insurance premiums. Judging from these figures, we can assume that quite a number of married women limit their working hours to control their income and thereby avoid tax and social insurance payments. These systems thus constitute a structural incentive toward working part-time.

Looking at the supply side, we have seen multiple factors leading women, and particularly married women, to part-time and other nonregular employment. Since, like other markets, the labor market settles at the point where supply and demand meet, let's consider this question of supply and demand next.

Does supply or demand exert more influence?

Are supply factors stronger or are demand factors? That is, has it been primarily the supply side of women workers themselves or the demand side of companies that has led to the current situation of so many Japanese women working part-time?

In a word, it is the company side that has exerted the decisive influence: companies have taken the leading role in employing women as nonregular workers, and women have accommodated themselves to that. Now let's look at the reasons why this is the case.

First, let's look at the results of a recent economic analysis. Ōsawa (2006) examines whether demand-side factors (companies) or supply-side factors (workers) exerted more influence in the increase in the number of part-timers and *Arbeit* (temporary workers) among young people and married women between 1992 and 2002. Table 8-6 outlines these findings. We see that in the case of part-time work, supply-side factors contributed 33.2 percent and demand-side factors

62.4—the demand side had nearly twice the impact of the supply side. In the case of *Arbeit*, the supply side contributed a negative 22.2 percent because the labor pool of young people shrank, while the demand side was overwhelmingly decisive at 124.1 percent.

Ōsawa's research was of both young people and married women, and the figures are a composite of the two groups, so we cannot say categorically that the findings apply to all married women. Married women make up a very large percentage of part-time workers, however, so the conclusion that demand-side factors are stronger than supply-side factors in their case still stands.

Let's now look at nonregular workers who reported that their employment status was an involuntary choice—namely, that they were unable to find a company that would hire them as a regular employee. If there are large numbers of such workers, that would clearly indicate that companies have the stronger influence.

Table 8-7 gives this information for women. Over 35 percent of contract and dispatched workers responded that they are in those positions although they originally wanted regular work. The figures for young part-time workers and married part-time workers are also quite high at 25.2 percent and 14.9 percent, respectively. None of the figures are over 50 percent, however, so for most women nonregular

Table 8-6 Factor analysis of the increase in part-time and *Arbeit* (temporary workers) (1992–2002)

(%)

	Contribution ratio of supply-side factors (workers)	Contribution ratio of demand-side factors (companies)
Part-time workers	33.2	62.4
Arbeit (temporary workers)	−22.2	124.1
Part-time workers + *Arbeit*	5.5	93.3

Notes: 1. The figures do not total 100 due to cross-terms.
2. Calculated based on Statistics Bureau, Ministry of Internal Affairs and Communications, *Employment Status Survey*.
Source: Ōsawa (2006, 178, fig. 13-3).

work was a voluntary choice. Nonetheless, quite a number of female nonregular workers did report that they wanted regular positions if possible, and we can assume from this that companies would not hire them as such. This means that the demand side exerted more influence than the supply side.

Nagase (2003) analyzed other data and found that 30 percent of married female part-time workers are doing part-time work as a second choice because no full-time work was available, as are 51 percent of never-married/divorced women. Both studies show, therefore, that a lower percentage of married women than of young and never-married/divorced women are in part-time work as a second choice. In contrast with young and never-married/divorced women who must earn their own living and so strongly desire regular work, many married women find part-time work adequate because of their husband's income. As a result, a lower percentage of such women are doing part-time work against their original wishes.

Based on these two analyses, we can conclude that female part-time and other nonregular workers are numerous in Japan because of strong demand-side (company) factors. The wishes of the supply

Table 8-7 Reason for taking nonregular employment: "Because no company would hire me as a regular employee" (2003)

(%)

Women	
Contract employees	35.5
Hired dispatched workers	39.9
Registered dispatched workers	37.0
Young part-time workers	25.2
Married part-time workers	14.9
Older part-time workers	12.2

Note: Figures represent the percentage of respondents who selected "because no company would hire me as a regular employee" from among the reasons for taking nonregular employment (multiple responses were permitted and respondents were asked to select all responses that applied).

Source: Based on Japan Institute for Labor Policy and Training (2006, 109, table 4-1-1).

side (female workers) also have an impact, however, so the large number of nonregular workers cannot be explained entirely by corporate factors.

Employment Type and Inequalities among Women

As has already been noted, clear inequalities exist between female regular and nonregular employees not only in wages but also in bonuses, promotions, employee benefits, and participation in social insurance programs. It is important to remember that about half of female workers are engaged in nonregular work. The desire of companies to save on labor costs by hiring these women plays strongly here.

It is also true, though, that some women, and particularly married women, want part-time and other nonregular work from the start. The short working hours allow them time for housework and childrearing, and the women have a better chance of achieving a good work-life balance. The majority of women engaged in nonregular work, including young as well as married women, seek such work of their own volition and indicate that they are quite satisfied with it. And many observers say that there is no need to be concerned that the work terms for nonregular workers are poor if the women desire such work themselves and are satisfied with it. A key recent example of this perspective is Satō and Koizumi (2007).

My personal view, however, is that the gap between regular and nonregular workers is not acceptable and must be reduced.

First of all, the high level of satisfaction—or lack of active discontent—among nonregular workers can be likened to the attitude found in those who have withdrawn altogether from the job market. Such individuals, unable to find employment in the bad economic times, have in the end resigned themselves to the situation and withdrawn from the world of work. Similarly, people resign themselves to part-time work, thinking that even if they were to look for a regular position they would not find one because the economy is bad. We can imagine such people responding, out of that fatalistic acceptance of their situation, that on the whole they are satisfied. No doubt many also convince themselves that they should be happy with their part-time position because they are lucky to have a job at all.

Another important consideration is that married female part-timers may be satisfied with their current work status, but no one can know what will happen to them in the future. Their husbands may die, or they may get divorced—as we saw in chapter 4, the divorce rate is climbing. The day might well come when these women are suddenly face-to-face with the negatives of being a non-regular worker—namely, low wages (and abrupt fall into poverty with a divorce), no social insurance, and a weak safety net. What good then is their "satisfaction" with nonregular work? We live in uncertain times. Yokoyama (2003 and 2005) recommends that women continue to work outside the home even after marriage because full-time homemakers can find themselves suddenly in poverty after a divorce and can find that their work skills have eroded if they have not worked through their childrearing years. Freeters and other young people cannot depend on their parents forever, as they will pass away at some point.

I also believe that nonregular employees see regular employees looking exhausted due to the long hours of work they have to put in and conclude that, even though the work terms for nonregular positions are indeed poor, it is better to work shorter hours at their own pace than to half kill themselves for the company. They like having less responsibility. While this offers some explanation as to why nonregular workers indicate a high level of work satisfaction, it leaves us asking whether it is acceptable for regular workers to have such inhumane work lives.

Finally, the principle of equal pay for equal work has not yet taken root in Japan. Even if a regular worker and a nonregular worker perform the same work, they receive far from the same pay simply due to their employment status. From the perspective of fairness, this is unacceptable. It is true that regular employees make a greater contribution to the company because they are charged with more responsibilities and also must work overtime, so it is logical for there to be some gap in wages. Nonregular workers also accept this to some degree. As we saw in this chapter, however, the wage gap is too great. Some even say that nonregular workers are more capable and contribute more than regular workers in this country. Japan needs to move in the direction of enacting legislation to make the hourly wage the same for full-time and part-time workers who are performing the same work, as the Netherlands has done. The fact that nonregular workers indicate considerable work satisfaction must not be used as an excuse to claim that Japan need not adopt the principle of equal pay for equal work. Making compensation packages fair is important for Japanese society overall. Without this, the inequalities between regular and nonregular workers will not diminish.

Chapter Nine

Conclusion

In these pages, we have analyzed inequalities among Japanese women—a sociological phenomenon that is gaining recognition throughout the nation. According to Ueno and Nobuta (2004, 52), the Japanese term *jojo kakusa* (literally, "woman-woman gap") was coined by Okutani Reiko, the president of a temporary staffing firm, to refer to the disparity between talented women who have exciting careers and unskilled women who have part-time or other nonregular positions. Although there is a huge gap between the philosophies of Ueno and Nobuta and of Okutani—the first two are Japan's leading feminists while Okutani has said that those who suffer *karōshi* (death from overwork) are responsible for their own fate—all three recognize the existence of inequalities among women in Japan today.

I agree with that assessment: there are real disparities among women in Japan today. And such a gap between the privileged and the underprivileged is present not just among women but among all people, including men. In chapter 1, we examined the gender gap and then, from chapter 2 on, a range of different inequalities among women. I have attempted to offer an in-depth analysis of a full spectrum of issues—inequalities between the highly educated and the lesser educated, between those married and those single, between those with children and those without, between full-time homemakers and working women, between those in the management track and those in the clerical track at their workplaces, and between those with regular employment and those with nonregular employment. What kinds of inequalities are there in each area?

Why have they arisen? Are they justifiable? These questions were taken up in detail in the various chapters so I will not summarize the findings here. In this concluding chapter, I would like instead to make six general points based on what we have examined in the rest of the book.

First, men have an impact on almost all inequalities among women. For example, the social class of full-time homemakers is decided based on their husband's status, income, and assets (chapter 2). The issues of marriage and divorce (chapter 4) and children (chapter 5) arise as a result of women's relationships with men. A slightly more complex example is that of married women with non-regular employment (chapter 8): there is a great difference between those who are covered by social insurance programs as their husband's dependents and those who enroll independently, and many married women reduce their work hours for reasons related to tax and social insurance.

Second, many inequalities among women are actually the product of the gender gap (chapter 1). We looked at the education gap (chapter 3) and noted that men and women take different academic courses in high school and university; men concentrate in the sciences, engineering, and social sciences, while women take humanities, arts, and home economics. In other words, if women do not intend to work outside the home, they have the freedom to enter departments and disciplines that are not very relevant in the working world. This education gap, however, has an impact on women's future employment (chapter 6) and on the issues of career tracking and promotion (chapter 7). The gender gap at companies that has resulted from the traditional practice of placing men in management-track positions and women on the clerical track has evolved today into the division of women into two camps: management track and clerical track. The gender gap, or discrimination against women, exists in corporate promotions as well; this can be interpreted similarly to the situation of career tracking.

These first two points reflect the major impact that men have on inequalities among women. My third point is that, on the other hand, some inequalities among women result from the choices made by the women themselves. These days more women want to attend and, are graduating from prestigious universities (chapter 3). And we have moved away from, an age when women could be divided in terms of education into two broad groups—the highly educated at one extreme and the lesser educated at the other. Now there are three groups—the ultra-educated, the highly educated, and the lesser educated. Ultra-educated women want a full career after graduation from a prestigious university, and they earn a comparatively high income. Women in the other two groups who have graduated from junior colleges or average four-year universities (the highly educated) or from high school (the lesser educated) may not necessarily perform very high-level work, but an increasing number of them are career-oriented and want to work throughout their lives.

The divide between women who want to pursue lifelong careers and those who do not is more pronounced today (chapters 6, 7, and 8), with the second group including full-time homemakers as well as women who resign from their jobs at marriage or childbirth and then return to the work force after their childrearing years. The kinds of women who fall into each of the two categories as well as the resulting inequalities have been detailed in earlier chapters.

The matter of disparity in household income depends on the level of the husband's income in the case of both full-time home-makers who have no income and married women with nonregular positions and thus low wages. Couples where both the husband and the wife are highly educated and working will enjoy a comparatively high household income, while couples where both members have a minimal level of education will have a low family income, particularly if the wife either does not work or has a nonregular position. The resulting gap in income between these two types of couples is quite substantial. And since marriages between those of the same educa-tion level make up the majority in Japan (chapter 4), the income gap between the two types is, in fact, growing. As a rather extreme exam-ple, consider the very large financial gap that would arise between a couple composed of two employed doctors and a couple where the husband is a taxi driver and the wife works part-time. This captures one aspect of inequality in Japan today.

The fourth point I would like to make is the major impact of marriage and childbirth on disparities among women and indeed on the overall course of a woman's life. As has been mentioned several times, women are faced with the decision of whether to continue their employment at the time of marriage or childbirth or to resign even if only during their childrearing years. The number of women who quit their jobs is declining, albeit slowly. Men, though, are virtually never faced with having to make such a decision; almost no men resign from their work because of marriage or children. Some may say that this constitutes an inequality of opportunity from the perspective of career-oriented women because only women are required to make this decision.

Each person is free to determine how he or she wants to live. I do not think that single women in their thirties are "loser dogs." It is also true, though, that most women want to have a romantic relationship and get married, to have children, and, if possible, to work too. They will face various obstacles, but tackling those challenges will give their lives meaning. People may fail sometimes, but another path forward opens quickly if they accept it when things do not work out; they should not resent others whose dreams are fulfilled.

The fifth point I would like to address is whether the disparities that exist among women are justifiable or not. While there clearly are inequalities, they do not require particular attention if there are rational reasons for them. Here it is important to distinguish between inequalities of result and inequalities of opportunity. (For a detailed discussion, see Tachibanaki [2004b and 2006].) Simply put, inequalities of result are differences in income and assets, or the fruits of people's economic endeavors, whereas inequalities of opportunity are differences that arise before engagement in economic activity—namely, differences in education, occupation, employment, and promotion. Equal opportunity is achieved by offering all people the chance to compete and ensuring there is no discrimination in the selection process.

When Japan was a poor nation, opportunities for education were not given to women; many families gave their sons as much education as possible and accepted that they were unable to offer that to their daughters. Now households in Japan have become more afflu-ent so families differentiate less and less between their sons and daughters in education. Moreover, women have an increased desire for education. From that perspective, this means that women are not at a particular disadvantage.

Rather, Japan is now in an age where the finances, education, and occupations of the parents heavily influence the educational attainment of all the children—both sons and daughters. Due to social class rigidity, both women and men today encounter inequal-ity of educational opportunity. For a detailed analysis, refer to Kariya (2001), Tachibanaki (2004b), and Fukuchi (2006).

Another example of inequality of opportunity is career tracking and promotion (chapter 7). Women are given the opportunity to select either a management-track or a clerical-track position when they join a company, so this is not a major problem. The issue is, rather, whether there are opportunities for employees to change tracks midcareer. Moreover, the clerical track may be phased out in the future, as the trend is toward replacing clerical-track employees with part-time or dispatched workers and toward having management-track employees perform clerical tasks at the same time as their core work duties.

The real problem lies in opportunities for women to be hired and promoted. Discrimination in hiring is gradually lessening in Japan thanks to the Equal Employment Opportunity Law, but it still persists. Penalties and monitoring must be strengthened so that gen-der discrimination at the time of hiring is eliminated. As has been mentioned throughout the book, it is also crucial that women dem-onstrate a clear desire to pursue a full career and that society support women by providing childcare facilities and other such measures.

Gender discrimination is a major factor behind the extremely low number of women in management positions; men have an advantage over women in promotion. Companies report that they have no women suitable for promotion; however, few women want to continue their corporate career and try for promotion when they know that such opportunities are not available to them. Also play-ing a role here is the traditional concept that the husband should be the breadwinner while the wife stays at home and takes care of housework and childrearing. Although I do not want to attribute the lack of female managers completely to women's lack of opportunity for promotion, it is true that gender discrimination has an impact here. Since Japan is becoming a gender-equal society, it should move toward eliminating discrimination in promotion. The Equal Employment Opportunity Law and similar measures are steps in that direction, but Japan still has far to go.

Sixth, and last, let's consider inequalities of result. These disparities can be measured by comparing wages, income, and assets—the results of an individual's economic activity (chapters 7 and 8). Of the three, income and assets are affected by factors unrelated to gender, such as interest rates, dividends, and land prices, so wages earned from work are the most appropriate for measuring inequalities of result for women.

Gender discrimination has a major impact on wages. Tachibanaki (1996) and Nakata (1997) have shown that this discrimination is considerable even if we control for other factors, such as education, occupation, and years of service at the company. Kawaguchi (2005) and many other experts, however, have noted that the degree of discrimination is decreasing, albeit gradually, and this is a positive development. Two issues remain, though. First, female advancement through the ranks at companies is improving at a very slow pace, as already mentioned. Inequalities of opportunity for promotion between men and women must be rectified, as there is a large wage gap between those promoted to the managerial level and those in nonmanagerial positions. Second is the disparity between regular and nonregular employees. There is a considerable—and expanding—wage gap between regular and nonregular employees (chapter 8). Inasmuch as women make up the majority of nonregular workers while most men are regular workers, the gender gap is an element in the disparity. There are many female regular workers, however, so that the wage gap can also be seen as caused by differences in employment status among women. The wage gap should thus be understood not as a gender disparity but as an inequality of result (wages) due to differences in employment status.

It is unfair for there to be wage disparities based on differences in employment status: there should be equal pay for equal work. Some say that there is no urgent need for such an "equal pay for equal work" policy in Japan because female part-time workers and other nonregular employees express little dissatisfaction with their lot. I, however, do not support that viewpoint, as explained in chapter 8.

In this book we have examined the various social inequalities that exist among women in Japan today. Some of the disparities are justifiable; others are not. My goal has been to emphasize the need to ensure equality of opportunity and to correct those inequalities of result that are not justifiable.

There are two additional observations that I would like to make here in regard to women and social inequalities. First, women have more opportunities than men do to change their social position. Through marriage, women can move up to a privileged social position, as captured in the Japanese phrase *tama no koshi* ("she married into money"). Of course, cases of *gyaku tama no koshi* ("he married into money"), where the man marries upward, are not unknown, but it is more common for women to do so.

It is an unfortunate fact, though, that more women than men are on the wrong side of social inequalities. Accomplished women used to be introduced frequently as the "first woman ever to hold such-and-such a post." This statement reveals that few women have equal standing to men. In the past, Japan did not extend equal opportunity to its women. Needless to say, Japan must work to further secure this for women. Once equal opportunity is achieved, a woman who works hard will gain high social standing. If a woman is successful in education, employment, and promotion, the path will be clear for her to take a top position in society.

Consider the example of a female prime minister. Japan has never had a woman prime minister so having a woman rise to that position would represent a major victory in terms of the issues discussed in these pages. Of course, whether a woman wants to serve as prime minister or other top figure depends on her values, and I am not trying to recommend this path in particular.

Second, whether they wish this or not, women are faced with more choices than men are at various junctures in their lives. One clear example is the option of becoming a full-time homemaker; this avenue is open to women but is essentially closed to men. Women have a wider range of options than men not just in terms of marriage, but also in terms of whether to have children and whether to work full-time or part-time if they work outside the home. Men can let many life decisions take their own course without thinking very deeply about them, but women must often make a conscious decision that takes into consideration a variety of factors and possible outcomes.

This book has shown that the choices a woman makes will have a major impact on her status and lifestyle and has also explicated the role that discrimination and social systems in Japan play in those choices. Japan faces the urgent task of giving its women equal opportunity and correcting inequalities of result that are not justifiable. Women can have flexible lives with a range of choices, though. Dare I suggest that women can have greater life satisfaction than men if they navigate those choices well?

References

Abe Y. 2006. "Fūfu no gakureki to tsuma no shūgyō" (The relationship between a couple's educational attainment and the wife's employment). In *Nihon no shotoku bunpai: Kakusa kakudai to seifu no yakuwari* (Income distribution in Japan: Evidence and policies for tackling widening inequality), ed. Oshio T., Tajika E., and Fukawa T., 211–236. Tokyo: Univ. of Tokyo Press.

Abe Y. and Ōishi A. 2006. "Tsuma no shotoku ga setai shotoku ni oyobosu eikyō" (The impact of the wife's income on the household's income). In *Nihon no shotoku bunpai: Kakusa kakudai to seifu no yakuwari* (Income distribution in Japan: Evidence and policies for tackling widening inequality), ed. Oshio T., Tajika E., and Fukawa T., 185–210. Tokyo: Univ. of Tokyo Press.

Akagawa M. 2000. "Josei no kaisōteki chii wa dono yō ni kimaru ka?" (Determining women's social status). In *Jendā, shijō, kazoku* (Gender, market, and family), ed. Seiyama K., 47–63. Vol. 4 of *Nihon no kaisō shisutemu* (Stratification system in Japan). Tokyo: Univ. of Tokyo Press.

———. 2004. *Kodomo ga hette, nani ga warui ka!* (Fewer children: What's wrong with that!). Tokyo: Chikuma Shobō.

Becker, G. 1981. *A Treatise on the Family.* Cambridge, MA: Harvard Univ. Press.

Fujita Y. 2001. "30 dai danjo ga kangaeru shussan ikuji no risuku" (The risks of having and raising children: The views of men and women in their thirties). In *Raifu saikuru to risuku* (Life cycle and risk), ed. Tachibanaki T., 33–56. Tokyo: Toyo Keizai.

Fukuchi M. 2006. *Kyōiku kakusa zetsubō shakai* (A dead-end society with a hopeless education gap). Tokyo: Yōsensha.

Hara J. and Seiyama K. 1999. *Shakai kaisō: Yutakasa no naka no fubyōdō* (Social stratification: Inequality in an affluent society). Tokyo: Univ. of Tokyo Press.

Harada Y. and Suzuki H. 2005. *Jinkō genshō shakai wa kowakunai* (No need to fear a population decrease). Tokyo: Nippon Hyōronsha.

Hashimoto K. 2001. *Kaikyū shakai Nihon* (Japan as a class society). Tokyo: Aoki Shoten.

———. 2003. *Kaikyū, jendā, saiseisan: Gendai shihonshugi shakai no sonzoku mekanizumu* (Class, gender, reproduction: Structural maintenance of modern capitalism). Tokyo: Tōshindō.

Higuchi Y. 2000. "Paneru dēta ni yoru josei no kekkon, shussan, shūgyō" (Dynamic analysis of women's marriage, childbirth, and employment using panel data). In *Gendai keizaigaku no chōryū 2000* (Current trends in economics 2000), ed. Okada A. et al., 109–148. Tokyo: Toyo Keizai.

Higuchi Y. and Japanese Ministry of Finance Policy Research Institute, eds. 2006. *Shōshika to Nihon no keizai shakai: Futatsu no shinwa to hitotsu no shinjitsu* (The low birthrate and Japan's economy and society: Two myths and one truth). Tokyo: Nippon Hyōronsha.

Japan Institute for Labor Policy and Training, ed. 2006. *Rōdō seisaku kenkyū hōkokusho 68: Koyō no tayōka no hensen, 1994–2003* (JILPT research report no. 68: Transition of diversification of employment between 1994 and 2003). Tokyo: Japan Institute for Labor Policy and Training.

Kariya T. 2001. *Kaisōka Nihon to kyōiku kiki: Fubyōdō saiseisan kara iyoku kakusa shakai e* (Education in crisis and stratified Japan: From the reproduction of inequality to an "incentive divide" society). Tokyo: Yūshindō Kōbunsha.

Katō H. 2001. *Jinkō keizaigaku nyūmon* (Introduction to population economics). Tokyo: Nippon Hyōronsha.

———. 2007. *Jinkō keizaigaku* (Population economics). Tokyo: Nikkei Publishing.

Kawaguchi A. 2005. "1990 nendai ni okeru danjokan chingin kakusa no shukushō no yōin" (Changes in the Japanese gender wage gap in the 1990s). *Keizai bunseki* (Economic analysis), no. 175:52–82.

Kohara M. 2001. "Sengyō shufu wa yūfuku na katei no shōchō ka? Tsuma no shūgyō to shotoku fubyōdō ni zeisei ga ataeru eikyō" (Is the full-time housewife a symbol of a wealthy family? The impact of the tax system on the employment of wives and income inequality). *Nihon rōdō kenkyū zasshi* (Japanese journal of labor studies), no. 493:15–29.

Maeda M. 2004. *Kosodate shiyasui shakai: Hoiku, katei, shokuba o meguru ikuji shiensaku* (Parenting-friendly society: Childcare support measures for daycare, the home, and the workplace). Kyoto: Minerva Shobō.

Miura A. 2005. *Karyū shakai: Arata na kaisō shūdan no shutsugen* (The underclass society: The emergence of a new social stratum). Tokyo: Kōbunsha.

Morita Y. 2003. "Ikuji kyūgyō hō to josei rōdō" (The Childcare Leave Act and female labor). In *Kigyō fukushi no seido kaikaku: Tayō na hatarakikata e mukete* (Institutional reforms for enterprise-based welfare provisions: Toward diverse work styles), ed. Tachibanaki T. and Kaneko Y., 87–108. Tokyo: Toyo Keizai.

Nagase N. 1997. "Josei no shūgyō sentaku" (Women's work choices). In *Koyō kankō no henka to josei rōdō* (Changing employment practices and the female labor force), ed. Chūma H. and Suruga T., 279–312. Tokyo: Univ. of Tokyo Press.

———. 2003. "Nihon no hitenkei rōdō: Josei raifu saikuru to shokugyō sentaku" (Atypical labor in Japan: Women's life cycle and occupational choices). In *Hatarakikata no mirai: Hitenkei rōdō no Nichibeiō hikaku* (The future of labor: A comparison of atypical labor in Japan, Europe, and the United States), ed. Ōsawa Machiko and S. N. Houseman, 263–299. Tokyo: Japan Institute for Labor Research.

Nakamura M. 1990. "Pātotaimu rōdō" (Part-time work). *Nihon rōdō kyōkai zasshi* (Monthly journal of the Japan Institute of Labor), no. 364:40–41.

Nakata Y. 1997. "Nihon ni okeru danjo chingin kakusa no yōin bunseki" (Analysis of the factors causing gender-based wage disparities in Japan). In *Koyō kankō no henka to josei rōdō* (Changing employment practices and the female labor force), ed. Chūma H. and Suruga T., 173–206. Tokyo: Univ. of Tokyo Press.

Naoi M. 1990. "Kaisō ishiki: Josei no chii shakuyō moderu wa yūkō ka" (Women's status consciousness: Is the borrowed status model effective?). In *Josei to shakai kaisō* (Women and social stratification), ed. Okamoto H. and Naoi M., 147–164. Vol. 4 of *Gendai Nihon no kaisō kōzō* (Social stratification in contemporary Japan). Tokyo: Univ. of Tokyo Press.

National Institute of Population and Social Security Research. 2007. *Wagakuni fūfu no kekkon katei to shusshōryoku, Heisei 17 nen dai 13 kai shusshō dōkō kihon chōsa, dai I hōkokusho* (Marriage process and fertility of Japanese married couples, report on the thirteenth Japanese national fertility survey, 2005, vol. I). Tokyo: National Institute of Population and Social Security Research.

National Institute of Population and Social Security Research. 2007. *Wagakuni dokushinsō no kekkonkan to kazokukan, Heisei 17 nen dai 13 kai shusshō dōkō kihon chōsa, dai II hōkokusho* (Attitudes toward marriage and family among Japanese singles, report on the thirteenth Japanese national fertility survey, 2005, vol. II). Tokyo: National Institute of Population and Social Security Research.

National Women's Education Center, ed. 2006. *Danjo kyōdō sankaku tōkei dēta bukku 2006* (Gender equality data book, 2006). Tokyo: Gyōsei.

Nitta M. 1993. "Pātotaimu rōdō no jittai" (Part-time work). *Jurisuto* (Jurist), no. 1021:33–38.

Ochiai E. 1997. *The Japanese Family System in Transition: A Sociological Analysis of Family Change in Postwar Japan.* Trans. Simul International. Tokyo: LTCB International Library Foundation. Distributed by I-House Press, in Tokyo.

Ogura C. 2003. *Kekkon no jōken* (Conditions for marriage). Tokyo: Asahi Shimbun.

Ojima F. 2003. "Gakkō kara shokuba e: Jendā to rōdō shijō" (From school to the workplace: Gender and the labor market). In *Jendā de manabu kyōiku* (Understanding education through gender), ed. Amano M. and Kimura R., 212–228. Kyoto: Sekai Shisōsha.

Ojima F. and Kondō H. 2000. "Kyōiku tassei no jendā kōzō" (Gender and educational attainment). In *Jendā, shijō, kazoku* (Gender, market, and family), ed. Seiyama K., 27–46. Vol. 4 of *Nihon no kaisō shisutemu* (Stratification system in Japan). Tokyo: Univ. of Tokyo Press.

Ōsawa Machiko. 1993. *Keizai henka to joshi rōdō: Nichibei no hikaku kenkyū* (Economic change and female labor: A comparative study of Japan and the United States). Tokyo: Nihon Keizai Hyōronsha.

———. 2006. "Keizai no gurōbaruka to tayōka suru koyō keitai" (Economic globalization and the diversification of employment types). In *21 seiki no josei to shigoto* (Women and work in the twenty-first century), ed. Ōsawa Machiko and Harada J., 175–189. Tokyo: Society for the Promotion of the University of the Air.

Ōsawa Machiko and Harada J., eds. 2006. *21 seiki no josei to shigoto* (Women and work in the twenty-first century). Tokyo: Society for the Promotion of the University of the Air.

Ōsawa Machiko and S. N. Houseman, eds. 2003. *Hatarakikata no mirai: Hitenkei rōdō no Nichibeiō hikaku* (The future of labor: A comparison of atypical labor in Japan, Europe, and the United States). Tokyo: Japan Institute for Labor Research.

Ōsawa Mari. 1993. *Kigyō chūshin shakai o koete: Gendai Nihon o jendā de yomu* (Beyond a corporate-centered society: Understanding contemporary Japan through the lens of gender). Tokyo: Jiji Press.

Oshio T. 2002. *Kyōiku no keizai bunseki* (Economic analysis of education in Japan). Tokyo: Nippon Hyōronsha.

Ōtake F. 2005. *Nihon no fubyōdō: Kakusa shakai no gensō to mirai* (Inequality in Japan: The illusion and future of social disparity in Japan). Tokyo: Nikkei Publishing.

Sakai J. 2003. *Makeinu no tōboe* (Howl of the loser dogs). Tokyo: Kōdansha.

Satō H. 1998. "Hitenkei rōdō no jittai" (The actual situation of atypical employment). *Nihon rōdō kenkyū zasshi* (Monthly journal of the Japan Institute of Labor), no. 462:2–14.

Satō H. and Koizumi S. 2007. *Fuantei koyō to iu kyozō: Pāto, furītā, haken no jitsuzō* (Unstable employment as mirage: The truth about part-time, freeter, and dispatched work). Tokyo: Keisō Shobō.

Shigeno Y. and Ōkusa Y. 1998. "Ikuji kyūgyō seido no josei no kekkon to shūgyō keizoku e no eikyō" (The effects of childcare leave programs on women's marriage and employment continuation). *Nihon rōdō kenkyū zasshi* (Monthly journal of the Japan Institute of Labor), no. 459:39–49.

Shirahase S. 2000. "Josei no shūgyō to kaikyū kōzō" (Women's employment and class structure). In *Jendā, shijō, kazoku* (Gender, market, and family), ed. Seiyama K., 133–155. Vol. 4 of *Nihon no kaisō shisutemu* (Stratification system in Japan). Tokyo: Univ. of Tokyo Press.

———. 2005. *Shōshi kōrei shakai no mienai kakusa: Jendā, sedai, kaisō no yukue* (The unseen gaps in an aging society: Locating gender, generation, and class in Japan). Tokyo: Univ. of Tokyo Press.

Suruga T. and Nishimoto M. 2001. "Kikon josei no saishūgyō ni kansuru jisshō bunseki" (Reemployment of married women: An empirical analysis). *Kikan kakei keizai kenkyū* (Japanese journal of research on household economics), no. 50:56–82.

Tachibanaki T. 1996. *Wage Determination and Distribution in Japan.* Oxford: Oxford Univ. Press.

———. 1997a. *Raifu saikuru no keizaigaku* (The economics of the life cycle). Tokyo: Chikuma Shobō.

———. 1997b. *Shōshin no shikumi* (The mechanism of promotion). Tokyo: Toyo Keizai.

———. 2000. *Sēfuti netto no keizaigaku* (The economics of safety nets). Tokyo: Nikkei Publishing.

———. 2002a. *Shitsugyō kokufuku no keizaigaku* (The economics of overcoming unemployment). Tokyo: Iwanami Shoten.

Tachibanaki T. 2002b. *Anshin no keizaigaku: Raifu saikuru no risuku ni dō taisho suru ka* (The economics of security: Dealing with risk throughout the life cycle). Tokyo: Iwanami Shoten.

————. 2004a. *Datsu furītā shakai: Otonatachi ni dekiru koto* (Emerging from a society of freeters: What adults can do). Tokyo: Toyo Keizai.

————, ed. 2004b. *Fūin sareru fubyōdō* (Sealed inequality). Tokyo: Toyo Keizai.

————. 2005. *Kigyō fukushi no shūen: Kakusa no jidai ni dō taiō subeki ka* (The coming end of employee benefits: How should we respond in this age of widening social disparities?). Tokyo: Chūōkōron-Shinsha.

————. 2006. *Kakusa shakai: Nani ga mondai na no ka* (A divided society: What are the issues?). Tokyo: Iwanami Shoten.

————, ed. 2007. *Seifu no ōkisa to shakai hoshō seido: Kokumin no jueki futan kara mita bunseki to teigen* (The size of government and the social security system: Analyses and proposals from the perspective of citizen benefits and burdens). Tokyo: Univ. of Tokyo Press.

Tachibanaki T. and Kimura M. 2008. *Kazoku no keizaigaku: Okane to kizuna no semegiai* (Family economics: Torn between money and family ties). Tokyo: NTT Publishing.

Tachibanaki T. and RENGO-RIALS (Japanese Trade Union Confederation [RENGO] Research Institute for Advancement of Living Standards), eds. 1995. *"Shōshin" no keizaigaku: Nani ga "shusse" o kimeru no ka* (The economics of promotion: What determines career advancement). Tokyo: Toyo Keizai.

Tachibanaki T. and Urakawa K. 2006. *Nihon no hinkon kenkyū* (A study on poverty in Japan). Tokyo: Univ. of Tokyo Press.

Tokyo Labor Research Institute, ed. 1994. *Josei rōdō kenkyū 9: Daisotsu josei no shokugyō sentaku kōdō to shokugyō seikatsu* (Research on women's labor no. 9: Occupational choices and lifestyles of university-educated women). Tokyo: Tokyo Labor Research Institute.

Tomita Y. and Wakisaka A. 1999. "Josei no kekkon shussan to sono shūgyō sentaku" (Women's employment during family formation). *Osaka Furitsu Daigaku keizaigaku kenkyū* (Osaka Prefecture University journal of economic studies), no. 45: 133–145.

Ueno C. 1990. *Kafuchōsei to shihonsei: Marukusu shugi feminizumu no chihei* (Patriarchy and capitalism: A Marxist-feminist approach). Tokyo: Iwanami Shoten.

Ueno C. and Nobuta S. 2004. *Kekkon teikoku: Onna no wakaremichi* (The marriage empire: Crossroads for women). Tokyo: Kōdansha.

Ueno C. and Ogura C. 2002. *Za feminizumu* (Feminism). Tokyo: Chikuma Shobō.

Wakisaka A. 1997. "Kōsu betsu jinji seido to josei rōdō" (Tracked personnel management systems and female labor). In *Koyō kankō no henka to josei rōdō* (Changing employment practices and the female labor force), ed. Chūma H. and Suruga T., 243–278. Tokyo: Univ. of Tokyo Press.

———. 2001. "Daisotsu josei no genjō to koyō kanri no henka" (University-educated women and changes in employment management). In *Daisotsu josei no hatarakikata: Josei ga shigoto o tsuzukeru toki, yameru toki* (Work modes of female university graduates: When women continue working, when women leave their jobs), ed. Tomita Y. and Wakisaka A., 1–20. Tokyo: Japan Institute of Labor.

Wakisaka A. and Okui M. 2005. "Naze daisotsu josei wa saishūshoku shinai no ka" (Why university-educated women do not return to work). In *Gendai josei no rōdō, kekkon, kosodate* (Current issues surrounding women at work and in the family), ed. Tachibanaki T., 184–210. Kyoto: Minerva Shobō.

Yokoyama Y. 2003. "Shūgyō shien seisaku no chōkiteki kōka" (The long-term impact of employment support policies). In *Kigyō fukushi no seido kaikaku: Tayō na hatarakikata e mukete* (Institutional reforms for enterprise-based welfare provisions: Toward diverse work styles), ed. Tachibanaki T. and Kaneko Y., 61–86. Tokyo: Toyo Keizai.

———. 2005. "Josei no kon'in jōtai to tenshoku saishūshoku kōdō" (Women's marital status and job-changing/reemployment efforts). In *Gendai josei no rōdō, kekkon, kosodate* (Current issues surrounding women at work and in the family), ed. Tachibanaki T., 147–165. Kyoto: Minerva Shobō.

Yoshikawa H. et al. 1995. *Kekkon* (Marriage). Tokyo: Univ. of Tokyo Press.

Index

A

Abe Y., 178

abortion, 163–66, 163 table 5-8.

Akagawa M., 44–46, 51, 45 table
2-1, 133; dominant status model,
44–47, 45 table 2-1

arranged marriages (*miai kekkon*),
103–4, table 4-4, 116–19, 117 fig.
4-5, 118 fig. 4-6, 173. *See also* love
marriage

assets: as determinants in social
class, 41, 44, 49

atypical work. *See under* nonregular
workers

B

"baby hatches," 164–65

Becker, G., 143, 177

birthrate: decline in, 13, 133–38, 134
table 5-1, 136 table 5-2, 140 (*see
also* fertility, completed); measures to raise, 163–68. *See also*
abortion

bonuses, 233–34, 234 fig. 8-3, 240–
41

C

career advancement. *See* promotion

career tracking, 195–212: changing
career tracks, 204–10, 206 fig.
7-3; and educational attainment,
26, 201–4; and gender, 24–27,
25 fig. 1-7; history of, 199–201;
and inequality, 207–12, 269;
prevalence by corporate size,
196–97, 197 fig. 7-1; prevalence
by industry, 198–99, 198, fig.
7-2; prevalence by work duties,
199–200, 200 table 7-1; and promotion, 23–24, 196; proposed
revision of, 210–212; trends in,
197–98, 197 fig. 7-1. *See also* clerical track; management track;
promotion; quasi-management
track; region-based management
track; specialized track

Chicago School, 143

Childcare Leave Act, 185–87

childcare leave programs: impact on
women's employment continuation after pregnancy/childbirth,
154–57, 154 fig. 5-2; prevalence
of, 185–87, 186 fig. 6-5